# Thailand's Macroeconomic Miracle

## Stable Adjustment and Sustained Growth

PETER G. WARR

BHANUPONG NIDHIPRABHA

THE WORLD BANK, WASHINGTON, D.C.
OXFORD UNIVERSITY PRESS, KUALA LUMPUR

996 The International Bank for Reconstruction
l Development / The World Bank
8 H Street, N.W., Washington, D.C. 20433

ributed exclusively in Asia and non-exclusively in the rest of the world by

rd University Press
an U1/15, Seksyen U1
m Glenmarie Industrial Park
0 Shah Alam
gor Darul Ehsan
ysia

World Bank Comparative Macroeconomic Studies series emerges from a research project ... reviewed the macroeconomic experiences of eighteen developing countries over a period roughly from 1965 to 1990. So that the studies might be published with relatively little delay, the books have been edited outside the World Bank's Office of the Publisher by the Macroeconomic Research Department.

*Cover design by Sam Ferro*

Peter G. Warr is the John Crawford Professor of Agricultural Economics at the Australian National University, Canberra, Australia. Bhanupong Nidhiprabha is Associate Professor in the Faculty of Economics at Thammasat University, Bangkok, and Research Fellow at the Thailand Development Research Institute, Bangkok, Thailand.

World Bank ISBN 0-8213-2654-6
Oxford University Press ISBN 983-56-0000-7

NOV 2 6 1996

*Library of Congress Cataloging-in-Publication Data*

Warr, Peter G.
 Thailand's macroeconomic miracle : stable adjustment and sustained
growth / Peter G. Warr, Bhanupong Nidhiprabha.
  p. cm.
 Includes bibliographical references.
 ISBN 0-8213-2654-6
 1. Structural adjustment (Economic policy)—Thailand.
2. Thailand—Economic policy. 3. Thailand—Economic conditions.
I. Nidhiprabha, Bhanupong, 1954– . II. Title.
HC445.W363 1996
338.9593—dc20
          95–13672
          CIP

W O R L D  B A N K

C O M P A R A T I V E  M A C R O E C O N O M I C  S T U D I E S

WITHDRAWN

# Thailand's

# Macroeconomic

# Miracle

## Stable Adjustment
## and Sustained Growth

For Suthida and Divina

# Contents

# Foreword

This volume is the product of an intensive World Bank study of recent macroeconomic policy that reviewed the recent experience of eighteen countries as they attempted to maintain economic stability in the face of international price, interest
rate, and demand shocks or domestic crises in the form of investment booms and
related budgetary problems. The project paid particular attention to the 1974–79
period (which included the first and second oil price shocks), the 1980–82 period
of worldwide recession and external debt problems for many developing countries, and the 1983–90 period of adjustment to economic difficulties and the re-
sumption of growth.

The objective of the project was to glean instructive lessons by analyzing the
stabilization and adjustment policies pursued by these countries and assessing the
outcomes. The authors of each country study were asked to deal with a common
set of questions concerning the nature of the shocks or crises: their origin and degree of seriousness; the fiscal, monetary, exchange rate, and trade policies adopted
in hopes of preventing permanent harm to the economy; and the results of the policies. No single computable macroeconomic model was used in the project, but the
framework of the open-economy macroeconomic model was followed to ensure
consistency in generalizing about policy results. This intensive study of many episodes generated ideas and suggested relationships showing the cause and effect
behind the policies, the nature of the shocks and crises, and the governmental response to them.

The overall findings of the project are presented in a synthesis volume by
I. M. D. Little, Richard N. Cooper, W. Max Corden, and Sarath Rajapatirana, *Boom,
Crisis, and Adjustment: The Macroeconomic Experience of Developing Countries.*

Thailand provides a case study of relatively successful adjustment. Despite
significant external economic shocks and some internal political instability, Thailand was less adversely affected by the turbulence of the 1970s and early 1980s
than virtually any other oil-importing developing country. The successful adjustment took the form of consistently high rates of economic growth, low inflation,
and only moderate growth of external debt. The present study provides details of
how this was accomplished. The role of economic policy is a central theme.

The results of the study show the importance of cautious macroeconomic policies, combined with reliance on market mechanisms as the principal means of resource allocation. While the Thai achievement of sustained economic growth

combined with macroeconomic stability is impressive, the policies which produced this outcome appear to be capable of being emulated by other developing countries, should they choose to do so.

Publication of this study was made possible by a generous grant from SIDA, the Swedish International Development Authority.

*Sarath Rajapatirana*
*Director, "Macroeconomic Policies, Crisis, and Growth*
*in the Long Run" Research Project.*
*Economic Adviser,*
*Operations Policy Group*

# Acknowledgments

The authors wish to acknowledge the contributions of the many individuals who have assisted in this study. Work on this manuscript began in 1986, when Peter Warr was a visiting professor in the Faculty of Economics at Thammasat University, Bangkok. At that time, Bandid Nijathaworn, then of Thammasat University, was a member of our team. In 1987 Bandid Nijathaworn left Thammasat to join the International Monetary Fund and subsequently the Bank of Thailand. We gratefully acknowledge his important contribution to the initial stages of our research, without implicating him in the many changes of direction and emphasis that occurred thereafter.

The World Bank project leaders—Richard Cooper, Max Corden, Ian Little, and Sarath Rajapatirana—were helpful and constructive at all stages of the research. Detailed comments and suggestions from Max Corden and Sarath Rajapatirana were especially helpful. Sarath Rajapatirana was a patient and constructive project coordinator. Many colleagues also provided helpful comments on earlier drafts and offered suggestions for the research. In particular, numerous valuable comments, suggestions, and corrections of factual errors were received from Ammar Siamwalla, president of the Thailand Development Research Institute. Two anonymous readers also provided many helpful comments and saved us from errors of fact and judgment. Other colleagues who assisted us with their comments included Vittorio Corbo, Peter Drysdale, Malcolm Falkus, George Fane, Ross Garnaut, Alan Meltzer, Dennis de Tray, James Reidel, and David Vines.

We had the benefit of research assistance from many able individuals. These included Zita Albacea, Sunee Budsaiyavith, Soonthorn Chaiyindeepum, Ahmed Hafi, Elsa Lapiz, Wimolmas Lulitanonda, Siriwan Pichitwonglert, Maneerat Pinyopusarerk, Kobkul Pitarachart, Agus Setiabudi, and Cao Yong. Monique Lumb provided much-valued secretarial assistance and Suthida Warr worked heroically to assist in assembling the final manuscript.

The assistance of all the above individuals, and any others we have neglected to mention, is greatly appreciated. We were not able to adopt all the suggestions we received, including many with which we were in general agreement. As always, final responsibility for what remains resides with the authors.

# Thai Names

The Western scholarly convention of referring to individuals and citing authors by their family names is awkward in the case of Thailand because the Thai custom is to identify individuals by their first names. These are the names by which Thais are most readily recognized, both within Thailand and abroad. Thai family names tend to be long and unfamiliar. Indeed, the use of family names at all is a relatively recent innovation. In this book we have followed the Thai custom by referring to Thai individuals and authors primarily by their first names. Thus, for example, the 1984 study by Chaiyawat Wibulsawasdi is cited as Chaiyawat (1984) rather than Wibulsawasdi (1984). When referring to Thai individuals in the text we have included family names as well as first names whenever it seemed that confusion might arise from stating first names only. In the bibliography, both the first names and family names of Thai authors are given in full, and the authors are listed alphabetically by their first names. The other names are listed in the usual order.

# Acronyms

| | |
|---|---|
| ASEAN | Association of Southeast Asian Nations |
| BAAC | Bank of Agriculture and Agricultural Cooperatives |
| BOI | Board of Investment |
| CAO | Changwat (provincial) administrative organization |
| CGD | Comptroller-General Department |
| DSR | debt service ratio |
| ERP | effective rate of protection |
| GDP | gross domestic product |
| GHB | Government Housing Bank |
| GNP | gross national product |
| GSB | Government Saving Bank |
| IFCT | Industrial Finance Corporation of Thailand |
| IMF | International Monetary Fund |
| LC | letter of credit |
| LIBOR | London interbank offer rate |
| LPG | liquefied petroleum gas |
| LTF | long-term flows |
| NAD | National Accounts Division (of the NESDB) |
| NCF | net claims on financial institutions |
| NCG | net claims on government |
| NDC | net domestic credit |
| NDPC | National Debt Policy Committee |
| NEDB | National Economic Development Board |
| NEPR | net export performance ratio |
| NESDB | National Economic and Social Development Board |
| NFA | net foreign assets |
| NIE | newly industrializing economy |
| NOL | net other liabilities |
| NSO | National Statistical Office |
| OECD | Organisation for Economic Co-operation and Development |
| OLS | ordinary least squares |
| OPEC | Organization of Petroleum Exporting Countries |
| SDR | special drawing right |
| SES | Socio-Economic Survey |

| SIFO | Small Industries Finance Office |
| SNA | standard accounting framework |
| STF | short-term flows |
| TDRI | Thailand Development Research Institute |
| TFP | total factor productivity |
| USAID | United States Agency for International Development |
| VAT | value added tax |

# Data Notes

- *Billion* is 1,000 million throughout.
- Dates indicated with a slash (1967/68) are fiscal years.
- *Dollars* are current U.S. dollars unless otherwise specified.
- The symbol — in tables means not available.
- n.a. means not applicable.

# Chapter One

# Introduction

The performance of the Thai economy in recent decades has been nothing short of stunning. In 1950, following an entire century of economic stagnation, Thailand was one of the world's poorest countries. Since then, its economy has experienced rapid growth, declining poverty, and macroeconomic stability. What is particularly impressive about this achievement is that it occurred in a volatile economic and political environment.

Like most developing countries, Thailand has had its share of internal and external economic and political shocks. Internally, it has suffered political turmoil throughout much of the postwar period. Authoritarian military governments alternated with democratic or semidemocratic regimes for brief periods, all in an atmosphere of military coups, attempted coups, threatened coups, and general political unrest. Paradoxically, Thailand maintained economic stability despite this political chaos.

Thailand has also been affected by strong external shocks. They have included: a perceived military threat from Vietnam in the 1960s; some side effects of the Vietnam war, among them a flood of American aid and military spending during the war, followed by its abrupt cessation; the boom in international primary commodity prices of 1972–73; the two massive petroleum price increases of 1973–74 and 1979–80; the high interest rates of the early 1980s; the world recession of the first half of the 1980s; and a foreign investment boom in the late 1980s. Moreover, Thailand has experienced a very large long-term decline in its terms of trade—from an index of 100 in 1970, to about 60 in 1990. Nevertheless, whereas many developing countries, including some of Thailand's Southeast Asian neighbors, were badly destabilized by these and even lesser shocks, Thailand showed surprising resilience.

From 1965 to 1990 the real gross national product (GNP) per capita in Thailand grew at an annual rate of 4.2 percent, compared with an average of 2.5 percent for low- and middle-income countries. Even more remarkable was the stability of Thailand's growth. In a pattern almost unique among oil-importing countries, Thailand's real output per head of population has not experienced a single year of negative growth since 1958 (figure 1.1). And between 1986 and 1990, the Thai economy was the fastest growing in the world. Although income distribution appears to have become more unequal over the past two decades (figure 1.2), the incidence of absolute poverty has declined significantly. The rate of inflation has been low, averaging only 3.8 percent from 1965 to 1990 compared with an average rate of 32 percent for all low- and middle-income developing countries, and its exchange rate has been stable. All this was achieved with only moderate growth of the external debt and with stable international reserves.

Considering the degree to which other economies were destabilized by internal and external shocks seemingly no more severe than those listed above, the Thai experience of stable growth seems almost miraculous. The thesis of this book, however, is quite the opposite. There was no miracle. Although its achievement was impressive, Thailand did not accomplish anything that other countries, similarly endowed with physical and human resources and experiencing similar shocks, could not have matched. The Thai achievement of stable growth could have been equaled or even bettered by others, had they been disposed to adopt the required policies. This study attempts to show how Thailand did it.

Such a study is of interest not only because it can shed light on Thai economic history, but also because it may hold important lessons for other developing countries. There are presumably an unlimited number of ways of adjusting poorly to external shocks, but far fewer possible ways of adjusting well. Although case studies of mismanaged adjustment in this or that country are clearly of value, particularly to specialists studying those countries, the choices made usually turn out to

**Figure 1.1. Per Capita GDP at Constant 1972 Prices, 1951–91**

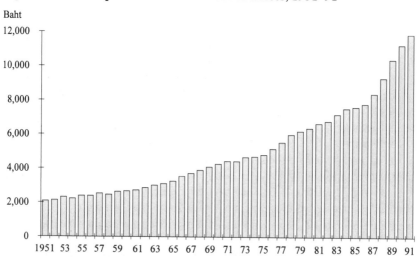

*Source:* National Economic and Social Development Board, Bangkok.

**Figure 1.2. Income Shares by Population Quintile, 1975–76 and 1988**

Income share (percent)

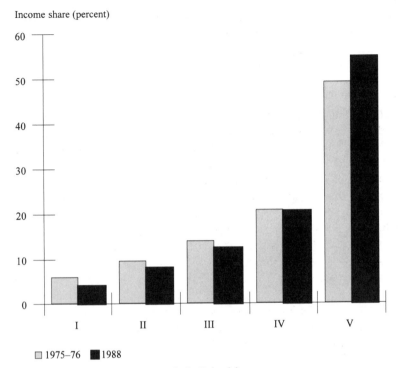

□ 1975–76 ■ 1988

*Note:* Quintile I is the poorest, quintile V the richest.
*Sources:* Suganya and Somchai (1988); Thailand, National Statistical Office (1988).

have a country-specific explanation. A detailed study of successful adjustment, where it has occurred, may have more useful lessons to offer. That is, the lessons of success may be more transferable than the lessons of failure.

Our central contention in this book is that Thailand was able to achieve economic stability despite its apparent political turmoil because it followed cautious economic policies. These policies were greatly influenced by the attitudes of the country's policymakers, most notably by the conservatism of its bureaucrats. These attitudes helped Thailand avoid major mistakes.

If valid, this conclusion has broad implications for the economic history of the world since 1970. As noted earlier, many developing countries were badly destabilized by the volatile events of the external environment surrounding them. Why not Thailand? If the answer is that Thailand followed good policies, then it presumably follows that others could in principle have responded similarly but that, for some combination of reasons—no doubt different in every case—they did not do so. But their destabilization was not an inevitable consequence of the shocks they experienced; it was at least in part a consequence of their own policy responses to those shocks. It could have been otherwise.

Part One of the book describes the economic and political setting in which Thailand's macroeconomic achievement took place. Part Two examines the shocks themselves and Thailand's adjustment to them.

Our study concentrates on the period from 1970 to 1990. An earlier starting point might have been chosen except for data considerations. The data series in the revised national accounts recently published by the Thai government begins with 1970. This revised data series, released in 1987, differs so much from previously available data that it is difficult to compare Thai economic data immediately before and after 1970. Data for the years before 1970 must be considered somewhat unreliable, and if it is possible to avoid using them it is advisable to do so. We end with 1990 because it was the latest year for which full statistical coverage was available at the time our study came to a close.

# Part One

---

# The Macroeconomic Policy Environment

# Chapter Two

# The Political and Historical Setting:
# The Paradox of Policy Stability

Throughout most of its modern history, Thailand has tolerated heavy military in-volvement in its political affairs. Thailand's political history since World War II has been punctuated by a succession of military coups and attempted coups, some-times followed by relatively democratic periods, sometimes not. In the two de-cades since 1970 the role of the military in civilian matters has become increasingly contentious because the country's growing urban, educated middle class has begun demanding democratic reform and a reduced role for the military in the country's economic as well as political affairs.[1]

It is hardly surprising that to outsiders Thai political life often seems unstable. The institutions governing the succession of political power in Thailand have in-deed experienced many crises, but these events should not be taken to mean that Thai political life is no more than an unruly succession of coups. The struggle for the top jobs is one matter, but policy formation is quite another, and there the un-derlying reality has been far more stable than the appearance. This stability stems in large part from fact that the Thais are united by a popular monarchy and by the religion of the majority, Buddhism. The present monarch is His Majesty King Bhumipol Adulyadej, who has reigned since 1946. Ethnic Chinese constitute a large minority group heavily concentrated in the capital, Bangkok. They are treat-ed as Thais, however, and the nation has clearly benefited from their entrepreneur-ial abilities. Unlike some of its neighboring countries, Thailand has experienced little racial conflict.

Despite many military coups or attempted coups, Thai policymakers have continued to follow similar basic political and economic philosophies. They have differed on distributional matters, but they have all been committed to economic growth and shared the belief that market forces combined with prudent public sec-tor infrastructure investment should be the principal means for achieving that end. Thailand's bureaucracies have played a particularly important role in maintaining the continuity of economic policy along these lines. But where did these conservative attitudes come from?

This chapter presents the political and historical context in which Thailand's economic adjustment has occurred over the past two decades. The chapter opens with a sketch of Thai political developments since the founding of Bangkok two centuries ago. It then addresses the question of why the conservative attitudes of Thailand's economic policymakers developed as they did.

## Thailand's Turbulent Political History

For the purposes of this discussion, the historical events of interest begin with the establishment of Bangkok as Thailand's capital in 1782, following the destruction of the former capital of Ayutthaya by Burmese forces in 1767.

### The Founding of Bangkok

The birth of the new capital coincided with the founding of the Chakri dynasty, which has reigned since that time. The present king is the ninth of the dynasty (thus known as Rama IX). These historical events help explain why Bangkok continues to play a prominent role in Thai public life and in the Thai imagination, a role that extends well beyond its being merely the national capital. Partly because of this history, Thailand's economic activity is heavily concentrated in this one city. Its position in this respect is unmatched in any other country of Thailand's size.

Although military considerations were the primary reason for the relocation of the capital from Ayutthaya to Bangkok, the move had important economic consequences. Whereas Ayutthaya is situated 80 kilometers upstream from the mouth of the Chao Phya River, Bangkok is right at the mouth and adjacent to the Gulf of Thailand. Being on the river, Ayutthaya was able to maintain significant maritime trade connections, but it would never have been able to engage in the commerce and international communication that the new capital fostered from its more favorable location.

### Avoidance of Colonization

Thailand avoided colonization by European powers in the nineteenth century by successfully playing off the British in Burma and India to the west and in Malaya to the south against the French in Indochina to the east and in Laos to the north. To preserve the independence of the central plains, however, particularly that of Bangkok, the government made major territorial concessions to both powers. The British took over what is now Penang in Malaysia, and the French gained much of present Cambodia and Laos. Under the Bowring Treaty signed by King Mongkut (Rama IV) and Great Britain in 1855, Thailand agreed to embark on some free trade in its economic policies. But unlike similar treaties the Western powers signed at about the same time with China and Japan, the treaty with Thailand was apparently entered into without much overt coercion from the British (Ingram 1971).

In Thai historical accounts, King Chulalongkorn, the fifth king of the Chakri dynasty (Rama V), who reigned from 1868 to 1910, is given credit for avoiding colonization, for establishing the Thai civil service, and for abolishing slavery. Although recent historical accounts claim that Thailand was able to avoid colonization more because of a convenient compromise between the British and French (Wyatt 1984), King Chulalongkorn had clearly recognized that internal financial stability was vital to keeping the European colonizers at bay. Any sign of Thai financial instability, it was feared, might have been used as a pretext for the European gunboats to attack Bangkok. The king engaged a British financial adviser, from the Bank of England, to consult on economic matters. Predictably, his advice was conservative. The British financial adviser continued to be an influential force in Thailand's economic affairs for many years, and the position was not abolished until the late 1950s. More important, the Bank of England became the conservative model for the establishment and operation of the Bank of Thailand following World War II.

Free trade policies promoted the expansion of agricultural exports but did not produce rapid economic growth. In the century following the Bowring Treaty, Thai economic growth barely kept pace with population growth (Sompop 1989), and there was virtually no structural change. Agricultural exports were the main source of both foreign exchange and government revenue. The agricultural growth was not driven by improved productivity but by the expansion of the cultivated land area (Ammar, Suthad, and Direk 1993). Land remained abundant until the 1960s.

*Constitutional Monarchy, 1932*

The period of absolute monarchy ended in 1932 with a coup d'état against King Prajadhipok (Rama VII). The king agreed to support a constitutional monarchy. Although the coup seems to have lacked public support, it was successfully portrayed by the new military leaders as a "revolution." A succession of military-dominated governments followed.

In 1939 a government edict changed the country's English-language name from Siam to Thailand. "Siam" is apparently a non-Thai word (possibly Khmer or Chinese) that came into use only after its formal appearance in the original nineteenth-century treaties with Britain and France; "Thailand" is a literal translation of the Thai-language name for the country. The change of name symbolized the abrogation of the old treaties and declared that the Thai state warranted a legal status on a par with that of the imperial powers of the world.

The Thai government allied itself with Japan during World War II, once invasion by Japanese forces became imminent. Thailand subsequently shared in the Japanese hyperinflation toward the end of World War II, and this inflation continued for several years after the war. This was the country's sole experience of sustained rapid inflation. The inflation came on the heels of the founding in 1942 of the central bank, the Bank of Thailand, which has rigorously pursued anti-inflationary monetary policies ever since—not unlike those of the Bank of England, on which it was modeled. Today the Bank of Thailand plays a central role in Thailand's macroeconomic policymaking environment.

## Establishment of the Bank of Thailand

The idea of creating a central bank in Thailand originated during the reign of King Chulalongkorn (Rama V).[2] Following his return from a tour of Europe, the king began a program to modernize the country. In 1904, Prince Mahisra Raj Haruetai, the minister of finance, set up the Book Club Association, the first banking office owned by a Thai national. The first bank to open an office in Bangkok had been the Hong Kong and Shanghai Banking Corporation, which began operation there in 1888. In 1914 the Ministry of Finance employed Sir Bernard Hunter, a British banker, to prepare a plan for upgrading the Book Club Association into a central bank. Although the study was undertaken, the plan was not implemented. Following the 1932 coup, the Book Club Association was transformed into a commercial bank named the Siam Commercial Bank.

In 1939 the plan to create a central bank was reactivated, and the government enacted legislation establishing the National Banking Bureau. Functioning somewhat like a central bank, the bureau was to receive deposits from government institutions and other banks, oversee exchange control, and manage government borrowing activities. It opened in June 1940 with Praya Sonauraraj as its first director.

During the Japanese occupation of World War II, Japan proposed three major monetary changes: the value of the Thai baht was to be fixed in relation to the Japanese yen at the exchange rate of 1:1; transactions between Japan and Thailand were to be conducted in Japanese yen; and a central monetary authority was to be established in Thailand with advisers and key personnel from Japan. Thailand adopted the first two proposals, although the new monetary alignment implied a 36 percent depreciation of the baht against the yen. Before the war, the Thai baht had been fixed to the gold standard at the exchange rate of 1 baht per 0.66567 grams of pure gold, 11 baht per pound sterling, and 100 baht per 155.7 Japanese yen. Thailand was obliged to accept the second proposal under the terms of the alliance, which prohibited trade with countries other than Japan and its occupied territories. Thailand rejected the third proposal, however, as it would have given Japan complete control of the Thai currency. To prevent Japan from exercising direct control over the country's financial affairs, the Thai government hastily enacted the Bank of Thailand Act in April 1942, establishing the bank as an independent institution. Eight months later, in December, the Parliament passed a bill outlining the bank's functions and method of operation. The Bank of Thailand was opened on December 10, 1942, with Prince Wiwat as its first governor.[3]

Constitutionally, the Bank of Thailand is governed by a Board, which originally comprised six members: the minister of finance, as chairman of the board; the governor and deputy governor; and another three members appointed by the king (this number of appointed members was expanded to five in 1946 and later to the current eleven members).

### World War II Inflation

During World War II, government expenditure increased, stimulating aggregate demand and exacerbating inflation. But this domestic source of inflation was small compared with the inflationary forces from outside—notably the effects of the Japanese occupation. The high inflation during the war was caused mainly by an expansion of the money supply, beginning with the Japanese occupation in 1941 and the 36 percent depreciation of the baht imposed by Japan. Since Thailand was forced to trade only with Japan and its occupied territories, the trade balance subsequently moved in Thailand's favor as Thai exports became somewhat cheaper in yen prices. Meanwhile, the value of imports did not rise as much because Japan could not supply Thailand with goods needed for the war effort. Thus, Thailand built up foreign reserves in yen, and the Bank of Thailand had to sell baht to exporters, thereby increasing the domestic money supply.

The monetary expansion was also assisted by an increase in direct Japanese military expenditure in Thailand following the establishment of the new 1:1 exchange rate. Between 1942 and 1945 Japanese military expenditure increased from about 2 million baht per month to 100 million baht per month (Bank of Thailand 1962).

Because fiscal policy could not be used to restrain government expenditure during wartime, the remaining instrument available to control inflation was monetary policy, specifically, credit control, a salary deposit scheme, the use of checks to pay for certain transactions, and forced saving.

CREDIT CONTROL. When the money supply rose sharply in June 1943, the government imposed credit controls. First, it raised the currency reserve ratio, with the result that the commercial banks had to raise their deposits with the Bank of Thailand. The precise ratio was to be announced from time to time by the Ministry of Finance, but whereas the ratio had previously varied from 3 to 5 percent, it was now to be varied within the range of 9 to 45 percent.

Second, the government required financial institutions to hold government bonds at varying ratios: commercial banks were to hold at least 40 percent of their total deposits received, and insurance companies were to hold 45 percent of their total investible funds, or 75 percent of their total premiums received; the holdings for other credit institutions were to be determined from time to time by the Ministry of Finance.

After barely three months, the decree was amended to limit the currency reserve ratio to a maximum of 25 percent; and to specify that the amount of government bonds to be held by commercial banks would be determined by the Ministry of Finance from time to time, except that the amount of bonds plus currency reserves deposited at the Bank of Thailand were not to exceed 50 percent of total deposits received. In addition, the government bonds held by insurance companies were to be 30 to 40 percent of total investible funds, or 50 to 70 percent of the total premiums received; again, the precise figure was to be announced by the Ministry of Finance from time to time. These credit control measures were in effect until November 19, 1946.

THE SALARY DEPOSIT SCHEME. In 1943 the government required high-ranking officials to have saving accounts with commercial banks, and their salaries were to be paid into those accounts. This was an attempt to reduce the amount of cash in circulation.

THE USE OF CHECKS. In April 1944 the government decreed that starting on May 1, 1944, any transactions of goods and services of more than 1,000 baht were to be paid for by check. Otherwise, there was to be a surcharge of 10 percent on the tax otherwise levied on that transaction. The purpose of this measure was to reduce the amount of money in public circulation, encourage the use of checks rather than bank notes, which became scarce during the war, and prevent the use of money to hoard goods for speculative purposes. The decree was in effect for only a few months before Parliament reconvened and rejected the bill. It is therefore difficult to assess the effectiveness of this policy in reducing the amount of cash in circulation.

FORCED SAVING. In February 1945 the government issued a decree titled Saving Bonds in Emergency, which demonetized the 1,000 baht bank note that had been issued during the war. Holders of these notes were to return them to the Bank of Thailand in exchange for saving bonds of equivalent value. The bond was redeemable after one year at an interest rate of 1 percent. This forced saving proved to be the most effective instrument for reducing the money supply. Following the decree, 371.5 million baht were withdrawn from circulation, which amounted to about one-third of the total currency then in public hands.

INTEREST RATE POLICY. The government also raised interest rates to restrict credit. On February 23, 1945, the government raised the prime rate from 4.5 to 8 percent per year. This measure proved ineffective, however, and the money supply continued to rise.

*Postwar Military Governments, 1946–63*

Following World War II, Thailand was ruled by a succession of conservative military-controlled governments. Phibul Songkhram was prime minister from 1948 to 1957, when he was forced into exile as the result of a coup sparked by charges of election rigging. The military strongman Field Marshall Sarit Thanarat then installed two prime ministers, first diplomat Phote Sarasin and then General Thanom Kittikachorn, but in 1958 he assumed the premiership himself. Sarit's government began with the arrest of scores of suspected communists and the dissolution of Parliament.

An event of considerable significance for subsequent Thai economic history was the arrival of a World Bank advisory mission in 1957 (Suehiro 1989). The report of this mission (World Bank 1959) influenced Thai economic policy in two important ways. First, it recommended a fundamental shift in the nature of public sector involvement in the economy: away from direct production, via the extensive and highly inefficient public enterprise sector that existed at that time, toward investment in the public infrastructure required for economic development, particularly roads, ports, electricity supply, and telecommunications. Second, the report recommended that the government change its method of promoting private sector investment.

The World Bank report found a receptive audience in the government of the time, particularly in Sarit himself, and significant changes in economic policy followed. There was a new surge of public investment in infrastructure and the newly formed National Economic and Social Development Board (NESDB) began formulating regular five-year development plans to guide these investments. Although most of the public enterprises then in existence remained in place, they became less significant as private sector economic activity in manufacturing grew. Also, the Board of Investment was created in 1958 to render assistance to private investors.

*The Thanom Military Government, 1963–73*

With Sarit's death in December 1963, power shifted to a new military alliance headed by Generals Thanom Kittikachorn and Prapas Charusathien. Thanom became the prime minister and Prapas assumed the powerful posts of the commander in chief of the army and the minister of interior. The new government was less rigid than its predecessor but continued to ban political parties and political gatherings. The administration was preoccupied with the security problems associated with the growing communist threat.

A new constitution was promulgated in June 1968 and an election was held in February 1969. Thanom continued as premier. The new government's main political weakness was its inability to control the large number of independent members of Parliament. In November 1971 a plan by the opposition to defeat the government in a vote of no confidence was uncovered and prompted Thanom to stage a coup against his own government. The constitution and the Political Parties

Act were abrogated, and the country was brought under the management of the National Executive Council headed by Thanom. In December an interim constitution was announced giving sweeping power to the government. Thanom continued as prime minister.

In the following months, the government became increasingly unpopular, partly because of its unwillingness to return to democratic rule. The military was also growing wary of Thanom and Prapas, who had built up lucrative networks in business and dominated the succession in the army. In October 1973 several students and former members of Parliament were arrested while distributing leaflets calling for democracy. They were charged with inciting public unrest. The arrests sparked a student protest at Thammasat University in Bangkok, which led to a bloody confrontation between students and soldiers. Many students were killed and the king personally intervened, asking Thanom and Prapas to leave the country. Under additional pressure from other members of the military, the two went into exile.

*Civilian Government, 1973–76*

The king appointed Sanya Dharmasakdi, rector of Thammasat University, as the new prime minister. The Sanya government prepared the way for a period of democracy and civilian government. With Thanom and Prapas no longer on the scene, the military had lost a good deal of its political strength, leaving the country with the opportunity to experiment with civilian-based politics. A new constitution was promulgated in October 1974. Unlike previous constitutions, this one incorporated many of the basic elements of a British-style parliamentary democracy. The Political Parties Act was liberalized, although the Communist party remained illegal. There were forty-three political parties registered for the general election held in January 1975.

The election returned to the House of Representatives 269 members belonging to twenty-two political parties. The Democrats headed the list with seventy-two elected members and managed to form a minority government headed by Seni Pramoj, who became Thailand's first elected prime minister. The new government was defeated in a vote of no confidence in March 1975, and the premiership went to Kukrit Pramoj, leader of the Social Action party, who had engineered the Democrats' defeat.

Some interesting policy initiatives were introduced under Kukrit's government. Thailand reestablished diplomatic relations with China, closed American military bases in the country, and introduced several welfare programs and measures that were to be emulated by subsequent governments. These measures included the rice price support program, the Tambon (district) development funds, and the policy for free medical care for the poor. Kukrit still found the army hostile, however, a problem that later democratic governments were to share. The military became increasingly impatient with the public demand for social change and the growing influence of left-leaning ideologies among students and labor. Kukrit also had to contend with in-fighting among members of government vying for cabinet portfolios. Under pressure from the military, Kukrit reshuffled cabinet members and finally dissolved Parliament in January 1976, when a motion to oust him in Parliament through a vote of no confidence was about to be launched.

The election of April 1976 was unusually violent. A number of farmers, students, and labor leaders who supported liberal political parties were killed. The Democrats again headed the list with 114 elected members. Kukrit's Social Action party won 56 seats but he himself failed to be reelected. The Democrats formed a four-party coalition government under the premiership of Seni Pramoj.

A split developed in the new coalition government when former premier Thanom Kittikachorn returned from exile as a Buddhist monk. Students mobilized in protest against the return of the former dictator, which many of them saw as a provocation to disorder. The situation became uncontrollable when civilian mobs and police stormed Thammasat University to silence the student protesters. On the morning of October 6, 1976, many students were killed and many more arrested. The Seni government was unable to keep order. That same evening, the military staged a coup, dissolved Parliament, and abandoned the constitution. This coup ended three years of civilian government marked by perpetual political turmoil and student unrest and put the premiership and the control of government back in the hands of the military.

The brief years of civilian government had coincided with significant economic changes. New interest groups had emerged and new policies initiated and implemented. An important new development was the involvement of the business class in politics. A number of bankers and well-known business people obtained ministerial portfolios and were able to influence the direction of economic policies. This was a radical departure from the previous periods, when control over policy was shared only by the military and the bureaucracy.

*Military Rule, 1976–79*

The new military strongman was Admiral Sangad Chaloryu, who launched the coup under the banner of the National Administrative Reform Council. The new government, backed by the military, was headed by an ultraconservative lawyer, Thanin Kraivichien. Thanin's strong anticommunist stand and nationalistic attitudes led him to adopt extreme policies, which alienated his government from the bureaucracy, the press, foreign allies, and factions in the army, particularly the army's young field commanders. The administration's emphasis had shifted back toward national security, law, and order and ignored the country's basic social problems. The military became increasingly embarrassed by Thanin's conservative vision. In October 1977 the military staged a coup to dismiss the man they had put into power.

Although Thanin made no major changes in economic policy during his one year of tenure, he did take the important step of empowering the Ministry of Finance to borrow directly from abroad. Foreign borrowing by the Thai public sector dates back to the first railway loans in the period of King Rama V, but Thanin relaxed the administrative procedures involved. It is not clear whether the decision was made to please the military or to facilitate expansion of public investment, but it led to a surge in both public expenditure and the country's foreign debt.

The 1977 coup was again led by Admiral Sangad, who headed the National Revolutionary Council, which took power. Nevertheless, the premiership was offered to an army general, Kriangsak Chamanand, whose soft diplomacy during the Thanin period had made him popular among many sections of the Thai community. The premiership, which was granted under an interim constitution, was to be limited to one year, during which Kriangsak was to prepare for national elections and civilian rule.

The military had been divided over the choice of the premiership succeeding Thanin. Kriangsak's leadership was known to have the backing of the young field commanders in the army and was favored by Washington and Peking because it was thought he could ease tensions in the region. His immediate task was to consolidate power within the military and to ease the tension that had built up during the Thanin period. To defuse the situation, Kriangsak personally sponsored an amnesty bill pardoning all those arrested in the October 6 incident of the previous year and lifting censorship of the press. He concurrently made himself defense minister and reshuffled the military to consolidate his power base. In addition, he appointed General Prem Tinsulanonda commander in chief of the army.

A new constitution was promulgated in November 1978 establishing two chambers in Parliament: an elected House of Representatives and an appointed Senate. The constitution gave limited power to the elected house and preserved military influence in the Parliament through the appointed Senate. The leader of the Senate, who was also leader of the Parliament, was to nominate candidates for the premiership for a vote in a joint sitting. This tacitly brought the prime ministership under the influence of the military and the bureaucracy, which dominated the Senate. The constitution was thus seen by many as a perpetuation of military rule.

*Quasi-Civilian Government, 1979–91*

In April 1979 a general election was held under the new constitution. No single party obtained a majority, and the Senate selected Kriangsak to continue in the premiership, leading a coalition government made up largely of pro-Kriangsak independents. The composition of the Kriangsak cabinet was a focal point for attack by the opposition because it reduced the role of the government's elected members. The regime ran into further problems in February 1980, when it announced a string of petroleum product price increases, which met strong public protest. The parliamentary opposition united over the issue and submitted a parliamentary motion calling for a vote of no confidence. The motion was openly supported by a number of members of Parliament. Unable to control the situation, Kriangsak resigned one day before the scheduled motion was to be debated.

The prime ministership was offered to General Prem Tinsulanonda, a respected army general, who was favored by the military and the main political parties. Prem became prime minister in March 1980. He was not an elected member of Parliament but was able to take the premiership under a constitutional provision that was to produce havoc 12 years later.

The distinctive feature of the Prem government was that power was shared by the political parties, the military, and the bureaucracy. Through the appointed Senate, the military and the bureaucracy controlled the premiership and screened important policies. The prime minister ensured that the bureaucracy maintained its influence in government by controlling three important cabinet portfolios: defense, finance, and interior. The other portfolios were shared among the coalition parties. Although the Prem administration experienced several political crises—which led to cabinet reshuffles, attempted coups, and unscheduled elections—the basic arrangement of power sharing described above remained undisturbed for eight years. Threats of a vote of no confidence and of embarrassing revelations regarding Prem himself led to his resignation in 1988.

Following the election of July 1988 Chatichai Choonhavan became prime minister, the first elected member of Parliament to attain this post since Seni Pramoj in 1976. The Chatichai government presided over the period of the most rapid economic growth in Thai history, but the government itself was widely regarded as corrupt, even by Thailand's generous standards. Civilians were appointed to key economic posts that the military leadership regarded as their own, and the atmosphere became increasingly tense.

## The 1991 Military Coup

In February 1991 the military leadership staged a sudden coup against Chatichai, installing a National Peace Keeping Council to run the country and abolishing the 1978 constitution. The coup leaders, Generals Suchinda Kraprayoon and Sunthorn Kongsompong, cited the corruption of the Chatichai government as the reason for the coup. A more likely reason, according to close observers, was that the Chatichai government had excluded the top military leaders from the benefits of government corruption.

The coup leaders installed a widely respected businessman, Anand Panyarachun, as prime minister. Elections were held early in 1992, and parties supporting the military won control of the Parliament. General Suchinda became prime minister even though he was not himself an elected member of Parliament and had publicly promised not to claim the office. Pro-democracy demonstrators were infuriated. They were led by the former governor of Bangkok, Major General Chamlong Srimuang, who staged a public hunger strike in protest at Suchinda's actions. The composition of the protesters reflected the rapid socioeconomic changes that had begun to take place in Thailand. Unlike the youthful student demonstrators of 1973 and 1976, the demonstrators in 1992 included a high proportion of affluent, middle-aged, middle-class professionals—many reportedly carrying mobile telephones and driving to the demonstrations after work in Volvos and BMWs—but a significant number were indeed veterans of the student demonstrations of the 1970s.

The chaos led in mid-May to a massacre of demonstrators by soldiers apparently acting under the orders of Suchinda himself. Suchinda was forced from office in disgrace. Further conflict was avoided when the king intervened and reappointed Anand Panyarachun prime minister, in preparation for fresh elections. These elections were held in September 1992 and produced a democratically elected civilian government.

*Political Instability?*

The preceding summary of Thailand's turbulent political history would hardly lead one to expect stability of either economic policy or performance to result. But, as later chapters demonstrate, that is exactly what happened. How can it be explained? The facts are indeed puzzling, but four points can be mentioned in partial explanation of this apparent paradox.

First, Thailand's political history has not been as volatile as it may seem. Although power has often changed hands through violence or the threat of violence, the various contending forces have had a great deal in common. In general, political leaders have had to be acceptable to the military, or at least to some powerful factions within it. Most potential political leaders either are or have recently been senior military men. The degree of military involvement in political affairs in Thailand has surprised many foreign observers, as has the public's tolerance of this involvement as a normal state of affairs. Strong military connections are indispensable for aspiring political leaders. This means that politicians espousing views that conflict strongly with the conservative outlook shared by most Thai military men can expect trouble.

Second, partly because of the military factor, Thailand's political parties are not separated by wide ideological differences. Despite the vigorous competition between them, the major parties all agree that it is vital to preserve Thai traditions and institutions, and especially to remain loyal to the present monarch, King Bhumipol. In these respects, the fact that Thailand was not colonized by European powers is clearly very important. Thai traditions and institutions were not eroded or discredited by the militarily superior Europeans in the way that they were in most former colonies. The Thai intelligentsia have little difficulty in identifying with their country's past.

Third, over the past thirty years, most political leaders in Thailand have perceived a potential military threat from communist Vietnam. This has had a unifying effect and encouraged caution in domestic and foreign policy. Thailand also experienced a domestic communist insurgency of its own, which it successfully suppressed.

Fourth, Thailand's conservative bureaucracy exhibits a surprising degree of independence from political control. Thailand has adopted essentially the British system of a permanent and professional civil service. As a result, the Thai bureaucracy perceives its long-term loyalty as being owed primarily to the king, representing the nation, rather than to the current government. This system is in contrast to that in Thailand's near neighbor, the Philippines, for example, which is modeled on the civil service system of the United States. There political appointees dominate the upper ranks of the bureaucracy, only to be replaced en masse when the administration changes.

## Sources of Economic Conservatism

The sustained conservatism of Thailand's economic policy can be traced to a number of factors. Five will be discussed: the desire to maintain a balance of trade, the impact of macroeconomic instability on the livelihood of policymakers, the policy attitudes of senior bureaucrats, the example of China in the 1940s, and the influence of the World Bank's recommendations in 1959.

### Maintaining a Trade Balance

Thai monetary policy prior to 1970 has its roots in the nineteenth century, when all of Thailand's neighboring countries were colonized by Western powers (see Ingram 1971: 170–74). Under the influence of British financial advisers, the country's leaders in Bangkok believed that a sound financial policy would leave the least possible excuse for foreign intervention on the grounds of financial irresponsibility. Thus they favored conservative monetary policies that gave high priority to achieving a balance of trade and to maintaining the value of the baht and its exchange rate with the pound sterling. With the fixed exchange rate system (at 11 baht per pound sterling), the Thai money supply was dependent on foreign reserves and hence on the country's trade position.

The legal mechanism used to control the money supply was the Currency Act of 1928, drafted by Sir Edward Cook, then financial adviser to Siam. Under the terms of the act, baht notes could not be issued unless the equivalent value in gold and pounds sterling was placed into the currency reserve. Thus, the value of the baht was backed 100 percent by the equivalent value of strong foreign liquid assets. Indeed, from 1928 to 1932 it was backed by more than 100 percent.

The composition of the currency reserves was later amended to include sterling securities, U.S. dollars, and dollar securities; however, the amount of gold, foreign exchange, and foreign securities with a maturity of less than one year was at no time to equal less than 60 percent of the total amount of baht issued. In effect, this put a ceiling on the printing of money such that it could not be more than 1.67 times the total foreign liquid assets held in the currency reserves. This principle was strictly adhered to, and in fact the ratio of currency reserves to baht in circulation never fell below 70 percent until World War II.

During the Japanese occupation of World War II, gold and foreign securities deposited in England and the United States were frozen by the Allies, and the value of the baht was not fully backed. In 1941 the government passed the Currency Emergency Act to allow Japanese yen and government bonds to be included in the currency reserves. Thus the rule governing the maintenance of foreign liquid assets came to be upheld by the Japanese yen instead. This provision allowed the money supply to increase rapidly in response to Japan's growing military expenditure in Thailand during the war.

After the war, the large part of the currency reserves that were held in Japanese yen were virtually worthless. Between 1946 and 1947 the ratio of total foreign liquid assets to the total amount of baht issued fell below 60 percent for the first time, and the government had to replenish the foreign assets in the currency reserves. It did so by restricting imports and introducing a multiple exchange rate regime (Corden 1967). At the same time, it curtailed the amount of baht in circulation to match the amount of currency reserves.

By 1958 the reserve position was again stable, and the government passed a new currency act, drafted by Prince Wiwat, then one of the government's financial advisers. It restored the monetary principle contained in the 1941 Currency Emergency Act, whereby foreign liquid assets must be maintained at a ratio of not less than 60 percent of the total amount of baht issued. This principle has been adhered to since that time (see figure 2.1).

**Figure 2.1. Ratio of Foreign Liquid Assets to Total Baht Issued, 1928–89**

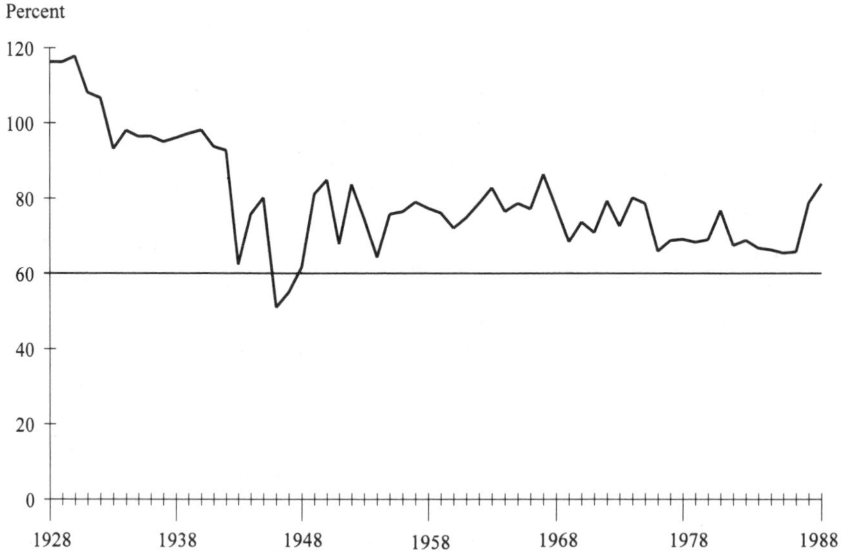

*Source:* Bank of Thailand.

*The Impact of Macroeconomic Instability on the Livelihood of Policymakers*

During the period of absolute monarchy, which lasted until 1932, the majority of senior civil servants in Thailand were members of the royal family or the nobility. Until 1875, they earned their living from collecting rents or from the use of land granted to them by the crown. The area of land granted was based on their position; this system was called *sakdina*. In return, they had to pay taxes on part of their earnings. Under Thailand's subsistence economy, this system provided its civil servants with an adequate and flexible income. The tax burden was proportional to their earnings. Exactly how much civil servants could earn per month is not known accurately because no records were kept, but it can be said that they were well-off. According to an old Thai saying, "It is better to have as patron a single civil servant than ten merchants."

The situation changed with the government reform initiated during the reign of King Chulalongkorn (Rama V). In 1875 tax collection and government budgeting came under central control. Thereafter, civil servants were paid fixed salaries and the *sakdina* was abolished. The salary adjustments were intermittent, however, occurring only when grievances arose, and they were not formally indexed to the cost of living. Indeed, systematic statistical measurement of the cost of living was not introduced until after World War II.

During the rule of King Vajiravud (Rama VI), from 1910 to 1925, the government's financial position weakened, owing to the expenditures required for the king's modernization program, as well as his own extravagance. In 1911 the king ordered that his second coronation proceed in grand style, with foreign dignitaries in attendance, and the affair cost about 4.5 million baht, or nearly 8 percent of the national budget of just over 60 million baht (Terwiel 1983: 295). In February 1912 this lavish spending provoked an unsuccessful plot to overthrow him.

Siam experienced its first financial crisis in the period 1919–22, when the international price of silver rose sharply. As a result, the value of the country's silver coin climbed beyond its face value, and this encouraged the melting down of coins for export. W. J. F. Williamson, the British financial adviser to the kingdom, recommended that the purity of silver coins be reduced, but this suggestion was rejected (Ingram 1971: 155). Instead, the government opted in November 1919 to revalue the baht from 13 to 9.54 baht per pound sterling. Another important event at this time was the fivefold increase in the price of rice, owing to the unprecedented overseas demand for Thai rice after World War I. Between 1914 and 1918 the average price of number 1 White Garden rice had ranged from 5.5 to 7.8 baht per picul (60 kilograms) and then in mid-1918 it soared to 34 baht per picul (Ingram 1971: 156). As a result, the real incomes of civil servants fell drastically in relation to those in commerce.

By the time King Prajadhipok (Rama VII) ascended the throne in 1925, the government was in serious financial trouble. The country was then hit by the Great Depression, and government revenue plummeted from 107 million baht in 1929—30 to 79 million in 1931–32 (*Statistical Year Book of Siam* 1933–35: 26). To prevent a financial crisis, the government began cutting its expenditure and raising additional taxes:

> In February 1932 the financial situation became such that the government, in panic, once more raised the tariff on all goods except those still restricted by treaty. As a result, the prices of many articles rose quickly—by amounts of 5 percent to as much as 20 percent in a month. Port dues, land and house taxes, and the excise duty on matches and cement were all increased. At the same time, hundreds of civil and military officials were retired, and 5 percent was deducted from the salaries of those remaining. (Thompson 1941: 549)
>
> In April 1932 a tax was imposed on all salaries above 600 Ticals (baht) per year. This fell hardest on the small-salaried intelligentsia and brought home to every one the seriousness of the government's financial plight. (Thompson 1941: 554).

Once again the real incomes of the civil servants were seriously affected, although this time the cause was not inflation but a reduction in their nominal incomes. These events culminated in the revolution of June 24, 1932, which brought the absolute monarchy to an end. Although the decline in the real incomes of the civil servants was not the direct cause of the revolution, their discontent made the upheaval more acceptable after it came. They clearly blamed the hardships they had experienced on the financial mismanagement of the government.

During and shortly after World War II, Thailand experienced its only period of sustained high inflation, the causes of which were outlined above. Accurate records from 1933 onward on the salaries of civil servants, the price of rice, and the cost-of-living index attest to the drastic effects the inflation had on the welfare of civil servants. Table 2.1 shows salaries for the lowest-ranking and the highest-ranking civil servants, in columns (1) and (2), respectively. For present purposes, the highest-ranking are of most interest. Rice prices are available from 1933 onward. A cost-of-living index is also available from 1948 onward. These two price series are shown in columns (3) and (4), respectively. They are the same until 1948, because the price of rice is used for both series, but diverge after that date. The last four columns show the real salaries of each of the two categories of civil servants, deflated by each of the two price series. These calculations are summarized in figures 2.2 to 2.4.

The story told by these records is very clear. The rapid inflation of World War II and its aftermath were a disaster for civil servants, especially for those at the top. Indeed, to this day the salaries of civil servants, in relation to the price of rice, have not returned to their prewar levels. Moreover, they have never recovered their former position in relation to the wages of lower-ranked civil servants. Not only did civil servants experience genuine economic hardship as a result of the rapid inflation of the 1940s, but corruption also became entrenched. The public standing of civil servants was thereby permanently damaged by these events.

**Table 2.1 A Comparison of Nominal and Real Monthly Salaries of Civil Servants, 1933–90**
(baht per month)

| Date of enforcement | Nominal monthly salaries | | Rice price index | Cost of living index | Real monthly salaries for lowest rank | | Real monthly salaries for highest rank | |
|---|---|---|---|---|---|---|---|---|
| | Lowest (1) | Highest (2) | (3) | (4) | (1)÷(3)*100 | (1)÷(4)*100 | (2)÷(3)*100 | (2)÷(4)*100 |
| 1933 | 20 | 1,000 | 100.0 | 100.0 | 20.00 | 20.00 | 1,000.00 | 1,000.00 |
| 12/28/1936 | 20 | 1,000 | 95.4 | 95.4 | 20.96 | 20.96 | 1,048.22 | 1,048.22 |
| 10/07/1939 | 20 | 1,000 | 106.4 | 106.4 | 18.80 | 18.80 | 939.85 | 939.85 |
| 10/24/1942 | 20 | 1,000 | 218.3 | 218.3 | 9.16 | 9.16 | 458.09 | 458.09 |
| 01/01/1948 | 30 | 1,200 | 2,275.2 | 2,275.2 | 1.32 | 1.32 | 52.74 | 52.74 |
| 05/18/1951 | 30 | 1,400 | 2,422.0 | 2,502.7 | 1.24 | 1.20 | 57.80 | 55.94 |
| 05/16/1954 | 30 | 1,400 | 2,807.3 | 3,071.5 | 1.07 | 0.98 | 49.87 | 45.58 |
| 11/01/1959 | 450 | 8,000 | 3,009.2 | 3,640.3 | 14.95 | 12.36 | 265.85 | 219.76 |
| 10/01/1967 | 540 | 8,600 | 5,064.2 | 4,438.9 | 10.66 | 12.17 | 169.82 | 193.74 |
| 06/01/1973 | 600 | 8,600 | 5,504.6 | 5,528.7 | 10.90 | 10.85 | 156.23 | 155.55 |
| 01/01/1974 | 750 | 9,855 | 7,486.2 | 6,816.5 | 10.02 | 11.00 | 131.64 | 144.58 |
| 10/09/1975 | 750 | 10,900 | 7,871.6 | 7,094.1 | 9.53 | 10.57 | 138.47 | 153.65 |
| 10/01/1978 | 900 | 12,690 | 9,529.9 | 8,780.0 | 9.44 | 10.25 | 133.16 | 144.53 |
| 01/01/1980 | 1,080 | 15,225 | 11,339.4 | 11,608.1 | 9.52 | 9.30 | 134.27 | 131.16 |
| 01/01/1982 | 1,255 | 17,745 | 14,110.1 | 13,871.9 | 8.89 | 9.05 | 125.76 | 127.92 |
| 01/01/1989 | 2,100 | 25,000 | 17,284.4 | 17,170.9 | 12.15 | 12.23 | 144.64 | 145.60 |
| 04/01/1990 | 2,350 | 30,600 | 18,183.5 | 18,308.5 | 12.92 | 12.84 | 168.28 | 167.14 |

Note: The cost of living index before 1948 was calculated on the basis of the rice price index.
Source: Thailand, Ministry of Finance (1990); and National Statistical Office, Statistical Yearbook of Thailand, various issues.

**Figure 2.2. Nominal Salaries of the Highest and Lowest Rank of Civil Servants, 1909–90**

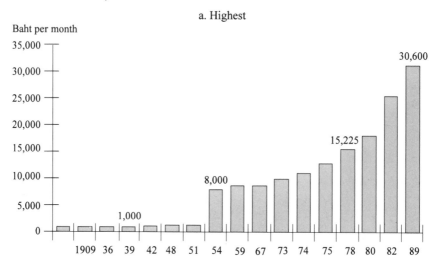

a. Highest

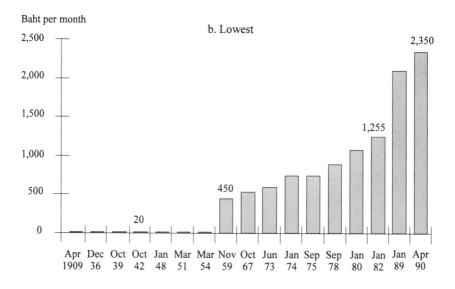

b. Lowest

*Source:* Table 2.1.

**Figure 2.3. Real Salaries of the Highest and Lowest Rank of Civil Servants Adjusted by the Rice Price Index, 1909–90**

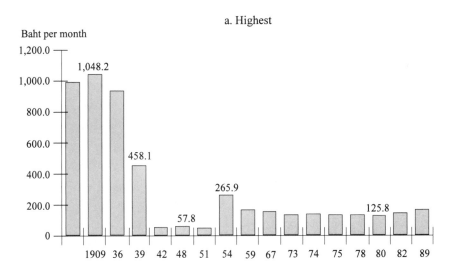

a. Highest

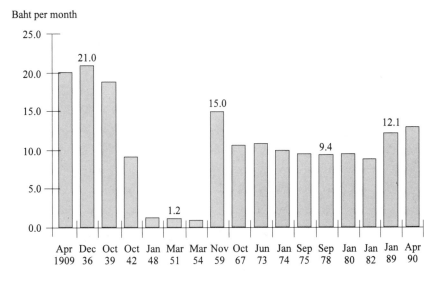

b. Lowest

*Source:* Table 2.1.

**Figure 2.4.  Real Salaries of the Highest and Lowest Rank of Civil Servants
Adjusted by the Cost-of-Living Index, 1909–90**

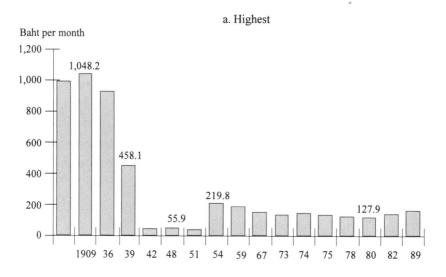

a. Highest

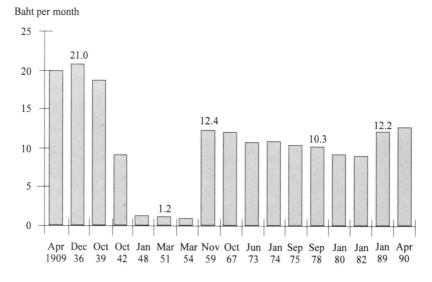

b. Lowest

*The Policy Attitudes of Senior Bureaucrats*

The preference for conservative economic policies among senior bureaucrats is particularly evident in Thailand's monetary affairs. Among those who espoused conservatism in monetary matters were two of the most influential governors of the Bank of Thailand: Prince Wiwat, who, as already mentioned, was the first governor of the bank and a long-time financial adviser to the government; and Dr. Puey Ungphakorn, the longest-serving governor of the central bank, who held office from 1959 to 1971.

In an August 1944 report to the finance minister on postwar monetary reconstruction, Prince Wiwat stated that it was urgent to restore the stability of the currency before World War II ended.[4] Inflation had to be slowed down, he argued, in order to restore the internal stability of the financial system. An informed student of history, he pointed to the hyperinflation in Germany after World War I as an example of the catastrophic consequences of failing to make such an adjustment immediately after a war. This warning, not made public in Thailand at the time, reflected Prince Wiwat's study for degrees in history in England and France between 1913 and 1920.

Dr. Puey Ungphakorn's conservative views are best revealed by his rule of thumb for managing the monetary policy of the Bank of Thailand. He described his rule in a lecture at Thammasat University in 1969: the rate of monetary growth, he stated, should be limited to 2 to 3 percent above the GNP growth rate.[5] In his view, economic stability was more desirable than rapid growth. This conservative monetary approach appears to have derived from Dr. Puey's egalitarian outlook and his belief that high inflation would lead to an inequitable distribution of wealth.

*The Example of China in the 1940s*

Until the Communist victory in China in 1949, connections between the Chinese business and professional elite in Thailand and China itself were very close. Many of the Chinese elite in Thailand were sent to China for their education. China fell to the Communists, however, following the ravages of World War II and the inability of the Kuomintang government to control the ensuing inflation. The Communists promised to stop the hyperinflation and subsequently did so, albeit brutally. What effect, if any, did these events have on postwar policymaking in Thailand?

Members of the ruling elite in Thailand were acutely aware of events in China, in part because their own country was also experiencing rapid inflation. Thus it would seem logical to suppose that they, along with Thailand's Chinese business owners, feared a similar Communist insurrection within Thailand. But the lack of clear evidence of such a connection suggests that any such link was probably minor. The domestic factors described above were apparently much more important.

*The Influence of the World Bank's 1959 Recommendations*

At the request of the Thai government, the World Bank sent a mission to Thailand in 1957–58 to help the authorities formulate a public development program. Many of the mission's recommendations (see World Bank 1959) were subsequently adopted. As discussed earlier, one suggestion was that the government should shift the emphasis in its economic activities from direct involvement in industrial production through public enterprises to the provision of public infrastructure. Additional recommendations relating to sound fiscal management and effective control of the banking system are especially important for the present discussion.

First, the World Bank mission recommended a strict procedure of budgetary appropriation and disbursement. Under earlier practices, politicians often failed to adhere to budgetary appropriations for particular purposes. Expenditures in excess of appropriations were usually debited against a suspense account until they received legal authorization in the future budget. The Budget Bureau was established in 1959 independently of the Ministry of Finance to control the budgeting of all government departments. The procedure for annual budget appropriations was governed by the Annual Appropriation Act, and extra expenditure was not allowed without the approval of Parliament. Budgetary accounting and fiscal reporting functions were consolidated and were required to provide the government with up-to-date information on its fiscal position.

Second, in the area of banking, the mission recommended that authority over the supervision and control of the commercial banks be transferred from the Ministry of Finance to the Bank of Thailand and that the control be tightened. Previously, the commercial banks had been rife with shady practices and with dubious political connections between the banks' executives and politicians. This led to the Commercial Banking Act of 1962, which empowered the Bank of Thailand to monitor and supervise the commercial banks. The new act also aimed at preventing the commercial banks from becoming involved in political dealings that could lead to irresponsible banking practices. For example, it banned commercial banks from lending money to their directors. It also required commercial banks to maintain cash reserve ratios between 5 and 50 percent of their total deposits, the actual rate to be announced by the Bank of Thailand. The ratio was eventually set at 6 percent of total deposits.

Third, the mission recommended that the currency reserve be used for development purposes and that the Currency Act of 1928 be revised to this end. That act had been passed to ensure sound management of the currency reserve and thus required at least 60 percent of the total baht issued and circulated to be backed up by an equivalent value of foreign liquid assets in terms of gold, foreign currency, or foreign securities with maturity of less than one year. The mission argued that although this principle had proved successful in earlier decades, it was was now too conservative. It recommended that the government be authorized to use the currency reserve for development of the country. In 1958 the government passed a new currency act relaxing the restriction on the maturity of foreign securities to a period of not less than three years. But the 60 percent rule governing money issued and circulated remained in place.

It must be emphasized that the World Bank's recommendations would not have been greeted with such approval had they not suited the purposes of the Sarit government. Nevertheless, the package of recommendations clearly had an effect, which was still apparent more than three decades later.

## Conclusions

This chapter has summarized Thai political history since the founding of Bangkok with a view to explaining the origins of the conservative outlook underlying Thailand's economic policies. Thai views on economic policy have their roots in the traditional attitudes of the country's ruling elites. The Thai aristocracy of the nineteenth and early twentieth centuries held a virtual monopoly on government affairs. Avoiding domination by the European colonial powers and maintaining the existing social order domestically were given overriding priority. Financial stability at home was seen as a necessary means to those ends. The government's domestic economic role was severely constrained by these attitudes, which continued well into the twentieth century.

At least until the late 1950s this conservatism had largely achieved its objectives, but it had also retarded Thailand's economic growth. As explained in chapter 3, output per capita over the entire preceding century had remained at a virtual standstill. The neglect of public infrastructure was without doubt a leading cause of the country's poor economic performance. The change of attitude in the late 1950s was to have dramatic economic consequences.

During the Japanese occupation of World War II and shortly thereafter, Thailand had its sole experience of hyperinflation. The effects were devastating for many groups, above all for the country's civil servants. This experience, which occurred almost at the same time as the founding of Thailand's central bank, had long-lasting effects on the attitudes of the country's economic policymakers, especially in regard to monetary policy. It is not surprising that their overriding policy concern in subsequent years was to avoid inflation.

# Chapter Three

# The Economic Setting: Structure and Performance of the Thai Economy

This chapter provides a profile of the contemporary Thai economy and its recent economic performance. It focuses on three main topics: Thailand's social character, market structure, and economic performance.

## Social Character

The discussion opens with the characteristics of the Thai population and some significant social indicators.

### Population

As of mid-1990, the population of Thailand was 56 million. Between 1980 and 1990 the population grew at an average annual rate of 1.8 percent, a reduction from 2.7 percent over the decade before. Population density was 107 persons per square kilometer of total area and 275 persons per square kilometer of cultivable land. In 1990 the urban population was 23 percent of the total, compared with 13 percent in 1965, and 69 percent of the population worked in agriculture, compared with 6 percent in industry and 25 percent in services. The corresponding data for 1965 were 82 percent in agriculture, 5 percent in industry, and 13 percent in services. The degree of urbanization in Thailand is unusually low among countries in its income group, and the importance of agriculture in total employment is high. Even more unusual is the degree to which the urban population is concentrated in a single city, Bangkok.

In 1990, 60 percent of the population were of working age (fifteen to sixty-four years), compared with 50 percent in 1965. Life expectancy at birth was sixty-three years for males and sixty-seven for females, which represented an increase of about nine years each from 1965. The crude birth rate and crude death rates in 1990 were 22 and 7 per thousand, respectively, compared with 43 and 12 per thousand, respectively, in 1965.

The majority of the Thai population is Buddhist, but Islam is an important force in the southern provinces. There is a large population of Chinese origin, which, as mentioned in chapter 2, is concentrated in Bangkok. Ethnic and religious conflicts have occurred but are of minor importance by international standards.

*Social Indicators*

Table 3.1 provides social data on Thailand in comparison with other selected Asian countries. Thailand's adult literacy rate in 1990 was 93 percent. In 1988–89 the percentage of persons in the relevant age groups who were enrolled in formal education were 86 percent in primary school, 28 percent in secondary school, and 16 percent in higher education. The low participation rate at the secondary school level is especially significant. In the Philippines, for example, the comparable statistic reported for 1988–89 was more than twice as high, at 73 percent. In 1965 the participation rates in Thailand were 78 percent in primary school, 14 percent in secondary school, and 2 percent in higher education. Thus it is clear that educational investment has been concentrated at the higher level, at the expense of secondary school education.

Thailand's infant mortality rate—not reported in table 3.1—was 27 per thousand live births in 1990, compared with 90 per thousand in 1965. The rate in the Philippines was 41 and 73 per thousand, respectively. In 1988 the percentage share of household income by quintile, beginning with the lowest level, was 4.0, 8.1, 12.5, 20.5, and 54.9. The percentage share of the highest 10 percent was 34.8. Comparable data for the Philippines (relating to 1985) were 5.2, 8.9, 13.2, 20.2, and 52.5, with the highest 10 percent having a 37.0 percent share. These data suggest a marginally more unequal distribution in Thailand than in the Philippines. The Gini coefficients reported in table 3.1 also suggest this conclusion (the higher the Gini coefficient, the more unequal the distribution). Thai data for 1981 suggest a somewhat less unequal distribution than the above Philippine data or the 1988 Thai data. Income inequality in Thailand appears to be widening. The data in table 3.1 also show that poverty in Thailand, as in most Asian countries, is particularly concentrated in rural areas.

## Market Structure

To understand the market structure of the Thai economy, one must look at the macroeconomic environment as well as the structure of the country's product, labor, and financial markets.

**Table 3.1 Basic Social Indicators for Thailand and Some other East Asian Countries, 1965–90**
*(percent unless otherwise indicated)*

| Country | Average annual growth of population 1980–90 | GNP per capita (U.S. dollars) 1990 | Average annual growth of real GNP per capita 1965–90 | Average annual rate of inflation 1965–90 | Life expectancy at birth 1990 (years) | Employment[a] (1986–89) Agriculture | Employment[a] (1986–89) Industry | Employment[a] (1986–89) Services |
|---|---|---|---|---|---|---|---|---|
| China | 1.4 | 370 | 5.8 | 2.1 | 70 | 74 | 14 | 13 |
| India | 2.1 | 350 | 1.9 | 7.7 | 59 | 63 | 11 | 27 |
| Indonesia | 1.8 | 570 | 4.5 | 24.7 | 62 | 54 | 8 | 38 |
| Korea, Republic of | 1.1 | 5400 | 7.1 | 13.1 | 71 | 18 | 27 | 56 |
| Malaysia | 2.6 | 2,320 | 4.0 | 3.6 | 70 | 42 | 19 | 39 |
| Philippines | 2.4 | 730 | 1.3 | 12.8 | 64 | 42 | 10 | 49 |
| Thailand | 1.8 | 1,420 | 4.4 | 5.1 | 69 | 70 | 6 | 24 |

32

| Country | Expenditure on education[b] (1989) | Secondary school enrollment[c] (1988–89) | Urban population[a] (1990) | Percentage urban population in largest city (1980) | Income distribution[d] | | Poverty: Percentage population below poverty line[d] | |
|---|---|---|---|---|---|---|---|---|
| | | | | | Lowest 20 percent share of total | Gini coefficient | Total | Rural |
| China | 2.4 | 44 | 33 | 6 | — | — | — | — |
| India | 3.2 | 43 | 27 | 6 | 8.1 | 0.42 | 48 | 51 |
| Indonesia | 0.9 | 47 | 31 | 23 | 8.8 | 0.31 | 39 | 44 |
| Korea, Republic of | 3.6 | 87 | 72 | 41 | — | 0.36 | 16 | 11 |
| Malaysia | 5.6 | 87 | 72 | 41 | 4.6 | 0.48 | 27 | 38 |
| Philippines | 2.9 | 73 | 43 | 30 | 5.5 | 0.45 | 58 | 64 |
| Thailand | 3.2 | 28 | 23 | 69 | 4.0 | 0.47 | 30 | 34 |

a. Percentage of total.
b. Percentage of GNP.
c. Percentage of age group.
d. Data relate to 1983 (India), 1987 (Indonesia and Malaysia), 1985 (Philippines), and 1988 (Thailand).
Source: World Bank, World Development Report 1992.

*Macroeconomic Environment*

Since the end of World War II Thailand has followed a fixed exchange rate policy, with the baht pegged to the U.S. dollar. The trading system is quite open, but the capital account is less so. Movements of foreign exchange and Thai currency out of Thailand are regulated, although some of these regulations have recently been relaxed. Large conversions of Thai currency into foreign exchange for the purpose of capital export require Bank of Thailand approval.

Until the early 1990s interest rates on both borrowing and lending transactions were regulated by ceilings set by the Bank of Thailand. Interest rates have remained at these ceiling levels throughout most of Thailand's recent economic history.

Wages are officially subject to minimum wage controls, but these controls are effective only within the public sector and among large business enterprises. Elsewhere—in agriculture, small industrial enterprises, and in much of the service sector—the minimum wages cannot be enforced. In any case, the minimum wages seem to follow market forces, remaining somewhat above the wages seen in the small private manufacturing enterprises.

As explained in chapters 1 and 2, Thailand has followed rather conservative macroeconomic policies for most of the past century and for all of the postwar period. Its central policy objectives have been to maintain a stable exchange rate backed by secure international reserves and, above all, to avoid domestic inflation. The postwar policy environment has also been influenced by the relative independence of the central bank, the Bank of Thailand.

The Thai macroeconomic experience since 1970 cannot be understood without considering the implications of its fixed exchange rate, partly controlled capital account, and domestic interest rate controls. These variables determine the extent to which the domestic money supply can be controlled by the Bank of Thailand. Monetary policies appear to have been countercyclical and stabilizing in the past (see chapter 8), which suggests that capital flows are not fully free. But capital market reforms of the early 1990s are expected to enhance capital mobility and hence reduce the Bank of Thailand's ability to exercise this stabilizing role.

*Product Markets*

Like most low- and middle-income developing countries, Thailand has favored product market policies that implicitly tax agriculture and subsidize industry. In the past, the government levied export taxes on several agricultural export commodities, but these have been slowly phased out. Rubber is now the only commodity subject to an export tax. Tariffs and quantitative import restrictions are used to protect part of the manufacturing sector. The production of these commodities is highly competitive, except in the one or two cases described below.

AGRICULTURAL TAXATION. Rice is by far the most important agricultural commodity and a leading earner of export revenue. Until recently, rice exports were taxed by a combination of instruments: the rice premium, which was a specific export tax; an export duty, which was an ad valorem export tax; and a reserve requirement, which was equivalent to an ad valorem export tax. The effect was to keep both consumer prices and prices received by farmers well below international prices. The combined effect of these policies was equivalent to a 31 percent export tax in 1970, using the f.o.b. export price as a base, and a 67 percent export tax in 1973–74, years of very high international prices, which then declined to 13 percent by 1984 (Chirmsak 1984). The rice premium was suspended in early 1986 in response to the low international prices for rice and has not been reinstated.

In addition to these policies, the government assigns export quotas to individual export agents. The effect is to introduce a noncompetitive element into the rice export market. Each year the government announces target prices for paddy, but these are generally understood to be cosmetic. Some farmers are able to sell at support prices above current market prices with funds derived from the Farmer Aid Fund, which are the funds originating earlier from the proceeds of the rice premium. The majority of farmers derive no benefit from this provision.

The notable exception to this general story of taxing smallholder agriculture for the benefit of urban consumers is sugar. Domestic sugar prices are held above international prices. In the mid-1980s, domestic prices were at least three times as high as international prices. The distribution of holding sizes in the sugar industry is not typical of Thai agriculture, in that there are a small number of large farms and a much greater number of small holdings. This distribution is more typical of Latin America than of Asia. The small farmers are dependent on the larger ones for their markets because the large farmers tend to hold the supplier contracts with the large sugar mills. Together, these large farmers and the mill owners form a powerful political lobby.

MANUFACTURING PROTECTION. Although parts of the manufacturing sector are highly protected and inefficient, in general the sector is competitive and less highly regulated than its counterparts in some of Thailand's Southeast Asian neighbors. Thailand does not practice free trade, but its protection levels are moderate and quite stable.

There have been several empirical studies of protection policies in Thailand, most of which have concentrated on estimating effective rates of protection (ERPs)—that is, the proportion by which the overall structure of protection raises the value added received by an industry per unit of output in relation to what it would be under free trade. Unfortunately, these studies have used different types of data, different product definitions, and different methodologies. Some have used official tariff rates, whereas others have used tariff rates estimated from customs duty collections or from price comparisons. It is therefore difficult to compare the results of these studies over time. Nevertheless, the studies do show a similar pattern over the past three decades (their results are summarized in tables 3.2 and 3.3): namely, that the protective system has been biased against the agro-based industries

**Table 3.2    Effective Protection of Industry Groups by Levels of Fabrication and End Uses, 1964–84**
*(percent)*

| Industry group | 1964 | 1969 | 1974 | 1984 |
|---|---|---|---|---|
| Processed food | 47.47 | −32.6 | −19.41 | 7.93 |
| Beverages and tobacco | 215.45 | 241.3 | 2280.55 | 26.50 |
| Construction materials | — | 47.4 | 46.91 | 17.38 |
| Intermediate goods, I | 82.02 | 2.8 | 15.91 | 17.63 |
| Intermediate goods, II | 60.09 | 79.1 | 48.53 | 241.84 |
| Consumer nondurable goods | 70.95 | 32.5 | 90.63 | 23.84 |
| Consumer durable goods | 63.87 | 69.1 | 200.62 | 19.29 |
| Machinery | 37.48 | 30.6 | 30.02 | 32.40 |
| Transport equipment | 118.00 | 34.9 | 353.88 | 45.70 |

*Source*: Estimated rates of protection (ERPs) for 1964 and 1969 were obtained from Juanjai, Supote, and Sorrayuth (1986). The ERPs for 1974 and 1984 were obtained from Narongchai (1977) and Paitoon, Rachain, and Nattapong (1989), respectively. The weights used to aggregate products for 1974 and 1984 were value added at market prices of 1975 and 1985, respectively, obtained from Thai input-output tables.

and toward the manufacture of both import-competing and non-import-competing goods. This is the typical pattern of protection found in developing countries.

Trairong (1970) studied Thailand's ERPs in twenty-three manufacturing industries in 1964 using input coefficients from Belgium and the Netherlands, which he derived from Balassa's standardized input-output table. From official tariffs and the 1962 Investment Promotion Act, Trairong concluded that the system of protection was biased toward consumption goods, followed by intermediate goods, and biased against capital goods (for an English-language summary, see Juanjai, Supote, and Sorrayuth 1986).

Narongchai (1973, 1977) used input-output coefficients obtained from industrial surveys to estimate the ERPs of fifty-eight industries in 1969 and eighty industries in 1971 and 1974. When tariffs were used as the main instrument of trade policy and industries were classified by trade orientation, his results showed that import-competing and non-import-competing industries received the highest protection over the study period.

Pairote's (1975) study was also based on input-output coefficients from industrial surveys, which he used to estimate the ERPs of fifty-eight industries in 1964 and eighty-two industries in 1971 and 1974. The results confirmed that the protection system over the period of study was inward-looking, favoring firms selling on domestic markets. Again, import-competing and non-import-competing industries received the greatest protection. The structure of protection was biased against export industries. When industries were classified by end uses and levels of fabrication, the incentive effects were strongly in favor of consumer goods, especially beverages and tobacco and transport equipment, followed by capital goods (Juanjai and others 1986).

And in a study by Paitoon, Rachain, and Nattapong (1989), ERPs in Thailand's manufacturing sector for 1981, 1984, and 1987 were estimated from input coefficients from the 180-sector input-output tables of 1982 and 1985. The protective instruments covered in the study were mainly tariffs, import surcharges, export taxes, tax rebates and refunds, and royalties. When industries were classified by trade orientation, the results showed that the effective protection was biased against export industries. The non-import-competing industries received the highest protection, followed by the import-competing industries. As table 3.3 shows, over the period 1969–87 the export industries received the lowest effective protection, followed by the import-competing industries, while the non-importing industries received the highest effective protection.

## Labor Markets

Thailand's labor markets can be divided into four principal sectors: the civil service, the public enterprises, large private firms, and small private firms. Average wages are

**Table 3.3  Effective Rates of Protection of the Manufacturing Sector Classified by Trade-Oriented Group, 1969–87**

*(percent)*

| Sector | 1969 | 1974 | 1984 | 1987 |
|---|---|---|---|---|
| Export group | –43 | –35 | 2 | 4 |
| Import-competing group | | | | |
|   Excluding tires and tubes | 54 | 63 | 21 | 39 |
|   Including tires and tubes | (648) | | | |
| Non-import-competing group | | | | |
|   Excluding cigarettes and sodas | 187 | 77 | 53 | 55 |
|   Including cigarettes and sodas | | (812) | | |

*Note*: Products are classified on the basis of Narongchai's studies (1973, 1977), into three groups: export oriented, import competing and nonimport competing, depending upon their trade orientation. A product is classified as export if its export level is greater than 10 percent of its domestic production and if its net export is positive. It is import competing if its import is greater than 10 percent of its total consumption and if its net import is positive. The rest are classified as non-import competing. The 1975 value added at market price of each industry are used as weights to estimate the aggregate ERP of each product group of all years.

*Source*: The figures for 1969 are calculated from Narongchai (1973), those for 1974 are calculated from Narongchai (1977) and those for 1984 and 1989 are calculated from Paitoon, Rachain, and Nattapong (1989).

higher in the first two sectors, but so are the educational requirements for the jobs they offer. The data on wages in Thailand are very unreliable. Under the Labor Relations Act of 1975, trade unions are not permitted in the civil service but are legal elsewhere in the economy. In practice, trade unions are strong only in the public enterprises, which have a long history of labor organization. Many of these firms enjoy monopolies in their industries and have only a single large plant, located in Bangkok. These features make it relatively easy for unions to organize the work force. Large private firms have a history of opposing the formation and operation of unions. In this, the firms have generally received government support. A variety of tactics, including physical intimidation, have been used against workers attempting to organize (Mabry 1984; Hewison 1989). The unions cannot expect much help from the government.

Small private firms, which make up almost all of agriculture, most of manufacturing, and almost all of the service sector, obviously employ the bulk of the work force. The employees are not organized because the cost of organizing workers in scattered small firms would be very high. Labor markets in this dominant part of economy are in general competitive, and wages appear to be flexible, in response to variations in labor supply and demand (Bertrand and Squire 1980).

The evidence presented by Bertrand and Squire (1980) does not support the "dual economy" hypothesis in regard to Thailand's labor markets. Minimum wage legislation exists but is effective only in the public sector and in some, but not all, of the large private firms. As noted above, the legislated minimum wages tend to be marginally above the wages paid by small private firms. The discrepancy is greatest among the youngest, least skilled employees.

Labor in Thailand is quite mobile, but for the most part recent migrations have moved in the direction of Bangkok, where the new jobs have been heavily concentrated. Nevertheless, seasonal migration among agricultural regions is also important (Chalongphob 1993). Although official statistics on unemployment rates are unreliable, open unemployment seems to be a rare phenomenon in Thailand, except among the most highly educated. Chalongphob (1993) provides a valuable discussion of the reasons for high rates of open unemployment among university graduates.

*Financial Markets*

In recent decades the Thai financial system has deepened considerably, with the ratio of financial assets to gross domestic product (GDP) increasing from 40 percent in 1960 to 120 percent in 1990 (Robinson, Yangho, and Ranjit 1991). The number of financial instruments available to both users and providers of funds remains limited, however. As in many other developing countries, Thailand's financial markets include both substantial organized and unorganized sectors. The organized sector can be broadly defined to include all legally registered institutions. The unorganized sector encompasses financial transactions that do not go through organized financial institutions; the most prevalent forms of such transactions are borrowing and lending among individuals and in the rotating credit societies.

Thailand's organized financial markets are made up of eight main financial institutions: commercial banks; finance, securities, and credit companies; specialized banks; development finance corporations; the stock exchange; insurance companies; saving cooperatives; and a variety of mortgage institutions. The commercial banks make up the largest component in terms of total assets, credit extended, and savings mobilized. In 1990 they accounted for 71 percent of total financial assets in the country. The second largest is the finance companies, which began operating in 1969. Thailand has three specialized banks—the Government Saving Bank (GSB), the Bank of Agriculture and Agricultural Cooperatives (BAAC), and the Government Housing Bank (GHB); and two development finance corporations—the Industrial Finance Corporation of Thailand (IFCT) and the Small Industries Finance Office (SIFO). These specialized institutions are either owned or partly owned by the government.

COMMERCIAL BANKS. The financial market is dominated by the activities of commercial banks, which absorb roughly three-fourths of all deposits placed with financial institutions. They are therefore the central actors in Thailand's financial system (Naris 1993). The current structure consists of sixteen local (Thai-owned) banks and fourteen foreign banks. The role of foreign banks is very limited. In 1990 they accounted for only 5 percent of bank assets. Foreign banks operate at a competitive disadvantage in relation to local banks. They must pay a withholding tax on dividends transferred abroad; they cannot be quoted on the stock exchange, since they are subsidiaries of overseas parent companies and thus cannot apply for the 30 percent concessional corporate tax rate; and, most important, they are prohibited from opening new branches. The 1962 Commercial Banking Act restricted entry to the banking business. Licensing permits are required, and only one permit has been granted since 1965. Of the sixteen local commercial banks, one is a state enterprise (Krung Thai Bank), one has the Crown Property Bureau as a major stockholder (Siam Commercial Bank), another is partly owned by the government (Sayam Bank), and one is owned by military organizations (Thai Military Bank).

Over the past two decades, Thai commercial banks have enjoyed remarkable growth. From 1972 to 1986, the total assets of the banking system increased more than twelvefold, registering an average annual growth rate of 19.5 percent. This growth was fueled largely by an expansion in deposits, which has made the structure of bank assets deposit based rather than equity based. Some experts have pointed to this aspect of the current structure as a weakness. The most popular instrument in the Thai banking system is the time deposit, which commands an average share of 73 percent of banks' total deposits. Bank lending, by contrast, is dominated by overdrafts, which account for an average of 50 percent of bank credit extended. The rest is made up of loans and bill discounting, which have average shares of 20 and 30 percent, respectively.

A significant feature of the commercial banking industry in Thailand is the high degree of concentration in ownership. Ownership is dominated by sixteen families of Chinese origin (Naris 1993). Thai monetary authorities consider this concentration to be a problem, and attempts have been made to diversify bank ownership. The stock exchange has been the main venue for transferring ownership. Special legislation has limited the number of shares a person may own. This legislation has proved ineffective, however, as banks have not been able to meet the deadlines for ownership diversification and the deadlines have had to be extended repeatedly.

The Thai commercial banking industry has a cartel-like structure with its sixteen banks organized loosely under the Thai Bankers Association, through which they collectively set the standard rates for service charges and loan rates. Because of this oligopolistic structure, it takes time for all the banks to agree on the same adjustment, particularly in the downward direction, with the result that interest rates (on loans and deposits) respond rather slowly to market conditions. As a collective body, however, Thai bankers possess substantial power in dictating the cost and the allocation of domestic credit and in influencing the effectiveness of monetary policies.

Within the banking system, firms vary greatly in size and market share. This feature is important to keep in mind in any attempt to understand the bank credit market in Thailand. At present, the market is led by four large banks whose market shares in deposits and credit totaled 70 percent in 1990. These four banks are the Bangkok Bank, the Siam Commercial Bank, the Thai Farmers Bank, and the Krung Thai Bank. They dominate the interbank loan market since they are the main suppliers of liquidity for smaller banks and the foreign banks. In addition, they are the leading players in foreign transactions and thus can exert a degree of control on the supply of foreign exchange. Important decisions regarding interest rates and other price-setting decisions in the money market are influenced by these four banks, through the Thai Bankers Association.

REGULATIONS. A number of government regulations affect the financial market, especially the banking industry. The main measures of this kind have been the regulations imposing interest rate ceilings for loans and deposits, the controls on new entry, agricultural credit policy, and compulsory bond holding for branch expansion. The Bank of Thailand adjusts the ceiling rates to keep the domestic rates in line with foreign rates, to alleviate liquidity problems, or to implement monetary policy. Another important stipulation is that the ratio of the banks' capital funds to risky assets must be kept above a compulsory minimum. This measure is designed to prevent excessive expansion of bank credit and thereby to ensure the soundness of the banking system. In some years, this measure has made it difficult for banks to reduce excess liquidity through loan expansion.

A novel feature of monetary policy that is administered through the banking system is the use of rediscount facilities. The basic objective here is to assist high-priority sectors by providing low-cost funds. The rediscount facility was introduced in 1960 to finance rice exports and since then has been extended throughout industry, agriculture, and construction.

Recent financial market reforms have relaxed the regulatory environment significantly. In June 1989 the Bank of Thailand lifted interest rate ceilings on time deposits with a maturity of more than one year. In March 1990 this relaxation was extended to time deposits of one year or less. At present, the only remaining ceilings are on savings deposits and on lending rates.

In May 1990 the capacity of commercial banks to engage in foreign exchange transactions without seeking prior approval from the Bank of Thailand was extended, and capital account transactions in general were subsequently liberalized. From April 1991, foreign exchange accounts could be opened with commercial banks in Thailand for up to $500,000 for individuals and up to $5 million for corporations. Thai citizens were permitted to transfer up to $5 million abroad for direct foreign investment purposes. Furthermore, Bank of Thailand approval is no longer required for the repatriation of investment funds, dividends, and loan repayments.

BANK FAILURE AND RESCUE OPERATIONS. Thailand's financial system has some history of bank defaults. Before 1966, there were two such defaults, in 1959 and 1960. Under the rescue operation, deposits were mobilized from other commercial banks to address the immediate liquidity problem of the troubled bank. The government, through the Bank of Thailand, then organized a new management team to take over the operation of the bank. This procedure has remained the central style of rescue operation until today.

Between 1979 and 1986 Thailand experienced two serious crises relating to finance companies and three cases of bank failure. The finance companies had problems with outright fraud, losses due to stock market speculation, loans without proper collateral, and excessive lending to one's own business or an affiliated one. The financial crises in 1979 and 1984 shook public confidence in local financial institutions and prompted the Bank of Thailand to launch a major rescue operation in 1984. The rescue, which introduced a management-pool style operation, brought ailing finance companies under close government supervision. In 1984, nine finance companies had their licenses withdrawn, seven were brought under the control of the Ministry of Finance, and nineteen were brought into the management pool.

Public confidence in local financial institutions was further shaken by a string of bank difficulties in 1984, 1986, and 1987. In each of these cases, the Ministry of Finance and the Bank of Thailand rescued the failing banks by injecting low-interest loans and reorganizing the management team. Several liquidity funds, which received contributions from other healthy commercial banks and finance companies, were set up in the process as a means of injecting the necessary finance into troubled financial institutions. Toward the end of 1985, a new commercial bank decree was approved by the cabinet that empowered the monetary authorities to deal more decisively with ailing financial institutions. The decree led to the establishment of the Fund for Rehabilitation and Development of Financial Institutions. This fund, which receives interest-free contributions from all financial institutions and is managed by the Bank of Thailand, is designed to be the basic form of concessional assistance to ailing financial institutions.

Private foreign borrowing is relatively free. Although a withholding tax on foreign borrowing exists, it appears to have little effect on the inflow of international credit. Since the mid-1970s, local commercial banks and large companies have used foreign borrowing as a means of adjusting their liquidity positions. This feature makes local liquidity highly responsive to changes in foreign interest rates and the exchange rate. It seems that when the foreign interest rate was high or when there was speculation about a baht devaluation, capital inflow tended to slow down. Capital outflows, while officially requiring Bank of Thailand approval, occur through quasi-legal channels such as transfer pricing. Domestic interest rates, constrained by the ceilings set by the Bank of Thailand, do not rise correspondingly. As a result, liquidity in the domestic money market is tight. The reverse is true when foreign interest rates are low or the baht is strong.

Thailand's financial system is therefore prone to excess liquidity when the world interest rate declines, and this excess liquidity tends to be prolonged. The problem is that local commercial banks have a rather limited portfolio choice because the country's capital markets are not well developed and capital outflow, in the form of investing in foreign assets, has in the past been tightly regulated. Most banks therefore hold substantial amounts of government bonds and investment in short-term money markets such as treasury bills and bonds in repurchase markets. Another factor prolonging excess liquidity is the rigidity in interest rate adjustment, as noted earlier.

THE STOCK MARKET. Since the establishment of the Securities Exchange of Thailand in 1975, the stock market has grown steadily. The market recovered from a crash in 1979, and the ratio of market capitalization to GDP increased from less than 4 percent in 1980 to 29 percent in 1990 (Robinson and others 1991: 22). Confidence in the market was increased by reforms instituted in 1984 to prohibit all insider-trading activities and to improve the supervisory and regulatory framework.

## Economic Performance

Thailand's economic performance can be assessed from indicators such as national income, inflation, balance of payments, foreign debt, and income distribution.

### National Income and Growth

A detailed statistical summary of Thailand's macroeconomic performance from 1970 to 1991 is provided in table 3.4. In 1990, GNP per capita (not shown in the table) was U.S.$1,420 and in the preceding twenty-five years GNP per capita grew at an average annual rate of 4.4 percent, in real terms. From 1965 to 1980, GDP (total, not per capita) grew at an average annual rate of 7.2 percent and then slowed

**Table 3.4  Macroeconomic Summary, 1970–91**

*(percent growth rate, unless otherwise indicated)*

| Year | Real GNP | Exports | Imports | Terms of trade (export/import unit value) (percent) | Inflation (percent) | Current account balance/GDP (percent) | Real money supply (M1) | Total debt GNP (percent) | Total debt service/exports (percent) | Exchange rate (baht/ U.S. dollar) |
|---|---|---|---|---|---|---|---|---|---|---|
| 1970 | 7.4 | 0.3 | 4.0 | 100.0 | 0.8 | -3.8 | 9.7 | 16.6 | 17.1 | 20.8 |
| 1971 | 4.6 | 10.7 | 1.2 | 101.0 | 0.4 | -2.5 | 11.0 | 17.2 | 18.9 | 20.8 |
| 1972 | 5.4 | 26.6 | 13.8 | 111.0 | 4.8 | -0.6 | 17.7 | 16.8 | 17.4 | 20.8 |
| 1973 | 9.1 | 33.2 | 36.1 | 155.0 | 15.6 | -0.5 | 17.9 | 14.3 | 15.3 | 20.4 |
| 1974 | 4.1 | 44.9 | 49.2 | 130.0 | 24.3 | -0.7 | 13.0 | 13.2 | 14.8 | 20.0 |
| 1975 | 5.0 | -7.8 | 3.8 | 116.0 | 5.3 | -4.1 | 11.0 | 15.5 | 15.1 | 20.0 |
| 1976 | 8.9 | 24.9 | 12.2 | 107.0 | 4.2 | -2.7 | 12.4 | 13.1 | 12.8 | 20.0 |
| 1977 | 9.8 | 14.9 | 30.3 | 101.0 | 7.1 | -5.7 | 9.0 | 14.8 | 16.7 | 20.0 |
| 1978 | 9.3 | 21.7 | 15.9 | 102.0 | 8.4 | -1.5 | 17.1 | 18.5 | 17.4 | 20.3 |
| 1979 | 5.9 | 29.4 | 38.4 | 105.0 | 9.9 | -7.7 | 17.0 | 20.2 | 19.1 | 20.4 |
| 1980 | 6.2 | 27.0 | 23.2 | 100.0 | 19.7 | -6.2 | 13.8 | 25.7 | 14.5 | 20.5 |
| 1981 | 5.2 | 14.1 | 14.3 | 87.0 | 12.7 | -7.1 | 6.5 | 31.0 | 14.4 | 21.8 |
| 1982 | 4.8 | 6.0 | -9.6 | 79.0 | 5.2 | -2.7 | 12.0 | 34.2 | 16.0 | 23.0 |
| 1983 | 7.1 | -4.6 | 20.1 | 85.0 | 3.8 | -7.3 | 10.3 | 35.0 | 19.1 | 23.0 |
| 1984 | 6.3 | 14.1 | 3.8 | 83.0 | 0.9 | -5.1 | 5.4 | 36.4 | 21.5 | 23.6 |
| 1985 | 3.0 | 10.5 | 4.6 | 80.0 | 2.4 | -4.1 | 8.4 | 46.9 | 25.3 | 27.1 |
| 1986 | 4.6 | 20.7 | -3.0 | 89.0 | 1.9 | 0.6 | 18.2 | 44.6 | 25.4 | 26.3 |
| 1987 | 9.7 | 28.8 | 39.0 | 89.0 | 2.5 | -0.7 | 24.9 | 35.9 | 17.1 | 25.7 |
| 1988 | 13.3 | 33.9 | 46.1 | 86.0 | 3.8 | -2.7 | 8.0 | 30.1 | 13.7 | 25.3 |
| 1989 | 12.4 | 27.7 | 29.8 | 83.0 | 5.4 | -3.6 | 11.7 | 28.2 | 12.4 | 25.8 |
| 1990 | 10.0 | 14.4 | 28.5 | 81.0 | 6.0 | -4.9 | 8.5 | 31.3 | 9.8 | 25.6 |
| 1991 | 8.2 | 22.5 | 12.6 | 77.8 | 5.7 | -8.6 | 13.8 | 39.0 | 13.1 | 25.5 |

*Source:* Bank of Thailand, *Quarterly Bulletin*, various issues; World Bank, *World Development Report*, various issues; International Monetary Fund, *International Financial Statistics*, various issues, and *World Outlook*, May 1993 (for 1991 GNP only); and Asian Development Bank, *Asian Development Outlook*, 1992 (for 1991 current account only).

43

somewhat to 5.6 percent in the period to 1987. Growth accelerated dramatically in the following four years, exceeding 10 percent in each year.

Agriculture accounted for 12 percent of GDP in 1990, industry for 39 percent, and services for 48 percent. The corresponding distribution for 1965 was agriculture 32 percent, industry 23 percent, and services 45 percent. In the Philippines during the same year, the contribution of agriculture to GDP was substantially higher (22 percent), even though Philippine agriculture absorbed a smaller proportion of the total work force.

From 1980 to 1990 aggregate GDP grew at an average annual rate of 7.6 percent, compared with 7.3 percent from 1965 to 1980. From 1980 to 1990 the annual growth rates of sectoral contributions to GDP were agriculture 4.1 percent, industry 9.0 (of which manufacturing accounts for 8.9 percent), and services 7.8 percent. From 1965 to 1980 the corresponding growth rates were agriculture 4.6 percent, industry 9.5 (of which manufacturing made up 11.2 percent), and services 7.4 percent. The slower growth of agricultural output than of either industry or services is especially important. Total factor productivity growth in Thai agriculture has been slower than elsewhere in the economy (Ammar, Suthad, and Direk 1993), but this is only part of the story. Agriculture has also been releasing vast resources to the rest of the economy through the process of structural change, described below.

Thai national income data before 1970 are considered to be questionable and the NESDB has released a revised national income series for the period since 1970. Thailand's annual rate of GNP growth from 1971 to 1991 calculated from this new series is shown in figure 3.1. The annual fluctuations around the average rate of growth of real GDP of 7.1 percent principally involved external phenomena. Domestic political events have had remarkably little apparent effect on aggregate economic performance. Thailand experienced an export commodity boom from 1972 to 1974. This boom affected Thailand mainly through the price of rice. Exports surged and economic growth rose sharply in 1973. This event was quickly followed by the first international oil price increases of 1973–74 induced by the Organization of Petroleum Exporting Countries (these increases are known as OPEC I). Since Thailand is a substantial petroleum importer, the rise in oil prices slowed Thai growth in 1974 and 1975. Recovery occurred from 1976 to 1978, but the second round of oil price increases of 1979–80 (OPEC II) slowed growth again.

Other oil-importing countries, including the Philippines, were devastated by these petroleum price increases, but Thailand experienced only a growth recession, from about 9 percent to about 6 percent. Having borrowed internationally to finance the increased cost of petroleum imports during the mid- to late 1970s, Thailand suffered again from the high international interest rates of the early 1980s. By 1985 serious macroeconomic problems were evident, as already mentioned.

The boom that began in 1987 surprised Thai observers as much as outsiders. The boom was apparently driven by three principal forces: the depreciation of the U.S. dollar in relation to other currencies and the fact that the baht was pegged to it, which made Thai exports more competitive internationally; foreign investment, especially from two of the present newly industrializing economies (NIEs), Taiwan

**Figure 3.1.  Real GNP Growth Rate, 1971–91**

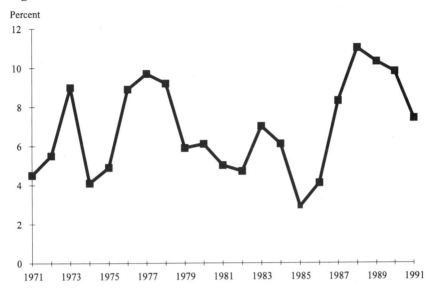

Percent

*Source:* Table 3.4 and authors' calculations.

and Hong Kong, which wished to avoid rising labor costs in their own countries; and continuing low international petroleum prices in relation to those of Thailand's export commodities.

In explaining Thailand's remarkable growth boom of the late 1980s, it would be easy to give too much weight to Thai-specific causes. Similar foreign investment-led booms were occurring in Malaysia and Indonesia, and even more significantly, in the southeastern corner of China, adjacent to Hong Kong and Taiwan. Country-specific factors did play a role, of course. The foreign investment did not flow to the Philippines. Its unreliable infrastructure, labor unrest, and high level of political uncertainty were enough to discourage it.

In focusing on Thailand's recent record of rapid growth, it is also easy to lose sight of the fact that Thailand's economic performance over the long term is very different from this. Long-term changes in Thai real income can be estimated from raw data provided in Sompop (1989). These estimates, expressed as real GDP per capita over the period 1870 to 1950, are shown in table 3.5. These data imply an average growth rate over this period of a mere 0.2 percent per year. Growth since World War II can be estimated more reliably. (Figure 1.1 shows this information for 1951–91, calculated from national income data provided by the NESDB.) In contrast with the century before, the average annual rate of growth of measured real GDP per capita over this period was 4.3 percent.

**Table 3.5    Estimated Gross Domestic Product, 1870–1950**
*(million of baht per year at 1950 prices)*

| Year | Agriculture | Manufacture | Services | GDP | Population (millions) | GDP per capita (baht per year) |
|------|------------|-------------|----------|--------|-----------|-------|
| 1870 | 2,417 | 678 | 2,524 | 5,619 | 5.775 | 973 |
| 1890 | 2,959 | 828 | 3,035 | 6,822 | 6.670 | 1,023 |
| 1900 | 3,222 | 883 | 3,274 | 7,379 | 7.320 | 1,008 |
| 1913 | 4,459 | 1,245 | 4,281 | 9,985 | 8.689 | 1,149 |
| 1929 | 5,735 | 1,603 | 5,749 | 13,087 | 12.058 | 1,085 |
| 1938 | 7,490 | 2,091 | 7,337 | 16,918 | 14.980 | 1,129 |
| 1950 | 10,196 | 2,794 | 9,559 | 22,549 | 19.817 | 1,138 |

*Source*: Calculated from data in Sompop (1989).

Although Thailand has experienced rapid economic growth over the past forty years, it is still a poor country today. For at least the preceding eighty years, and one presumes much longer, economic stagnation rather than sustained growth had been the norm. Figure 3.2 illustrates this point for the period 1870–1990. The figure combines Sompop's data on real GDP per capita for the period 1870–1950 (from table 3.5, re-based to 1972 prices) with the NESDB data for the period since

**Figure 3.2.  Per Capita GDP at Constant 1972 Prices, 1870–1990**

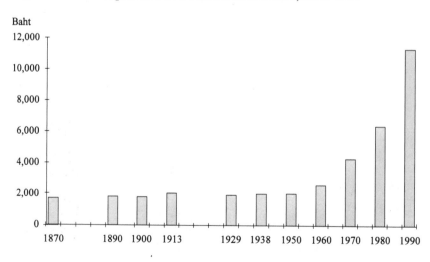

*Source:* Sompop (1989) and National Economic and Social Development Board, Bangkok.

1951, the latter series summarized at intervals of ten years. Economic growth, rapid or otherwise, is quite a recent experience in Thai history.

*Structural Change*

Figures 3.3, 3.4, and 3.5 show the long-term patterns of structural change in Thailand, expressed as the share (at constant prices) of agriculture and manufacturing in GDP and also the share of the agricultural labor force in total employment.

In 1985 manufacturing overtook agriculture as a share of Thailand's GDP. The decline in agriculture's share of GDP coincided with an expansion of industry's GDP share. The share of services in GDP barely changed (figure 3.3), but still exceeded industry's share. Agriculture's share of the total labor force also declined but its fall lagged well behind agriculture's declining share of national income (figure 3.5). The slow decline in agriculture's share of employment was matched by a rise in the services share, but not in that of industry (table 3.5). Table 3.6 shows that the share of services in Thai national output is unusually high.

*Exports, Imports, and the Terms of Trade*

Thailand's external terms of trade (the ratio of the average international prices of its exports to those of its imports) are shown in figure 3.6. From 1965 to 1990

**Figure 3.3. Sectoral GDP Shares, 1965 and 1990**

Percent (current prices)

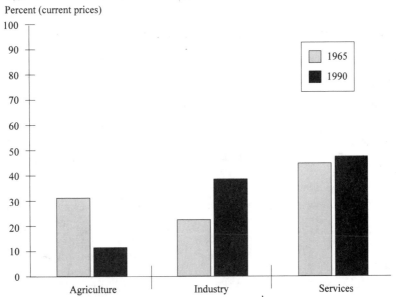

*Source:* World Bank, 1992.

**Figure 3.4. Sectoral Labor Force Shares, 1965 and 1986–89**

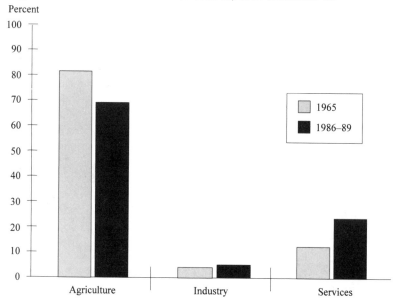

*Source:* United Nations Development Programme, 1992.

Thailand's terms of trade apparently declined from an index of 100 to an index of 65. The index surged upward following the 1973 commodity price boom and then fell significantly with each of the two OPEC petroleum price shocks (in 1973–74 and 1979–80).

The long-term decline in the terms of trade tapered off in the 1980s, and the growth rate of Thailand's merchandise exports accelerated through this period. The composition of these exports moved away from primary commodities and toward manufactured goods (table 3.7). By 1985 the total exports of manufactured goods exceeded those of primary goods, and by 1990 exports of textiles and clothing alone well exceeded those of rice, Thailand's traditional export commodity.

Until the late 1970s, most of Thailand's export industries were agro-based and included rice milling, frozen seafood, and canned fruit, which use agricultural products as raw materials. From 1980 onward, these exports became more diversified, with the addition of canned fish and crustaceans, garments, rubber sheets and rubber products, wood products, jewelry, and footwear. The new export industries—most notably, garments and footwear—tend to be labor-intensive.

We now present a new measure of the export performance of an industry that is designed to reveal the degree to which that industry is competing successfully in international markets. Our index of trade performance is based on earlier work of Balassa and others on "revealed"comparative advantage but is intended to improve upon these earlier measures. We call it the net export performance ratio (NEPR):

$$(3.1) \qquad N_j^T = \frac{(X_j^T - M_j^T)/X_j^W}{X_*^T/X_*^W}$$

where $N_j^T$ denotes Thailand's NEPR for industry $j$; $X_j^T$ and $M_j^T$ denote Thailand's gross exports and gross imports of commodity $j$, respectively; $X_j^W$ denotes world exports of commodity $j$; $X_*^T$ denotes Thailand's total exports of all goods; and $X_*^W$ denotes total world exports of all goods. Thus the index measures the degree to which Thailand's net exports of commodity $j$, as a share of world exports of that commodity, exceed or fall short of Thailand's share of world exports in general.

Table 3.8 shows the value of the NEPR for sixteen industries from 1970 to 1989. The annual trade data are summarized by computing the NEPR ratios over five-year periods to minimize the effect of random year-to-year variations in trade data. According to these analyses, Thailand's agricultural exports continue to perform well. Textiles are also becoming important in this respect, and furniture and nonmetallic

**Figure 3.5. Agricultural Share of GDP Compared with Agricultural Share of Labor Force and Manufacturing Share of GDP, 1960–90**

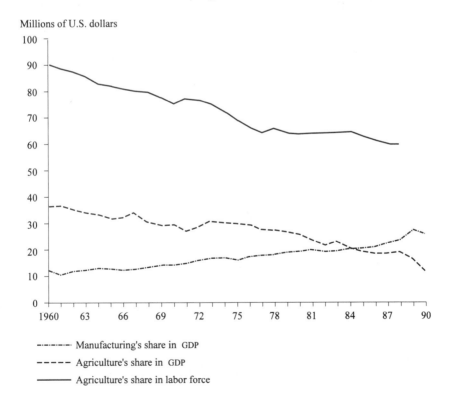

Millions of U.S. dollars

--·--·-- Manufacturing's share in GDP

- - - - - Agriculture's share in GDP

———— Agriculture's share in labor force

*Source:* National Economic and Social Developing Board, Bangkok.

**Table 3.6    Structure of Production: Distribution of Gross Domestic Product, 1965–90**

*(percent)*

| Country | Agriculture | | Industry | | Manufacturing | | Services | |
|---|---|---|---|---|---|---|---|---|
| | *1965* | *1990* | *1965* | *1990* | *1965* | *1990* | *1965* | *1990* |
| China | 44 | 27 | 39 | 42 | 31 | 38 | 17 | 31 |
| India | 44 | 31 | 22 | 29 | 16 | 19 | 34 | 40 |
| Indonesia | 56 | 22 | 13 | 40 | 8 | 20 | 31 | 38 |
| Korea, Republic of | 38 | 9 | 25 | 45 | 18 | 31 | 37 | 46 |
| Philippines | 26 | 22 | 28 | 35 | 20 | 25 | 46 | 43 |
| Malaysia | 28 | 19 | 25 | 42 | 9 | 32 | 47 | 39 |
| Thailand | 32 | 12 | 23 | 39 | 14 | 26 | 45 | 48 |

*Note*: Manufacturing is a component of industry. Except for rounding errors, the shares of agriculture, industry, and services should sum to 100.

*Source*: World Bank, *World Development Report* 1992.

manufactured products show a steadily improving export performance. The relative performance of less highly processed wood products has declined.

At least part of Thailand's export growth can be attributed to changes in policy, but the degree to which this is so is the subject of some controversy. It is true that

**Figure 3.6.  Overall Terms of Trade Index, 1961–90**

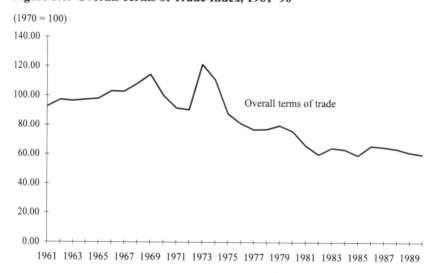

(1970 = 100)

*Source:* Bank of Thailand.

**Table 3.7  Growth and Structure of Merchandise Exports, 1965–90**
(percentage of total)

| Country | Annual growth rate of exports | | Fuels, minerals, and metals | | Other primary commodities | | Machinery, transport, and equipment | | Other manufacturing | | Textiles and clothing | |
|---|---|---|---|---|---|---|---|---|---|---|---|---|
| | 1965–80 | 1980–90 | 1965 | 1990 | 1965 | 1990 | 1965 | 1990 | 1965 | 1990 | 1965 | 1990 |
| China | — | 11.0 | 15 | 10 | 20 | 16 | 9 | 17 | 56 | 56 | 29 | 27 |
| India | 3.0 | 6.5 | 10 | 8 | 41 | 19 | 1 | 7 | 47 | 66 | 36 | 23 |
| Indonesia | 9.6 | 2.8 | 43 | 48 | 53 | 16 | 3 | 1 | 1 | 34 | 0 | 11 |
| Korea, Republic of | 27.2 | 12.8 | 15 | 2 | 25 | 5 | 3 | 37 | 56 | 57 | 27 | 22 |
| Malaysia | 4.6 | 10.3 | 34 | 19 | 60 | 37 | 2 | 27 | 4 | 17 | 0 | 5 |
| Philippines | 4.6 | 2.5 | 11 | 12 | 84 | 26 | 0 | 10 | 6 | 52 | 1 | 7 |
| Thailand | 8.6 | 13.2 | 11 | 2 | 86 | 43 | 0 | 20 | 3 | 44 | 0 | 16 |

*Source:* World Bank, *World Development Report* 1992.

51

**Table 3.8    Net Export Performance Ratios, by Industry, 1970–89**

| Export | 1970–74 | 1975–79 | 1980–84 | 1985–89 |
|---|---|---|---|---|
| Agriculture | 5.54 | 6.16 | 6.43 | 4.43 |
| Tobacco | −0.74 | −0.57 | −0.46 | −0.35 |
| Textiles | 0.20 | 1.24 | 1.77 | 2.16 |
| Wood products | 1.29 | 0.93 | 0.30 | 0.42 |
| Furniture | −0.16 | 0.15 | 0.57 | 1.05 |
| Paper | −0.96 | −0.98 | −0.86 | −0.50 |
| Printing | −0.99 | −0.61 | −0.53 | −0.38 |
| Rubber | −0.65 | −0.49 | −0.33 | 0.04 |
| Chemicals | −2.20 | −2.07 | −1.74 | −1.44 |
| Petroleum | −2.27 | −1.69 | −1.56 | −1.43 |
| Nonmetallic manufacturing | −0.74 | −0.49 | −0.22 | 0.09 |
| Metal products | −0.68 | −0.75 | −0.67 | −1.27 |
| Machinery | −2.18 | −1.95 | −2.06 | −1.75 |
| Electrical machinery | −1.23 | −0.95 | −0.71 | −0.40 |
| Transport | −1.28 | −1.25 | −0.88 | −0.74 |
| Other manufacturing | −0.05 | −0.10 | 0.27 | 0.76 |

*Source:* Computed from United Nations trade data provided by the International Economic Data Bank, Australian National University.

export taxes were reduced from 1976 onward and that some export industries, including textiles and sugar, received assistance from the Bank of Thailand through loans under concessional terms channeled through the commercial banks. Generous terms were also offered for the repayment of concessional export credits. Nevertheless, these policy changes could hardly have generated the growth of manufactured exports that actually occurred.

The rhetoric of Thailand's development plans has led some observers to assume mistakenly that export promotion policies produced the export expansion. Beginning with the Third Plan (1972–76), export promotion was indeed stressed over import substitution in the plan documents, but this change of language reflected more an effort to keep up with intellectual fashion than a policy commitment. The protection of inefficient manufacturing sectors actually increased during this period, as it did through the remainder of the 1970s. The relationship between the government's various instruments of industry policy and the performance of the industries receiving assistance is explored in greater depth in chapter 4.

Between 1974 and 1981 the volume of merchandise exports grew at 11.3 percent, whereas real GDP and the volume of merchandise imports grew at 7.1 and 6.6 percent, respectively. Between 1970 and 1982, agricultural exports as a share of total merchandise exports declined from 71 percent to 64 percent. Nonagricultural primary exports declined from 15 to 7 percent and manufactured exports grew from 14 to 29 percent. Over the same period, total merchandise exports as a proportion of GDP grew from 10 to 19 percent. Roughly two-fifths of this growth was accounted for by primary exports and three-fifths by manufactured exports.

From 1986 to 1990 manufactured exports continued to flow rapidly. Led by the growth of manufactured exports, total merchandise exports grew at an average rate of 25 percent from 1986 to 1990. In the decade to 1990 the share of manufactured exports in total exports more than doubled from 30 to 60 percent. As a share of GDP, the total exports of goods and nonfactor services also doubled over the same decade, from 17 to 35 percent. Exports of textile products exceeded the value of rice exports for the first time in 1985, and only two years later were more than twice as important as rice exports.

Three features of the destinations of Thailand's exports are notable. First, a high proportion goes to developing countries (38 percent compared with an average of 27 percent for lower middle-income countries). Second, of the developing countries, a good number are the fast-growing East Asian countries. Third, of the exports going to industrial countries, an unusually high proportion goes to Japan (26 percent), which also has enjoyed a high long-term growth rate.

Data on the composition of Thailand's imports show a declining relative importance of consumer goods, matched by a steadily rising share of intermediate goods and, to a lesser extent, capital goods (Warr 1993). These changes reflected Thailand's rapidly developing but still early industrialization, which greatly increased the demand for imported intermediate goods. Imported petroleum products consist primarily of crude oil. Their share in total imports rose steeply with the petroleum price increases of 1973–74 and 1979–80 and declined again with the price declines of the 1980s. Some import replacement also also took place, as domestically produced natural gas increasingly replaced imported crude oil through the 1980s (Praipol 1993).

## Inflation

Thai economic policy has been shaped by a strong aversion to inflation. This is especially true of the monetary policies implemented by the Bank of Thailand since World War II. To what extent has this goal been achieved? Figure 3.7 shows the annual rate of inflation for the period since 1938. The data for 1938–48 are based on rice prices, and those for the period since 1948 are from cost-of-living surveys.

After a rapid increase during and shortly after World War II, inflation has remained below 5 percent, except for two brief surges associated with the petroleum price increases of the 1970s. Even then, inflation was quickly brought under control by stringent monetary contractions. It is well known in Thai financial circles

**Figure 3.7.  Inflation Rate, 1938–90**

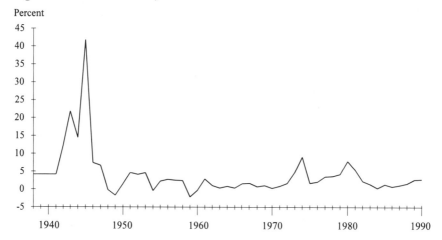

*Source:* Bank of Thailand.  See also data discussion in chapters 2 and 3.

that the Bank of Thailand will contract monetary policy whenever inflation rises above 6 percent and will persist with this policy until the rate falls below 6 percent. Thailand's monetary policy therefore has considerable credibility. Inflationary expectations do not become a serious obstacle to restraining inflation. Thailand's record of monetary management is clearly impressive.

*External Debt*

Thailand avoided the severe debt crises experienced by many developing countries in the 1980s, although by Thailand's conservative standards its levels of debt were still a problem. In 1990 total debt service as a proportion of exports of goods and services was moderately high by East Asian standards (table 3.9). The stock of debt in relation to GDP and the annual volume of exports was large but manageable, because of the high volume of exports. Nevertheless, the level of debt was such that Thailand could ill afford a significant decline in the value of its exports.

Thailand's adjustments to the oil price shocks of the 1970s and the high interest rates of the early 1980s were financed to a large extent by foreign borrowing. Such a policy is sustainable as long as the borrowed funds are invested wisely, so that the loans can be repaid. Thailand has managed to follow this dictum, but the Philippines, for example, failed in this respect, while Indonesia, which is more heavily indebted than either of these two countries, appears to have used the borrowed funds in productive ways.

**Table 3.9    Total External Debt and Total External Debt Ratios, 1980 and 1990**

| Country | Total external debt (millions of U.S. dollars) | | Total external debt as percentage of export of goods and services | | Total external debt as percentage of GNP | | Total debt service as percentage of exports of goods and services | |
|---|---|---|---|---|---|---|---|---|
| | 1980 | 1990 | 1980 | 1990 | 1980 | 1990 | 1980 | 1990 |
| China | 7,972 | 52,555 | 22.1 | 77.4 | 1.5 | 14.4 | 4.6 | 10.3 |
| India | 20,560 | 70,115 | 136.0 | 282.4 | 11.9 | 25.0 | 9.3 | 28.8 |
| Indonesia | 20,888 | 67,908 | 94.2 | 229.4 | 28.0 | 66.4 | 13.9 | 30.9 |
| Korea, Rep. of | 29,749 | 34,014 | 130.6 | 44.0 | 48.7 | 14.4 | 19.7 | 10.7 |
| Malaysia | 5,195 | 19,502 | 44.6 | 55.9 | 28.0 | 48.0 | 6.3 | 11.7 |
| Philippines | 17,386 | 30,456 | 212.5 | 229.2 | 49.5 | 69.3 | 26.5 | 21.2 |
| Thailand | 8,257 | 25,868 | 96.3 | 82.0 | 25.9 | 32.6 | 18.7 | 17.2 |

*Source*: World Bank, *World Development Report*, various issues.

## Balance of Payments

As in all countries operating with fixed exchange rates, Thai economic policy discussion is dominated by a concern about the balance of payments. This preoccupation is almost certainly excessive, but it does act as a restraint on policies that would imply unsustainable external deficits. Thailand's international reserves are satisfactory, in relation to its level of imports and GDP (summarized in table 3.10). In 1990 these reserves were equivalent to 4.4 months of import coverage, compared with 1.5 months for the Philippines, 3.2 months for Indonesia, and 1.9 months for India. For many African countries, reserves are equivalent to less than one month's import coverage.

## Foreign Investment

In the late 1980s Thailand became a major recipient of direct foreign investment. The magnitude of this foreign investment boom is shown by figure 3.8, and data on the net inflows and the regions they came from can be seen in table 3.11. By 1991 the composition of this foreign investment had shifted away from Thailand's traditional sources—Japan, the United States, and Europe—and toward the countries of Northeast Asia. In 1990 Northeast Asia accounted for 60 percent of the $2 billion total net direct foreign investment in Thailand, the Association of South-

**Table 3.10    Current Account Balance and Reserves, 1970 and 1990**
*(millions of U.S. dollars)*

|  | Current account | | | | | |
|---|---|---|---|---|---|---|
|  | *After official transfers* | | *Before official transfers* | | *Gross international reserves* | |
| *Country* | *1970* | *1990* | *1970* | *1990* | *1970* | *1990* |
| China | −81 | 12,000 | −81 | 11,935 | — | 34,476 |
| India | −385 | −9,304 | −591 | −9,828 | 1,023 | 5,637 |
| Indonesia | −310 | −2,369 | −376 | −2,430 | 160 | 8,657 |
| Korea, Rep. of | −623 | −2,172 | −706 | −2,181 | 610 | 14,916 |
| Malaysia | 8 | −1,672 | 2 | −1,733 | 677 | 10,659 |
| Philippines | −48 | −2,695 | −138 | −3,052 | 255 | 2,036 |
| Thailand | −250 | −7,053 | −296 | −7,235 | 911 | 14,258 |

*Source*: World Bank, *World Development Report 1992*.

east Asian Nations (ASEAN) 13 percent, Europe 10 percent, and the United States 12 percent. Japan alone represented only 30 percent, compared with 44 percent in 1986. Rising in importance were Hong Kong (23 percent), Taiwan, China (6 percent), and Singapore (13 percent). These three sources together accounted for 40 percent of the total, well exceeding investment from Japan.

**Figure 3.8.  Net Incoming Private Foreign Direct Investment, 1971–91**

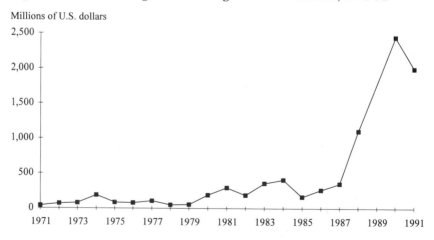

*Source:* Bank of Thailand.

**Table 3.11    Direct Foreign Investment into Thailand, Net Flows, 1980–85 to 1991**

*(millions of U.S. dollars)*

| Source | 1980–85[a] | 1986 | 1987 | 1988 | 1989 | 1990 | 1991 |
|---|---|---|---|---|---|---|---|
| ASEAN | 14 | 14 | 21 | 65 | 109 | 252 | 253 |
| Europe | 45 | 30 | 67 | 111 | 196 | 198 | 196 |
| North America | 84 | 51 | 71 | 128 | 209 | 232 | 237 |
| Northeast Asia | 103 | 159 | 188 | 831 | 1,160 | 1,683 | 1,179 |
| Other | 22 | 9 | 5 | 4 | 97 | 77 | 130 |
| Total | 268 | 263 | 352 | 1,139 | 1,771 | 2,442 | 1,995 |

a. Average per year.
*Source*: Bank of Thailand.

Faced with rising labor costs that were making labor-intensive manufacturing less profitable, firms in established NIEs began looking for new places to invest. Thailand was seen as an attractive host. By 1989 this source of investment had helped boost Thailand's total foreign investment (net direct investment plus portfolio investment) to $3.2 billion (the direct investment was $1.8 billion and the portfolio investment $1.4 billion). This total accounted for 15 percent of Thailand's gross fixed investment. Although foreign investment has become important for Thailand, domestic investment remains far more important (Bank of Thailand 1992).

*Income Distribution and Poverty*

Although the distribution of income and the incidence of poverty are significant factors in Thailand, little analytical work has been done on this subject. Most of the studies in this area have been descriptive works based almost entirely on a single set of flawed and incomplete data compiled during periodic socioeconomic surveys (SES) conducted by the National Statistical Office (NSO). Because the sampling procedures and definitions used by the NSO have changed repeatedly—and there is in any case no standard definition of poverty threshold levels of income—it has been difficult to make comparisons across time. Furthermore, the economic determinants of Thailand's income distribution have yet to be investigated in detail. The question remains, what broad conclusions, if any, can be drawn about the changing distribution of income in Thailand?

The SES data on the distribution of income over the period from the mid-1970s to the late 1980s were presented in figure 1.2. We concentrate on this interval because the NSO statistical definitions were reasonably constant during that time. The proportion of total income received by the poorest one-fifth of the population de-

**Table 3.12    Poverty Incidence and Economic Growth, 1975–76 to 1988**

| Poverty | 1975/76 | 1981 | 1986 | 1988 |
|---|---|---|---|---|
| *Lines (baht per capita per year, constant prices)* | | | | |
| Urban | 2,961 | 5,151 | 5,834 | 6,203 |
| Rural | 1,981 | 3,454 | 3,823 | 4,076 |
| *Incidence* | | | | |
| *Community (percent)* | | | | |
| Municipal areas | 12.5 | 7.5 | 5.9 | 6.1 |
| Sanitary areas | 14.8 | 13.5 | 18.6 | 12.2 |
| Villages | 36.2 | 27.3 | 35.8 | 26.3 |
| *Region* | | | | |
| Bangkok and vicinities | 7.8 | 3.9 | 3.5 | 3.5 |
| Central | 13.0 | 13.6 | 15.6 | 12.9 |
| North | 33.2 | 21.5 | 25.5 | 19.9 |
| Northeast | 44.9 | 35.9 | 48.2 | 34.6 |
| South | 30.7 | 20.4 | 27.2 | 19.4 |
| Whole kingdom | 30.0 | 23.0 | 29.5 | 21.2 |
| Average growth rate of real GNP over preceding period (percent per year) | 5.9 | 7.5 | 5.2 | 11.5 |

*Source*: The poverty incidence data for 1975/76, 1981, 1986, are from Suganya and Somchai (1988) and those for 1988 from Medhi, Pranee, and Suphat (1991). In both of these studies poverty incidence was calculated by applying the rural poverty lines to sanitary areas. The GDP growth rates are calculated from table 3.4.

clined over this period, whereas the proportion received by the richest quintile rose. In other words, the distribution of income became more unequal.

Although increased inequality is generally considered to be undesirable, in this case the widening inequality does not necessarily imply that the poor became worse off, because average incomes also increased over the same period. The share of total income received by the poorest quintile fell from 6.1 to 4.5 percent over the period 1975–76 to 1988, but total Thai income rose in real terms from 5,200 to 9,500 baht per capita in constant 1972 prices, which represents an increase of about 83 percent. According to this calculation, the absolute real income of the poorest quintile rose by 35 percent (from 317 to 428 baht per capita, again in constant 1972 prices), even though the richest quintile gained proportionately three times as much: the income of this group rose from 2,564 to 5,216 baht per capita, or 103 percent.

Absolute poverty can also be assessed by measuring the proportion of the population whose incomes fall below a designated poverty line. Despite the arbitrary nature of any such cutoff point, the change in poverty incidence, so measured, may not be especially sensitive to the particular point that is selected. Measurements of this nature (see Suganya and Somchai 1988; Medhi, Pranee, and Suphat 1991; and table 3.12) indicate that absolute poverty in Thailand is principally a rural phenomenon, with the heaviest concentrations in the Northeast region. As for changes in the incidence of poverty over time, the SES data suggest that from 1976 to the early 1980s the incidence of poverty declined but then worsened until the mid-1980s, when it declined again.

This fluctuating pattern raises some important questions about the impact of growth on poverty. It is obvious that over the long term sustained economic growth is a necessary condition for poverty alleviation; no amount of redistribution could turn a poor country into a rich one. But it is not obvious that growth favors poverty reduction in the short run. Indeed, observers of the Thai economy have frequently asserted the opposite: that economic growth has failed to benefit the poor and may even have harmed them.

When the data on economic growth are plotted against the trends in poverty reduction, however, it becomes clear that—over this period, at least—the faster the growth, the greater the poverty reduction (figure 3.9). Rapid growth from 1976 to 1981 coincided with a decline in the incidence of poverty. Reduced growth caused by the world recession in the early to mid-1980s coincided with a worsening inci-

**Figure 3.9. Poverty Reduction and Economic Growth, 1975–88**

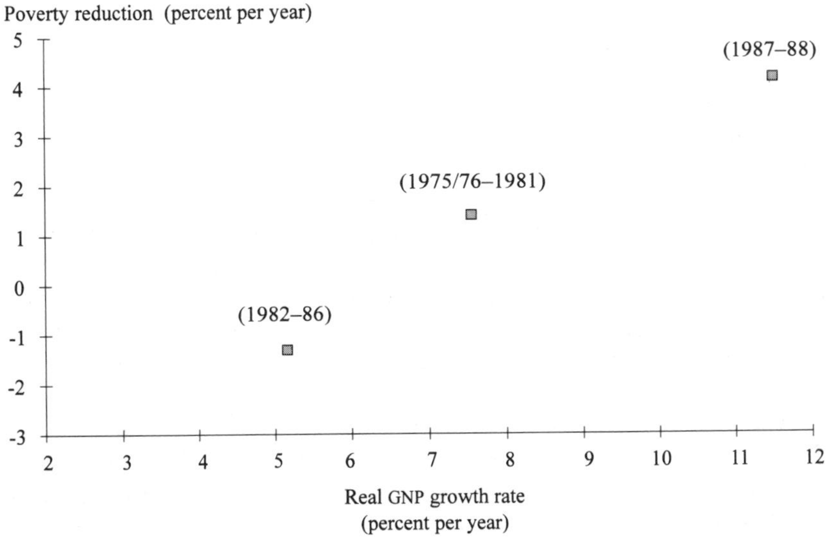

Poverty reduction  (percent per year)

Real GNP growth rate
(percent per year)

*Source:* Table 3.12.

dence of poverty up to 1986. The economic boom of the late 1980s coincided with a markedly reduced incidence of poverty. Of course, it would be absurd to say that rapid growth, and nothing more, is the answer to poverty, and equally absurd to deny that any increase in relative inequality could become a serious social problem. At the same time, the evidence provides no support for the suggestion that rapid economic growth is bad for the poor in absolute terms. On the contrary, the rate of growth may be the single most important determinant of the rate at which poverty declines, even in the short run.

### Appendix: Thailand's Macroeconomic Data Base

The macroeconomic data from Thailand can be divided into two groups: those from the period up to 1954 and those from 1954 to the present time.

*Macroeconomic Data up to 1954*

Official estimates of Thailand's GDP are available only from 1946. These were prepared by the National Income Division, National Economic and Social Development Board (NESDB). These data are shown in table 3.13. Official estimates of GDP at constant prices are available only from 1951; estimates for earlier years (that is, 1870, 1890, 1900, 1913, 1929, 1938, and 1950) can be found in Sompop (1989). These data were calculated at 1950 prices and are shown in table 3.5. The long-term structural change implied by Sompop's data for the period before 1950 and the NESDB data for the period since 1951 are summarized in figure 3.10. The picture that emerges from these data is one of a stagnant economy before 1950 and a rapidly modernizing one thereafter.

The historical series constructed by Sompop was an attempt to study the way the Thai economy was affected by the open international trade environment that resulted from the Bowring Treaty of 1855. On the production side, Sompop estimated the gross value added of each sector. In the sectors where hard data were available, his estimates were based on the actual output minus intermediate transactions. These sectors were rice, rubber, teak, and tin. Estimates for the remaining sectors (other crops, manufacturing, and services) were obtained by extrapolating backward, assuming a constant proportion of value added to GDP in those sectors: 1950 was used as the benchmark year and estimates were adjusted to take into account population growth. Sompop's estimates may therefore understate the degree to which structural change actually occurred.

The accuracy of Sompop's estimates depends on the level of disaggregation and the available data. For the years before 1918, no data are available on the output of other crops and other activities and therefore his estimates may be the only available source of information on these sectors. After 1918, however, data on the output of other crops (such as maize, cotton, tobacco, pepper, and livestock) begin to appear

**Figure 3.10. Shares of Agriculture, Manufacturing, and Services in GDP at Current Prices, 1870–1990**

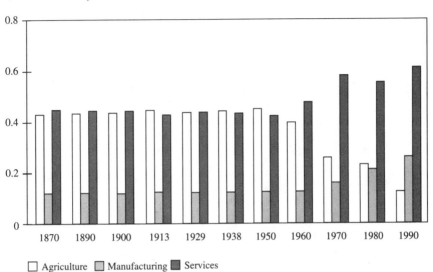

in the Statistical Yearbook of Thailand and can be used to improve Sompop's estimates. According to Sompop, real GDP (at 1950 prices) during the periods 1870–1913 and 1913–50 grew by only 1.3 and 2.2 percent, respectively, despite the expansion of the infrastructure and Thailand's transformation from a subsistence to a market economy in those years. Thus the question may arise as to whether the results would change if the estimation was based on the expenditure approach.

The official estimates of GDP in the earlier years were highly inaccurate. The estimates for 1946–50 were prepared by Joseph S. Gould, national income adviser, who used the expenditure approach. But according to Paul B. Trescott, Gould's calculations understated the actual levels of income and product. He in turn produced "best guess" estimates, which were published in Ingram (1971: 222). Nevertheless, there was only a 5 percent difference between Trescott's estimates and the official ones. Data for the subsequent years were estimated by the National Income Division of the NESDB, but frequent revisions in the 1950s and 1960s made the sequence of statistics intermittent and incompatible year by year. In 1989 GDP estimates were extensively revised and a new series, from 1970 to 1987, published. Table 3.13 shows only the revised estimates from the official sources as compiled by Wilson (1983) for the years 1946–69, and the NESDB new series from 1970.

**Table 3.13  National Income at Current Market Prices, 1946–89**

| Year | Agriculture (million baht) | Manufacturing (million baht) | Services (million baht) | GDP (million baht) | GNP (million baht) | Population (million) | GDP per capita (baht) | GDP per capita growth (%) | GNP per capita (baht) | GNP per capita growth (%) |
|---|---|---|---|---|---|---|---|---|---|---|
| 1946 | 6,272 | 1,146 | 2,915 | 10,333 | 10,333 | 17 | 597 | — | 597 | — |
| 1947 | 9,549 | 1,641 | 4,649 | 15,839 | 15,839 | 18 | 881 | 48 | 881 | 47.7 |
| 1948 | 11,211 | 1,706 | 5,540 | 18,457 | 18,457 | 19 | 997 | 13 | 997 | 13.1 |
| 1949 | 13,332 | 2,545 | 6,322 | 22,199 | 22,199 | 19 | 1,165 | 17 | 1,165 | 16.8 |
| 1950 | 14,650 | 3,239 | 7,706 | 25,595 | 25,595 | 20 | 1,304 | 12 | 1,304 | 12.0 |
| 1951 | 14,139 | 2,901 | 11,170 | 28,210 | 28,220 | 20 | 1,395 | 7 | 1,396 | 7.0 |
| 1952 | 12,944 | 3,288 | 13,289 | 29,521 | 29,549 | 21 | 1,417 | 2 | 1,419 | 1.6 |
| 1953 | 14,018 | 3,714 | 14,496 | 32,228 | 32,164 | 21 | 1,502 | 6 | 1,499 | 5.7 |
| 1954 | 12,830 | 3,778 | 15,436 | 32,044 | 31,997 | 22 | 1,450 | -3 | 1,448 | -3.4 |
| 1955 | 16,568 | 4,648 | 18,232 | 39,448 | 39,334 | 23 | 1,733 | 20 | 1,728 | 19.4 |
| 1956 | 16,586 | 4,970 | 19,533 | 41,089 | 40,929 | 23 | 1,753 | 1 | 1,746 | 1.0 |
| 1957 | 16,990 | 5,510 | 22,948 | 45,448 | 45,195 | 24 | 1,882 | 7 | 1,871 | 7.2 |
| 1958 | 19,099 | 5,229 | 22,843 | 47,171 | 47,021 | 25 | 1,897 | 1 | 1,891 | 1.0 |
| 1959 | 18,964 | 5,831 | 25,651 | 50,446 | 50,310 | 26 | 1,969 | 4 | 1,964 | 3.9 |
| 1960 | 21,463 | 6,759 | 25,762 | 53,984 | 53,885 | 26 | 2,046 | 4 | 2,042 | 4.0 |
| 1961 | 23,111 | 7,727 | 28,132 | 58,970 | 58,877 | 27 | 2,167 | 6 | 2,164 | 6.0 |
| 1962 | 23,689 | 8,997 | 31,107 | 63,793 | 63,695 | 28 | 2,274 | 5 | 2,271 | 4.9 |
| 1963 | 24,564 | 9,653 | 33,862 | 68,079 | 68,039 | 29 | 2,354 | 4 | 2,353 | 3.6 |
| 1964 | 25,008 | 10,435 | 39,224 | 74,667 | 74,589 | 30 | 2,504 | 6 | 2,501 | 6.3 |
| 1965 | 29,383 | 11,978 | 42,942 | 84,303 | 84,292 | 31 | 2,742 | 10 | 2,742 | 9.6 |
| 1966 | 36,921 | 13,910 | 50,459 | 101,290 | 101,282 | 32 | 3,195 | 17 | 3,195 | 16.5 |
| 1967 | 34,641 | 16,663 | 56,990 | 108,294 | 108,462 | 32 | 3,335 | 4 | 3,340 | 4.5 |
| 1968 | 36,616 | 17,851 | 62,307 | 116,774 | 117,046 | 34 | 3,481 | 4 | 3,489 | 4.4 |
| 1969 | 40,321 | 20,141 | 68,104 | 128,566 | 128,792 | 35 | 3,724 | 7 | 3,731 | 6.9 |
| 1970 | 38,163 | 23,503 | 85,719 | 147,385 | 147,606 | 36 | 4,146 | 11 | 4,152 | 11.3 |
| 1971 | 36,666 | 26,934 | 89,817 | 153,417 | 153,279 | 37 | 4,167 | 1 | 4,163 | 0.3 |

| 1972 | 43,130 | 31,311 | 95,635 | 170,076 | 169,467 | 38 | 4,434 | 6 | 4,418 | 6.1 |
|---|---|---|---|---|---|---|---|---|---|---|
| 1973 | 61,523 | 42,643 | 117,944 | 222,110 | 221,238 | 40 | 5,560 | 25 | 5,538 | 25.4 |
| 1974 | 75,420 | 53,475 | 150,311 | 279,206 | 279,112 | 41 | 6,756 | 22 | 6,753 | 21.9 |
| 1975 | 81,521 | 56,636 | 165,162 | 303,319 | 303,306 | 42 | 7,155 | 6 | 7,155 | 6.0 |
| 1976 | 92,460 | 68,186 | 185,870 | 346,516 | 345,632 | 43 | 8,019 | 12 | 7,999 | 11.8 |
| 1977 | 99,970 | 81,432 | 222,127 | 403,529 | 402,252 | 44 | 9,115 | 14 | 9,086 | 13.6 |
| 1978 | 119,638 | 97,658 | 270,930 | 488,226 | 484,604 | 45 | 10,797 | 18 | 10,717 | 17.9 |
| 1979 | 134,148 | 117,611 | 307,102 | 558,861 | 552,636 | 46 | 12,120 | 12 | 11,985 | 11.8 |
| 1980 | 152,852 | 139,936 | 365,721 | 658,509 | 653,115 | 47 | 14,023 | 16 | 13,908 | 16.0 |
| 1981 | 162,987 | 169,461 | 427,747 | 760,195 | 748,160 | 48 | 15,880 | 13 | 15,629 | 12.4 |
| 1982 | 156,839 | 176,360 | 486,803 | 820,002 | 807,072 | 49 | 16,786 | 6 | 16,521 | 5.7 |
| 1983 | 185,628 | 194,344 | 530,082 | 910,054 | 903,353 | 50 | 18,381 | 10 | 18,246 | 10.4 |
| 1984 | 175,190 | 218,050 | 580,172 | 973,412 | 961,961 | 51 | 19,245 | 5 | 19,019 | 4.2 |
| 1985 | 169,895 | 224,456 | 620,048 | 1,014,399 | 996,802 | 52 | 19,583 | 2 | 19,243 | 1.2 |
| 1986 | 178,140 | 258,644 | 658,584 | 1,095,368 | 1,072,931 | 53 | 20,679 | 6 | 20,255 | 5.3 |
| 1987 | 205,592 | 299,327 | 748,228 | 1,253,147 | 1,230,753 | 54 | 23,262 | 12 | 22,847 | 12.8 |
| 1988 | 250,384 | 373,326 | 883,267 | 1,506,977 | 1,482,207 | 55 | 27,420 | 18 | 26,969 | 18.0 |
| 1989 | 266,379 | 453,258 | 1,056,341 | 1,775,978 | 1,752,574 | 55 | 32,174 | 17 | 31,750 | 17.7 |

*Source:* Constance M. Wilson, Thailand: A Handbook of Historical Statistics, G. K. Hall & Co., Boston, Mass., 1983. National Economic and Social Development Board, National Income of Thailand: New Series 1970–1987, Bangkok (1989). National Economic and Social Development Board, National Income of Thailand (1991), unpublished report. National Statistical Office, Statistical Yearbook of Thailand, various issues.

## Macroeconomic Data since 1954

Since the early 1950s Thailand has built up quite a good data system, by the standards of developing countries. The National Income Accounts have been published since 1954. There are regular economywide surveys on employment, agriculture, industry, household income, and expenditure. Information on interindustry transactions in the form of input-output tables has been available periodically since 1980. The data on public sector finance are generally available and are of good quality. Data on international trade, finance, and prices are comprehensive and are published regularly. Data on financial flows (flow-of-fund tables) are also compiled.

The system by which Thailand compiles macroeconomic data was described in detail in an earlier study (World Bank 1979). The purpose of that report was to assess the reliability and the adaptability of the available macroeconomic data to meet the needs of planning and policy analysis. The World Bank report comprehensively reviewed the methods employed for deriving national accounts and identified a number of areas for potential improvement in the method of data compilation. An important conclusion of the World Bank report, which has direct bearing on the present study, was that although the existing macroeconomic data system in Thailand is superior to those of most countries at a similar stage of development, the quality of the data could be substantially improved with a better data base and with refined estimation methods.

The data used in the present study were assembled from a variety of sources, the main ones being the national accounts, the Bank of Thailand's *Quarterly Bulletin*, the government's labor force survey, and the consolidated public sector account. Most of these data are consistently and systematically prepared. The main issue that must be raised concerns data quality. There are a number of weaknesses in the existing data system that should be borne in mind, particularly those relating to the national accounts and the public sector accounts.

THE NATIONAL ACCOUNTS. The national accounts are prepared annually by the National Accounts Division (NAD) of the NESDB. The structure of the accounts conforms closely to the old United Nations standard accounting framework (old SNA). The main problems with the current system are that a rather weak data base is used for preliminary estimation and the estimation procedures are oversimplified. These difficulties are most evident in the derivation of sectoral value added at constant prices, estimates of private consumption and of changes in stocks, and in the treatment of external transactions in the national accounts. Most serious are the resulting biases in the estimation of sectoral value added,which range from 11 to 36 percent in nominal terms. According to the World Bank report cited above, the current national accounts understate true GDP by about 5 to 10 percent.

The recommendations outlined in the World Bank report were taken up in a major revision of national accounts data by the NAD of the NESDB. The revised series for 1970–84, for example, made use of proper weighted averages and indicators and better interpolation techniques. A commodity balance approach was adopted, deflation procedures were improved, and double deflation was used to arrive at the constant price GDP series. In another major change, several economic activities were reclassified to achieve greater consistency and to avoid double counting.

We were fortunate to have access to these unpublished revised data. Briefly, the level of GDP at constant prices in the new series is 5.4 percent higher than the old one, whereas the level of GDP at current prices in the new level is 3.7 percent higher than the old series. This marginally brings up the average overall growth rate (for 1970–74) from 6.5 percent in the old series to 6.6 percent.

The estimated growth rate for agriculture in the new series is lower than in the old series for 1971–76 but is higher for 1977–84. Exactly the reverse is seen for manufacturing. In summary, the new data suggest that the overall performance of the Thai economy under the Second and the Third plans was overestimated, while its performance under the Fourth and Fifth plans was underestimated. The most dramatic change is in the composition of sectoral output. According to the revised national accounts series, the share of agriculture fell below that of manufacturing in 1979, and since then the relative importance in production has shifted to manufacturing.

It is important to take note of the main weaknesses in the old data series, since they may have an impact on one's interpretation of Thailand's macroeconomic performance and problems. First, the level of GDP in manufacturing, construction, transportation, and services was understated (by 11 to 36 percent in nominal terms). Second, the level of GDP in banking was consistently overstated because interest payments to households were erroneously included in banking value added. Third, estimates of private consumption and government consumption were understated. Fourth, estimates of net changes in stocks in all likelihood included errors in the underlying production and consumption data. And fifth, estimates of net factor income from abroad were incorrect because of the erroneous treatment of net wages and salary payments.

PUBLIC SECTOR DATA. The fiscal data used in this study were drawn from three main sources: the Comptroller-General Department (CGD), the Bank of Thailand's *Quarterly Bulletin*, and the national income accounts. The data are on the whole reliable since they are based mostly on actual transactions. The CGD assembles most of the expenditure data by public sector agencies. The Bank of Thailand collects raw data on public finance from various sources and tabulates them in a more refined form. The bank also compiles the consolidated public sector accounts. In preparing the national income accounts data, the NESDB draws heavily on the data compiled by the CGD and the Bank of Thailand in estimating the fiscal activities of the government.

The main drawback of the public sector data is that expenditure items are not always assigned to the same categories and thus are difficult to compare across time. Another problem arises in the accounting of nonbudgetary expenditure and in the estimation of public sector deficits. Theoretically, nonbudgetary expenditures refer to all expenditures not financed by budgetary resources. The basic data comprise the consolidated expenditures of the public sector compiled by the Bank of Thailand. But the consolidated data cannot be directly compared with the value added concept of GDP because they include recurrent expenditures of state enterprises that represent intermediate inputs. Another difference is that the consolidated data pertain to the fiscal year (October to September) whereas the national accounts data are for the calendar year.

It is notable that the national accounts approach and the consolidated expenditures approach give a different impression of the size of nonbudgetary expenditure and public sector deficits. The size of public sector deficits suggested by the national accounts, which do not include the recurrent expenditure of state enterprises, is slightly higher than the figures implied by the consolidated data. This finding is somewhat surprising. The ratio of public deficits to GDP as reflected by the national income accounts also appears large. This may indicate that estimates of public expenditure in the national accounts are overstated. Previous studies of public sector resource management in Thailand have tended to rely on the consolidated data since they provide a basis for assessing the overall size of resource consumption by the public sector. The figures, however, cannot be conveniently related to the existing body of the national income accounts data. In this study, we rely primarily on the Bank of Thailand data.

# Chapter Four

# The Policy Setting:
# Role of the Public Sector

The role of the public sector in Thailand is best understood by examining its institutional framework and the the ways in which it intervenes in the economy. These interventions can be seen in the country's development plans, the fiscal system, sectoral and trade activities, financial market regulations, labor market regulations, the public provision of infrastructure, and the public enterprises.

Although Thai economic policies have been far from laissez-faire, the prevailing view in Thai political circles is that the government should play only a limited role in the economy. This attitude is strikingly different from that generally prevailing in other developing countries. The origins of these attitudes in Thailand were discussed in chapter 2.

By the 1980s, the role and the influence of the public sector—particularly of the core agencies controlling macroeconomic policy—had increased. Although the private sector remained the central source of economic dynamism, the government had become more active in economic affairs. This could be traced in part to a change in political leadership and the perceived macroeconomic difficulties the economy faced, but most of all to the changing intellectual climate in the Thai bureaucracy, which had begun to favor a more active economic role for the government. The government was also responding to demands by the educated general public for the government to take a more vigorous role in initiating and coordinating economic development.

Although the performance of public enterprises had been criticized by the 1959 World Bank report (see chapter 2) and by others, these enterprises remained more or less intact, and the main growth of public sector activity was not in these areas. Instead, the composition of public sector activity shifted away from direct involvement in industrial production toward the provision of public infrastructure and services.

## The Institutional Framework

The foundations of the current system of administration were laid a century ago, during the reign of King Chulalongkorn. The system was modeled along British lines, but it modified the traditional functions of court into a hierarchical system of government agencies, with administrative power assumed principally by the central government. Senior civil service posts were held exclusively by members of the aristocracy. This structure was also undoubtedly influenced by the centralized political structure prevailing at that time. Many elements of this administrative centralization have survived, surprisingly without radical change, to this day.

As noted in chapter 2, an equally important legacy of the Thai bureaucratic system established in the nineteenth century was the attitude that the civil service owes its loyalty primarily to the king, representing the Thai state, rather than to the current government. This attitude is deeply embedded and has been a strong force behind policy stability—some would say inertia—even in the presence of radical political change.

The public sector in Thailand consists of the central government, the local governments, and the state enterprises.

### Central Government

By far the largest public body is the central government. It is made up of twelve ministries, the Office of the Prime Minister, the Office of University Affairs, and seven independent government agencies, including the Parliament and the Bureau of Crown Property. Apart from supervising the work of departments, offices, and publicly funded agencies directly under them, the central government supervises the work of local governments and state enterprises.

The finance of central government is separated into budgetary and nonbudgetary transactions. The national budget requires the approval of the Parliament. Its expenditure is supported by incomes from six main sources: tax revenue; contributions from state enterprises; fines, fees, and proceeds from the sale of goods; domestic borrowing; the issue of new currency; and the use of treasury cash balances. The first three items are budgetary revenues whereas the next three are concerned with the financing of budgetary deficits. Note the absence of foreign borrowing as a source of budgetary finance. Receipts from foreign loans do not appear in the budget, and their control is treated separately.

Nonbudgetary transactions refer to fiscal transactions outside the annual budget. They take two basic forms: expenditure financed by external grants and loans, and expenditure financed by advances from the state treasury deposits. The latter is a special case and requires parliamentary approval, in the form of a special act. Expenditure financed by foreign borrowings is nonbudgetary and therefore does not require this approval.

Three regulations regarding central government expenditure are notable. First, in any fiscal year, the magnitude of any budgetary deficit may not exceed 25 percent of the expected revenue. Second, direct foreign borrowing by the Ministry of Finance in any fiscal year must be within 10 percent of the expenditure budget. And third, foreign loans for state enterprises that are guaranteed by the Ministry of Finance in any year must not exceed 10 percent of the expenditure budget.

### Local Governments

Local governments are the administrative arm of the central government in the provinces. Their administration is the responsibility of the Ministry of Interior, through the Local Administration Department. At present, local governments consist of 126 municipalities, 795 sanitary districts, 72 Changwat (provincial) administrative organizations (CAOs), the Bangkok Metropolitan Administration, and the Pattaya City Administration. The main administrative power rests with the CAOs, whose heads, except in the cities of Bangkok and Pattaya, are appointed rather than elected. Provincial governors are civil servants appointed by the Ministry of Interior. With this direct line of command, the central government is able to control local government administration. Clearly, the Thai system of government is highly centralized.

Local governments have relatively small weight in public sector finance—less than 5 percent in terms of expenditure. Their main source of income is the revenue from local taxes, revenue from taxes shared with the central government, own income from property, fines, fees and permits, contributions from the central government, and domestic borrowings. Foreign borrowing by local governments is legally possible but must be organized on their behalf by the Ministry of Interior. In practice, no such borrowing has ever taken place.

### Key Actors and the Existing Policy Framework

In Thailand's system of government, ministers are formally responsible for macroeconomic policy decisions. In reality, key decisions tend to be made by civil servants in four core agencies: the NESDB, which is the government's main economic planning agency; the Fiscal Policy Office of the Ministry of Finance; the Bank of Thailand; and the Bureau of the Budget (see figure 4.1, in which the core agencies are shaded). Policy decisions at the ministerial level, made either by an individual minister or by ministers acting collectively, usually as a cabinet, rely on information and analyses made available to them by the departments concerned and the core agencies. The directors of these core agencies ordinarily sit in the Council of Economic Ministers. This council is not a constitutional or even legally mandated body, but a subcommittee of the Council of Ministers (the cabinet). It does not have permanent status, nor is its membership constant.

Before they are discussed at the ministerial level, policy options are formulated through coordination and consultation between departments and experts from the core agencies. In recent years, the role and the influence of the core agencies have increased significantly as the government has become increasingly reliant on

**Figure 4.1. Policymaking Structure**

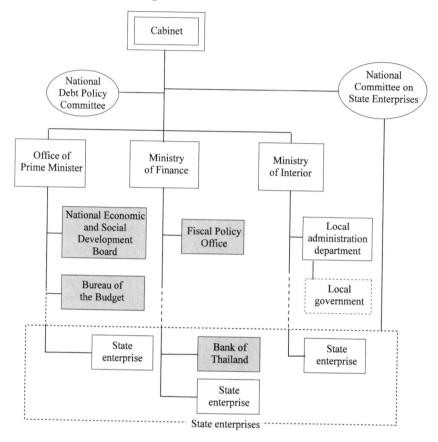

*Source:* Authors' compilation.

them for opinions and analyses. The heads of these core agencies are the central actors in formulating Thailand's macroeconomic policies.

## The Development Plans

Thailand's development plans are best described in relation to the economic conditions existing at the time they were formulated. The documents setting out the development plans are significant, even though they are not in themselves particularly important as instruments of actual policy. Because circumstances change from those anticipated when the plans are drawn up, departures from the plans are both inevitable and desirable. Nevertheless, they do show the way in which policy imperatives were perceived at the time the plans were formulated.

During the 1950s the government became considerably more active in economic affairs. This was in part the result of a change in political leadership and of the heavy influx of U.S. economic aid following the Second World War. In 1950 the National Economic Council was established to provide the government with staff services in economic studies and the analysis of fiscal and monetary problems. In 1954 the government introduced national accounting and passed the first Industrial Promotion Act, which marked the beginning of active government participation in industry. One of the recommendations of the 1957 World Bank mission, discussed in Chapter 2, was that a permanent planning agency be set up to undertake economic studies and to prepare national development plans.

Planning for economic development was formalized in 1959 when the National Economic Development Board (NEDB)—now known as the National Economic and Social Development Board—was established. Since then, seven national development plans have been drawn up. The underlying philosophy of economic planning in Thailand is a commitment to a market economy. Planning has been directed mainly toward securing a smooth functioning of markets with a minimum of direct government intervention or controls.

The First Plan (1961–66) was essentially a public expenditure program that accounted to a moderate degree for the source of revenue and the outlays of the government. The main objective of the plan was to encourage economic growth in the private sector through the provision of basic infrastructure. The principal thrust of government involvement was therefore concentrated on expanding infrastructure facilities in transport, communications, power, social and public services, and agriculture.

Economic growth during the First Plan period was both rapid and broadly based. The annual GDP growth rate averaged 8.1 percent. In sectoral terms, infrastructure and construction recorded the highest average annual growth rates, at 22.3 and 17.8 percent, respectively. Agricultural output also expanded rapidly, at an average rate of 6.2 percent. These rates were impressive by international standards. Much of this achievement was owed to favorable internal and external trends at the time. New attitudes of the government regarding expanded public expenditure, favorable world demand for Thai products, and U.S. military spending in the country did much to promote the success of the plan. During this period, capital expenditure increased at an average annual rate of 18 percent while prices remained fairly stable. Despite an unfavorable trade balance, the overall balance of payments was in surplus because of the massive inflows of foreign capital in the forms of loans and grants. Despite an accelerated population growth rate of 3.5 percent per year, per capita income rose on average by 4.8 percent per year.

The Second Plan (1967–71) was still largely a public expenditure program. It incorporated manpower planning but made no attempt to direct resource allocation among sectors. The Second Plan continued the First Plan's task of building infrastructure, particularly in those areas considered conducive to development. The pattern of public expenditure under this plan revealed the government's increased emphasis on the slower growth areas, especially the rural sector.

The growth of real GDP during the Second Plan was less impressive than it had been during the First. The average growth rate of real GDP was 7.5 percent. Output continued to expand rapidly in infrastructure and services while industry maintained a steady growth rate, averaging 10.1 percent per year. The slowdown in overall economic performance during this period was partly related to the slowdown in foreign investment and U.S. military spending. From 1969 to 1971 the balance of payments moved into a deficit position for the first time ever, also as a result of the decline in direct foreign investment.

Some commentators also pointed to the "disappointing" performance of agriculture, which grew at an average annual rate of "only" 4.5 percent. The decline in agricultural growth was due in part to the droughts in 1967 and 1968 and in part to fluctuations in the world price of major export commodities. This was also a period when the expansion of the agricultural land base virtually ceased (Ammar, Suthad, and Direk 1993) and agriculture was shedding labor to the rest of the economy. It has continued to do so—at an increasing rate—ever since. The 4.5 percent growth of agricultural output per year was therefore a more than satisfactory outcome and was in any case high by international standards.

The Third Plan (1972–76) reflected a moderate shift of emphasis in development thinking. Although still aiming for higher growth, the Third Plan set specific priorities for reducing the growing disparities between urban and rural areas, and between sectors. This shift reflected a growing awareness among NESDB planners of the increasing problems of regional disparity and poverty in the rural areas. The emphasis of the plan was not only on improving public infrastructure and maintaining economic stability, but also on achieving a more equitable distribution of income and social services.

Growth during the Third Plan period was disappointing, however, because of the first OPEC oil crisis of 1973–74, the resultant world economic slump, and the continued decline in U.S. military spending. The GDP growth rate averaged 6.2 percent. Again, this aggregate slowdown was attributed mainly to the performance of agriculture, which grew by "only" 3.9 percent per year. The increase in capital investment by the government continued the momentum of expansion in the country's infrastructure. In spite of the growth of industrial production (about 8.6 percent per year), it was evident that industry was concentrated in Bangkok, was capital-intensive, and thus was not generating sufficient employment. Nevertheless, migration from rural areas to the capital continued to be rapid. It was widely thought that the benefits of industrial expansion were not reaching the majority of the populace. Moreover, it was recognized that the impressive aggregate growth since the First Plan had been achieved at the expense of a rapid deterioration in Thailand's land, forest, water, and marine resources.

The Fourth Plan (1977–81) was intended to address these problems by restructuring the national economy. Its immediate objective was to revitalize the economy from the effects of world economic recession and to implement desired structural adjustments. The plan's objectives for the next five years were formulated in terms of eight development goals: the development and conservation of economic resources and environment; diversification and increased efficiency of production in rural areas; the development of industry; the promotion of exports, imports, and tourism; the development of principal cities and the improvement of Bangkok; and the dispersion of basic services, the dispersion of social services, and social development. The plan spelled out in detail the methodologies, targets, and funding that would be used to reach each of these objectives. At the heart of the plan was an attempt to switch from a growth orientation toward greater social awareness and an emphasis on economic readjustment.

The performance of the economy during the Fourth Plan period was again affected by changing world economic conditions, particularly the rising price of oil following the second OPEC oil price shock (1979–80), high international interest rates, and declining demand and prices for Thailand's commodity exports. In spite of the unfavorable external conditions, the economy did expand satisfactorily. The growth of real output averaged 7.1 percent per year over the plan period. This achievement was partly a result of the government's attempts to maintain the growth momentum by expanding public investment despite a drastic deterioration in domestic savings. The enlarged domestic investment-saving gap was reflected in a serious trade imbalance, and as income from other sources failed to compensate for this deficit, Thailand's balance of payments remained in deficit throughout the Fourth Plan period. As a consequence, foreign indebtedness increased substantially.

To deal with these problems, the Fifth Plan (1982–86) continued to give high priority to economic restructuring, to maintaining economic and financial stability, and to improving the quality of life of the rural poor. This was meant to be achieved by placing more emphasis on the quality of growth rather than the rate of growth. In the process, a reform of the public development administration system was to be carried out to facilitate rapid economic development. The growth momentum was thought to lie with industrial development, whose share of output was projected to reach that of agriculture by the end of the planning period. The main thrust of industrial policy was the promotion of export-oriented industries and the dispersion of manufacturing industries to provincial areas. Such a dispersion was seen as a way of achieving a balance of growth between urban and rural areas. The ambitious Eastern Seaboard Development Scheme, to be located close to the seaside resort of Pattaya, was to have been a central component of this policy. In later years this scheme had to be curtailed substantially.

The years 1982–86 coincided with slowed growth as a result of the world recession of the early 1980s. Largely as a result of the international oil price increases of the 1970s and early 1980s, Thailand's external terms of trade deteriorated from an index of 100 in 1973 to 51 in 1985 and 56 in 1987. Although Thailand had avoided the economic collapse that these external events had produced in other developing countries—including its near-neighbor the Philippines—by 1985 it was experiencing serious macroeconomic problems.

To begin with, the current account deficit in the balance of payments was persisting at the unsustainable level of 5 percent of GDP. The investment-savings gap had reached a similar magnitude. This represented mainly a decline in savings as a proportion of GDP from 20 to 22 percent in the late 1970s to 16 to 17 percent in 1985. In addition, foreign exchange reserves, as a proportion of GDP, had fallen from 12 percent in 1970 to 3 percent in 1985. This required a $500 million standby loan from the International Monetary Fund (IMF) in mid-1985. Its renewal was negotiated a year later.

At the same time, the external debt had risen to $16 billion, which was equivalent to 40 percent of GDP and 146 percent of exports. About $12 billion of this amount was long-term debt, of which $8 billion was public or publicly guaranteed. An additional $4 billion of short-term debt was held mainly in the private sector. The debt-service ratio in 1985 was about 26 percent, up from 17 percent in 1980.

To make matters worse, the government's budget deficit had remained at more than 5 percent of GDP over the previous five years. Total public expenditure for central and local governments and state enterprises was about 40 percent of GDP. The central government just managed to finance its current expenditures from its revenues. Virtually all capital expenditures were financed by borrowing. General government savings had fallen from 3.7 percent of GDP (average of 1970 to 1977) to less than 1 percent in 1985.

The overall rate of growth of GDP in real terms was lower in the 1970s than the 1960s, and lower still in the 1980s. Growth in the years 1985 and 1986 was the lowest of any two consecutive years since the 1950s; but this was a decline from a long-term real rate of growth of almost 7 percent to "only" 5 percent.

The Sixth Plan (1987–91) was drafted in response to the above problems. Its objectives were to

- Promote economic growth to at least 5 percent per year in real terms.
- Improve the administrative structure of the government and review its role. (The private sector was to play a greater role and thereby reduce the burden of the government.)
- Increase the mobilization of domestic saving from both private and public sectors from the target of 18.2 percent under the previous plan to 23.7 percent.
- Continue the privatization process and improve the administrative efficiency of the state enterprises. (The proportion of their foreign borrowing was also to be reduced.)
- Use fiscal and monetary measures to support economic growth and reduce the deficit in the trade and current accounts. (An important fiscal measure was to be the restructuring of the taxation system, which was to increase government revenues and to attract foreign investment.)

From 1986 onward Thai macroeconomic policy adjusted sharply to the imbalances described above. The adjustments included a large fiscal contraction. The fiscal deficit was transformed into a surplus equivalent to 1.3 percent of GDP in fiscal 1988 and to 4.9 percent in 1990. Cuts in public investment expenditure were a major component of this adjustment. Fixed capital formation in the public sector declined by three percentage points of GDP from fiscal 1985 to 1988 (to 5.8 percent of GDP). Simultaneously, Thailand experienced an export boom, concentrated in manufactures.

The boom appears to have been a consequence of two mutually reinforcing events, neither of which can reasonably be attributed to deliberate acts of policy on the part of the Thai government: a 30 percent depreciation of Thailand's real effective exchange rate from 1986 to 1990, resulting from the baht being pegged to a depreciating U.S. dollar; and the international relocation of light manufacturing industries from elsewhere in East Asia—especially Taiwan (China), Hong Kong, Korea, and Singapore, where labor costs were rising rapidly. The magnitude of the boom was as much a surprise to the Thai economic planners as to anyone else. But the reduction in expenditure on basic infrastructure—including roads, ports, and telecommunications—threatened the medium-term sustainability of the boom because these facilities were becoming badly congested.

**The Fiscal System**

The fiscal system can be examined from two perspectives: its methods of raising revenue and handling expenditures.

*Raising Public Revenue*

Responsibility for tax policy rests with the Ministry of Finance, specifically the Fiscal Policy Office. Tax revenue comes from both central and local taxes. In 1990 the ratio of total tax revenue (central and local) to GDP was 20 percent, which is low by international standards. The bulk of tax revenue comes from central government taxes.

Between 1970 and 1990 government revenue in relation to national income increased from 13 to 20 percent of GDP (table 4.1). The composition of tax revenues has changed markedly since the 1960s. Indirect taxes remain by far the most important component, while international trade taxes (import and export taxes) have declined in importance as a share of total taxes but not as a share of GDP. This change has been balanced by increases in the relative importance of income-based and consumption taxes. There is less emphasis on international trade taxes because Thailand has virtually eliminated export taxes and has reduced its average import taxes. An expansion in the volume of imports in relation to GDP partly offset this effect. Because of this shift, the present tax system has become more dependent on indirect domestic taxes. It is significant that, despite the increasing importance of income-based taxes (personal and corporate), direct tax revenues remain of limited importance by international standards.

The main features of the current tax system may be summarized as follows:

- The system is dominated by indirect taxes with a low elasticity to GDP and a small revenue base. As a result, the average tax rate tends to decrease automatically as GDP increases.

**Table 4.1 Composition of Government Revenue by Major Sources, 1970–90**
*(percent)*

| Source | 1970 | 1975 | 1980 | 1985 | 1990 |
|---|---|---|---|---|---|
| Total revenue | 100.0 | 100.0 | 100.0 | 100.0 | 100.0 |
| Income taxes | 11.7 | 16.1 | 17.7 | 21.9 | 24.8 |
| Indirect taxes | 79.1 | 72.4 | 74.9 | 68.3 | 68.9 |
| Other government revenue | 9.2 | 11.5 | 7.4 | 9.8 | 6.3 |
| Income taxes | 11.7 | 16.1 | 17.7 | 21.9 | 24.8 |
| Personal | 6.9 | 6.9 | 7.6 | 12.4 | 10.1 |
| Corporation | 4.8 | 9.2 | 10.1 | 9.6 | 14.2 |
| Petroleum | 0 | 0 | 0 | 0 | 0.4 |
| Indirect taxes | 79.1 | 72.4 | 74.9 | 68.3 | 68.9 |
| Import duties | 28.8 | 21.5 | 20.4 | 19.1 | 22.6 |
| Export duties | 4.5 | 3.6 | 3.5 | 0.7 | 0.0 |
| Business taxes | 19.7 | 20.3 | 19.2 | 18.4 | 21.9 |
| Sales taxes | 16.2 | 18.7 | 22.3 | 23.4 | 17.5 |
| Other taxes | 9.9 | 8.2 | 9.5 | 6.7 | 6.8 |
| Total revenue/GDP | 12.8 | 13.0 | 14.5 | 15.8 | 20.1 |

*Source*: Bank of Thailand, *Monthly Bulletin*, various issues; Customs Department; and Controller-General's Department.

- Personal income tax rates are progressive and have an income elasticity greater than unity. The progressive tax schedule, however, has limited effects on the top income earners because many types of income—including income from bequests and income from interest on bank deposits—are exempt from taxation. As a result, the ratio of tax to assessable income is not steeply progressive.
- Corporate income tax has limited importance, for close to half of all corporations declare losses for tax purposes. In 1984 less than 1 percent of all corporations paid 77 percent of corporate taxes. Without substantial improvements in collection, corporate income tax will remain an unreliable revenue measure.
- Domestic consumption taxes (business and excise taxes) have a regressive structure, and the tax base is small. At present, state enterprises do not pay business tax, and the excise tax covers only nine commodities. This feature makes revenue mobilization costly to the general public as tax rates need to be adjusted upward frequently for revenue purposes. The tax burden is therefore passed on to all consumers regardless of their income positions.
- The relative importance of international trade taxes has declined because the government continues to liberalize trade through tariff reforms and the

abolition of export taxes. Still, tariff rates vary greatly, ranging from 5 to 60 percent ad valorem.

- Direct government transfers play a small role in Thailand's fiscal structure, in part because the country does not have a welfare system. Furthermore, most of the transfers occur among public sector agencies and not between the government and households.

In January 1992 the government implemented a new value added tax (VAT) system. The new tax was designed to overcome some of the problems identified above. The cascading effect of the existing business tax system—the fact that the tax rate effectively increases along the chain of production—was stressed as a reason for implementing the VAT. The rate of the VAT was set at 7 percent, but many industries were exempted, including all of agriculture and any industries producing inputs for direct use in agriculture, such as fertilizer, animal feeds, and pesticides. Businesses with a total annual revenue of less than 600,000 baht (approximately $24,000) were also exempt. Exporters were entitled to a refund of the VAT on proof that the goods had been exported.

Despite the VAT reform, the existing tax system hinders effective revenue mobilization. An important policy issue at present is how to improve the existing tax system so that revenue can be raised more effectively without jeopardizing private incentives and without creating further inequality in the distribution of income.

*Public Expenditure*

There has been a steady shift over time in the allocation of public expenditure between current and capital expenditure (table 4.2). Thailand's badly congested public infrastructure in the early 1990s is partly a reflection of this trend. From 1985 to 1990 public expenditure as a proportion of GDP declined by a full five percentage points—from 20 to 15 percent. Thus in the late 1980s the government experienced record budgetary surpluses, as is apparent from a comparison of tables 4.1 and 4.2.

## Sectoral and Market Interventions

Until the late 1960s, the role of the public sector was confined largely to tax collection, public provision of a limited range of public services, and the commercial operation of the public enterprises. As the economy expanded, the authorities came to see the price system as a distorted and unreliable guide to resource allocation. As a result, direct intervention by the public sector increased. Some of the measures taken were meant to modify the pattern of resource utilization while some purposely added distortions in order to effect a change in the distribution of economic benefits. These interventions have taken place in five important areas of

## Table 4.2 Composition of Government Expenditure, 1970–90
*(percent)*

| Expenditure | 1970 | 1975 | 1980 | 1985 | 1990 |
|---|---|---|---|---|---|
| Total expenditure | 100.0 | 100.0 | 100.0 | 100.0 | 100.0 |
| | | | | | |
| *Economic classification* | | | | | |
| Current | 68.4 | 77.6 | 78.0 | 83.5 | 81.8 |
| Capital | 31.6 | 22.4 | 22.0 | 16.5 | 18.2 |
| | | | | | |
| *Major functional classification* | | | | | |
| Economic services | 29.1 | 25.3 | 18.8 | 15.3 | 17.5 |
| Social services | 26.3 | 29.1 | 29.3 | 29.5 | 31.2 |
| Defense | 17.5 | 17.9 | 20.2 | 21.6 | 18.9 |
| | | | | | |
| *General administration* | | | | | |
| And services | 14.1 | 14.7 | 14.6 | 12.9 | 14.1 |
| Unallocatable | 12.9 | 13.0 | 17.0 | 20.8 | 18.3 |
| Total expenditure/GDP | 17.1 | 14.9 | 18.4 | 19.7 | 14.8 |

*Source*: Bank of Thailand, *Monthly Bulletin*, various issues.

the economy: agriculture, industry, the energy sector (through petroleum pricing policy), trade, exchange rate policy, and regulation of financial and labor markets.

### Interventions in Agriculture

The main impetus behind Thailand's economic growth in the 1960s and the 1970s was the growth of agriculture. By the late 1970s, however, the land frontier was exhausted and agriculture's contribution to production had declined (Martin and Warr 1990, 1994). Nonetheless, agriculture remains the largest source of employment and the largest provider of income for the majority of the population. In the early 1990s, more than half of all Thai households still drew their principal incomes from agriculture.

Although agricultural growth has come mainly from private initiative, government intervention, particularly in the pricing system, has had a considerable impact (Ammar and Suthad 1989). The most important intervention, and the one with the longest history, had been the taxation of rice exports, which in its modern form began immediately after the Second World War and was suspended in 1986. Over these decades, the heavy export tax on rice had depressed rural incomes by reducing the farmgate prices of paddy and the rural wage rate (Chirmsak 1984). It also impeded technological change by altering the price-cost ratio in the rice sector. A high export tax (15 percent of the f.o.b. price) is still levied on rubber (Ammar and others 1993).

The compulsory rice reserve scheme that began in 1973 (a period of rice shortage) and ended in 1982 had a similar effect. Under the scheme, exporters were required to sell to the government a proportion of their rice (fixed in relation to the amount of rice exported) at a price set lower than the domestic price. This system was designed to provide the government with a cheap supply of rice for resale to the general public. The policy was thus similar to an ad valorem export tax and it further depressed farmgate prices for paddy.

The government has also imposed periodic export quotas on agricultural products. In the past, both rice and maize were occasionally subjected to such controls. At present, they apply only to cassava, since the government has agreed to limit exports of this product to the European Economic Commission. The Ministry of Commerce is responsible for the allocation of export quotas, and its allocations from year to year are often politically motivated.

Apart from rice, maize, cassava, and rubber, agricultural products subject to government regulation have included swine, castor oil seeds, and tobacco. In most of these cases, government regulations have introduced monopolistic elements into the markets that have reduced economic efficiency. In the swine market, for example, a condition for setting up a private slaughterhouse is that property rights on land and buildings be transferred to the local government, in accordance with the Animal Slaughtering and Meat Sale Control Act of 1960. In this way, public slaughterhouses, which are managed by local governments, gain a monopoly on the market.

*Interventions in Industry: Protection and Export Promotion*

The structure of Thailand's protection policy was discussed in chapter 3 under "Product Markets." Aside from this, the main feature of government intervention in industry has been the promotion of private investment, administered through the Board of Investment (BOI), which was established in 1959. The BOI uses a combination of various investment promotion schemes, tariff policies, tax regimes, and trade and price controls to direct the pattern of private investment. During the 1960s and the early 1970s, industrial policies strongly favored import substitution. Import tariffs were raised significantly to protect local industries, and the strongest incentives were directed at the production of final products based on imported intermediate and capital goods.

With the passage of the Investment Promotion Act of 1972, the emphasis of industrial promotion policy then supposedly shifted away from import substitution toward exports. Export promotion has since become the central theme of efforts to promote private investment in industry. At least, that has been the expressed intention. The 1977 Investment Promotion Act modified the 1972 act and introduced the promotion of trading companies.

Prospective investors must first apply for promotion privileges and obtain a BOI promotion certificate. A list of industries eligible for promotion privileges is drawn up by the BOI using the national development plan as a broad framework. The incentives offered typically include tax and tariff exemptions, a guarantee of government protection from nationalization and from direct competition by state enterprises, and guarantees of rights of profit and of capital repatriation. The range of incentives differs between the industries, depending on priority rankings in the promotion policy. The promotion policy as practiced has been criticized for its frequent changes, the BOI's use of its discretionary powers in granting promotional privileges, and the extent of the incentives offered, which often differ among firms within the same industry.

In addition to the BOI, the Ministries of Industry, Commerce, and Finance, as well as the Bank of Thailand, formulate and administer policies that directly affect industrial development and are ostensibly aimed at export promotion. The Customs Department provides a scheme for the exemption from or refund of import duties paid on inputs used in the production of goods for export. Because of administrative obstacles to and delays in the actual payment of drawbacks, few exporters actually claim the refunds to which they are entitled. The exemption scheme is also said to be administered in a discretionary manner. The Fiscal Policy Office of the Ministry of Finance operates a comprehensive tax refund system, called tax rebates, for all taxes incurred in the production of goods subsequently exported. These taxes are estimated on a case-by-case basis using input-output methods and information on the cost structure of the exporter. The rebate is paid in the form of tax credit certificates, which can be used against other tax liabilities. The Bank of Thailand provides export-oriented firms with a rediscount facility at subsidized interest rates. The Ministry of Commerce provides technical assistance through its Export Service Center.

The Ministry of Industry controls the establishment and expansion of factories and production plants and the use of local contents in production. At present, twenty-three categories of industry are subjected to factory control, and four industries—motor vehicle assembly, motorcycle production, electric wire and cable, and steel production—are subject to minimum local content requirements.

Like many other countries, both developed and less developed, Thailand has favored supporting infant industries thought to be capable of becoming successful exporters after a short period of protection. An important question to consider is the extent to which this policy contributed to Thailand's record of economic growth, which was led by manufactured exports.

We explore this issue by examining the statistical relationship between the trade performance of industries and the government's interventions to promote them. Our index of trade performance is the net export performance ratio of each industry, as described in chapter 3 and summarized in table 3.8. We are especially interested in the behavior of this index over time and its correlation with measures of industrial policy interventions. The analysis focuses on five instruments of intervention that can be quantified from available data: industry protection, the allocation of subsidized loans through the Industrial Finance Corporation of Thailand (IFCT), the promotion of industries through the Board of Investment, the allocation of tax exemptions by the Customs Department, and the allocation of tax rebates by the Fiscal Policy Office of the Ministry of Finance. The effectiveness of these instruments is assessed on the basis of the export performance of Thailand's leading industries.

Sixteen industries were selected for the analysis. To allow for the fact that these industries vary in size, we divided each industry's allocation of the instrument shown by its share of total value added, summed across all sixteen industries (table 4.3). Thus, an industry for which the resulting ratio exceeds unity receives a higher share of the total export promotion incentive concerned than its share of total value added, and so forth.

Table 4.4 shows the correlation coefficients between the measures of export performance and each of the above five measures of industrial policy interventions. Table 4.5 shows the correlation between the changes over time in each industry's trade performance and the changes in each of the five policy instruments. The results show that export performance is negatively related to all five measures. Moreover, the change over time in net export performance is negatively related to the change in all five instruments. Industries whose export performance worsened over time received increasing levels of support, but those whose performance improved tended not to receive such support.[1]

In the case of import protection, these results are hardly a surprise. Protection is explicitly an incentive to import-competing production and a disincentive to exporting. More surprising is the even higher negative correlation in the case of the BOI instruments and the tax rebates as well. Far from being instruments of export promotion, the IFCT loans, Customs Department tax drawbacks, Fiscal Policy Office tax rebates, and especially the BOI investment promotion schemes are similar to industry protection in their allocation across industries. At the industry level, it is clearly the poor performers that are promoted by these measures.

The political economy behind these results is presumably that industries that are well organized for lobbying purposes put proportionately more resources into the behavior that secures bureaucratic support than industries that are less well organized. But the former are not necessarily performing well in economic terms—our results suggest the reverse. Thus policy measures intended to promote exports are captured by the system of rent-seeking and in fact support roughly the same poorly performing industries as are favored by the system of protection.

*Petroleum Pricing Policy*

Thai economic growth in recent decades has been associated with industrialization, farm mechanization, urbanization, and the greatly increased use of transport services. Consequently, energy demand has grown rapidly: from 1974 to 1990 the rate was in excess of 12 percent per year. At the time of the first oil shock, imported petroleum products accounted for 86 percent of total commercial energy used, but

**Table 4.3  Instruments of Policy by Industry, 1960–90**

| Industry | Effective rates of protection (percent) | | | Share of total IFCT approved loans | | | Share of total BOI promoted projects | | Share of total tax drawback funds | | | Share of total tax rebate funds | | |
|---|---|---|---|---|---|---|---|---|---|---|---|---|---|---|
| | 1974 | 1984 | 1987 | 1960–79 | 1980–85 | 1986–90 | 1983–85 | 1987–89 | 1986 | 1987 | 1989 | 1986 | 1987 | 1989 |
| Agriculture | 5 | 9 | 13 | 0.94 | 1.14 | 1.49 | 0.86 | 0.70 | 0.06 | 0.04 | 0.02 | 0.07 | 0.06 | 0.05 |
| Tobacco | 2,067 | 7 | 10 | 0.18 | 0.01 | 0.00 | — | — | — | — | — | — | — | — |
| Textiles | 46 | 23 | 25 | 0.44 | 0.31 | 0.24 | 0.18 | 0.22 | 2.32 | 2.46 | 2.33 | 2.06 | 2.03 | 1.93 |
| Wood products | –42 | 58 | 65 | 0.46 | 2.06 | 1.37 | 0.71 | 2.13 | 0.16 | 0.20 | 0.14 | 0.42 | 0.59 | 0.6 |
| Furniture | 183 | 1 | 2 | 0.36 | 0.91 | 1.10 | — | — | — | — | — | — | — | — |
| Paper | 10 | 29 | 36 | 4.06 | 2.34 | 2.65 | 0.52 | 2.80 | 1.88 | 1.12 | 0.84 | 0.99 | 1.20 | 1.23 |
| Printing | –2 | –2 | 2 | 0.72 | 0.23 | 0.56 | 0.38 | 2.08 | — | — | — | — | — | — |
| Rubber | 48 | 7 | 14 | 0.32 | 0.40 | 0.94 | 1.52 | 1.74 | 8.22 | 8.43 | 7.39 | 1.84 | 1.77 | 2.07 |
| Chemicals | 52 | 35 | 45 | 3.45 | 2.87 | 2.24 | 1.93 | 1.62 | 0.49 | 0.37 | 0.61 | 0.76 | 0.65 | 0.72 |
| Petroleum | –10 | 5 | –6 | 0.26 | 0.07 | 0.56 | — | — | — | — | — | — | — | — |
| Nonmetallic | 88 | 20 | 24 | 3.54 | 4.46 | 1.47 | 3.38 | 0.98 | 0.69 | 0.95 | 0.67 | 0.58 | 0.64 | 0.72 |
| Metal products | 29 | 13 | 20 | 1.66 | 2.61 | 4.47 | 2.48 | 1.13 | 1.01 | 0.64 | 0.95 | 1.34 | 0.94 | 1.14 |
| Machinery | 5 | 23 | 25 | 0.00 | 1.94 | 1.87 | 0.49 | 1.54 | 0.68 | 0.30 | 1.77 | 1.63 | 2.52 | 6.11 |
| Electrical machinery | 217 | 21 | 26 | 2.95 | 0.25 | 1.01 | 3.00 | 2.59 | — | — | — | — | — | — |
| Transport | 151 | 40 | 153 | 0.33 | 0.20 | 0.08 | — | — | 0.08 | 0.18 | 0.12 | 0.10 | 0.14 | 0.35 |
| Other manufacturing | 498 | 18 | 18 | 0.97 | 1.15 | 0.15 | 0.99 | 1.31 | 0.21 | 0.23 | 0.28 | 0.92 | 0.98 | 0.54 |

*Note:* All industry shares are expressed in relation to the industry's share of total value added.

*Source:* IFCT approved loans data: from the Bank of Thailand. Data for value added is taken from National Income of Thailand, Office of the National Economic and Social Development Board, Bangkok. Effective rates of protection are drawn from the data underlying tables 3.2 and 3.3.

**Table 4.4  Correlation Coefficients across Industries: Trade Performance and Industrial Policy, 1970–89**

| Period | Effective rate of protection | | | IFCT loan allocation | | | BOI projects | | Tax drawbacks | Tax rebates |
|---|---|---|---|---|---|---|---|---|---|---|
| | 1974 | 1984 | 1987 | 1960–69 | 1980–85 | 1986–90 | 1983–85 | 1987–89 | 1986–89 | 1986–89 |
| 1970–74 | -0.06 | -0.02 | -0.08 | -0.16 | -0.03 | -0.02 | -0.24 | -0.39 | -0.16 | -0.46 |
| 1975–79 | -0.07 | -0.11 | -0.14 | -0.18 | -0.09 | -0.08 | -0.26 | -0.47 | -0.12 | -0.39 |
| 1980–84 | -0.06 | -0.16 | -0.15 | -0.16 | -0.11 | -0.11 | -0.23 | -0.52 | -0.11 | -0.40 |
| 1985–89 | -0.04 | -0.14 | -0.15 | -0.17 | -0.15 | -0.25 | -0.28 | -0.52 | -0.03 | -0.35 |

*Source:* Calculated from data on NEPR by industry in table 3.8 and levels of policy instruments by industry in table 4.3.

**Table 4.5  Correlation Coefficients across Industries: Changes in Trade Performance and Changes in Industrial Policy**

| Change in NEPR over the period: | Change in EPR | | | Change in IFCT loan allocation | | | Change in BOI promoted projects |
|---|---|---|---|---|---|---|---|
| | 1974–87 | 1974–84 | 1984–87 | 1960–79 to 1986–90 | 1960–79 to 1980–85 | 1980–85 to 1986–90 | 1983–85 to 1987–89 |
| 1985–89/ 1980–84 | -0.09 | -0.09 | 0.01 | -0.34 | -0.13 | -0.27 | -0.19 |
| 1980–84/ 1975–79 | -0.10 | -0.10 | 0.07 | -0.46 | -0.27 | -0.26 | -0.43 |
| 1975–79/ 1970–74 | 0.06 | -0.06 | 0.17 | -0.38 | -0.40 | -0.03 | 0.20 |

*Source:* Calculated from data in tables 3.8 and 4.3.

by 1985 this had fallen to 44 percent. The changes in energy use have been a consequence of structural changes in the Thai economy, international price changes, and government pricing policy. Thailand remains the fifth largest net importer of petroleum products among developing countries, after Brazil, India, the Republic of Korea, and the Philippines.

The government taxes petroleum products at widely different rates. Gasoline is heavily taxed, diesel oil and liquefied petroleum gas (LPG) are moderately taxed, and fuel oil and kerosene are scarcely taxed at all. Locally refined products, by far the most important, are taxed through a combination of excise taxes, municipal taxes, and a variable levy known as the "oil fund." There is no import tax on crude oil. Imported refined products are taxed by means of import duties, business and municipal taxes, and the oil fund levy. Changes in the oil fund levy make it possible for the government to regulate retail prices of petroleum products independently of ex-refinery and import prices.

In 1973 the ex-refinery rates of tax were about 100 percent on gasoline, slightly lower on LPG and about 30 percent on fuel oil. These tax rates were reduced after the first oil shock in an effort to keep retail petroleum prices down. The political importance of petroleum product pricing is shown by the subsequent events: the increase in the tax on petroleum products in 1980, which had been allowed to fall through the 1970s, led directly to the fall of the Kriangsak government (see chapter 2). The new government, led by General Prem Tinsulanonda, promptly reduced the taxes on petroleum products to about two-thirds of their average levels under the previous government.

Petroleum taxes have been an important source of revenue for the Thai government: they rose from about 7 percent of total tax revenue in 1974 to 13 percent in 1980, and since 1981 have remained at about 10 percent (Praipol 1993). Excise taxes account for about 85 percent of this revenue and import taxes for most of the remainder. The oil fund revenues have been used in part to subsidize the use of fuel oil by the Electricity Generating Authority. The net contribution to central government revenue has been small. These subsidies became especially important after the second oil price shock. From time to time, subsidies from the oil fund have been granted to all petroleum products, except gasoline. In 1990 the retail price of gasoline was about 100 percent above import prices, the price of LPG was 30 percent higher, and that of kerosene and fuel oil was roughly at import parity.

## Quantitative Restrictions on International Trade

Apart from tariffs and export taxes, the trade regime in Thailand includes a number of restrictive measures such as quantitative import and export controls. At present, there are import bans on eighteen commodities, and special permission is required to import another thirty. The Ministry of Commerce imposes and supervises the import controls. Commodities under control include those produced in the socialist countries, weapons and strategic firearms, rice, and sugar. The controls on rice and sugar are designed to prevent reimporting after the products have been exported.

Export controls are placed on thirty-eight commodities, sixteen of which are outright bans. The export controls are meant to ensure domestic supplies for local consumption at low prices. Items such as paper, pesticide, sheets of flat iron, polyfiber, and cement are regulated to ensure that local supplies are available.

Under the Price Setting and Antimonopoly Act of 1979, the Ministry of Commerce also administers price controls on "essential products." In 1986 thirty-four commodities came under price control. Such control has helped to keep down the cost of living, but it has been at the expense of shortages of these products in retail stores.

*Exchange Rate Control*

Exchange rate management is in the policy domain of the Bank of Thailand, but input from the Ministry of Finance is important. From 1955, when the multiple exchange rate system was abolished (Corden and Richter 1967) until the devaluations of 1981, the baht was maintained at more or less fixed parity with the U.S. dollar (20 to 21 baht per U.S. dollar). The main argument for this peg was the stability and the confidence it was believed to provide. Between 1955 and 1977, the dollar depreciated in relation to other currencies and the baht-dollar rate was adjusted five times, but these adjustments were all very small.

The volatility of the dollar and the enlarged trade deficits in the late 1970s following the second oil shock prompted the Thai government to reconsider its exchange rate policy. Although much of Thailand's trade is denominated in U.S. dollars, less than 20 percent of its export and import transactions are with the United States. Pegging to the overvalued dollar in the late 1970s had merely increased the country's balance of payments deficits. In March 1978 the Bank of Thailand announced that the baht would no longer be tied to the dollar but to a basket of currencies in which the dollar would be a major component. The new system was, however, short-lived. In November 1978, a system of daily fixing was introduced, in effect putting the baht back into parity with the dollar, at 19.8 baht per dollar.

In 1979 and 1980, Thailand encountered severe trade deficits, which reached a record 4.6 percent of GDP. The deficits resulted from an artificially strong dollar—to which the baht was still pegged and which had mitigated against Thai exports—and a strong growth in domestic spending. In response, the government devalued the baht twice in 1981, bringing the rate to 23 baht per U.S. dollar. The government also abandoned the daily fixing system. Such a drastic move, particularly the second devaluation, which then was the largest in recent history (8.7 percent), proved to be politically unpopular and led to the resignation of a deputy finance minister. To build up confidence in the baht after two successive devaluations, the government introduced a currency swap in 1981 to guarantee that those bringing in foreign funds would not have to pay back more than the amount they had borrowed from abroad when their loans came due.

The abandonment of the daily fixing system was tantamount to returning to the old single-rate, fixed exchange system. In 1984 the baht was again devalued—this time by 14.5 percent—to curb the growing trade deficit. The fixed exchange rate system was also abandoned and replaced by a supposedly flexible exchange rate system, under which the baht is tied to a basket of currencies. This switch was to provide greater flexibility in the management of the country's foreign exchange. It is obvious that the basket is heavily dominated by the U.S. dollar. Approximate parity to the U.S. dollar has been maintained in spite of the dollar's realignment in relation to other currencies. This matter is explored further in chapter 9.

*Financial Market Regulations*

Regulation in the financial market is the responsibility of the Bank of Thailand, with the approval of the Ministry of Finance. Financial regulations act both to stabilize the economy and to preserve the commercial viability of the financial system. The present regulations have four distinctive features.

First, entry to the financial industry, through the opening of new financial institutions—commercial banks, finance companies, and insurance companies—as well as branches of foreign banks, is regulated by the Ministry of Finance through licensing permits. In the case of commercial banks, this control, which is strictly enforced, is aimed at insulating the existing institutions from new competition in order to ensure their long-term viability and stability. In recent years, this tight control, together with the government's unwillingness to let ailing commercial banks collapse, has proved costly: government protection enabled mismanaged banks to continue their operation at public expense.

Second, until recently the Bank of Thailand regulated interest rates, by fixing the maximum deposit rates and maximum lending rates. Since June 1989 controls on the rates for time deposits have been relaxed. Commercial banks have been encouraged to vary their own rates voluntarily within the bounds prescribed in response to their liquidity positions. Individual banks, fearing that they would lose their market shares, competed for deposits by offering the ceiling rates for deposits. In situations of excess liquidity, this reduced bank profits. As a result, liquidity problems were prolonged until the Bank of Thailand eventually intervened, by adjusting the ceiling rates. The ceiling rates can thus be seen in part as a device for limiting the banks' capacity to exploit their oligopolistic power.

A third novel feature is that Thailand has no direct controls on capital inflows, whereas until recently capital outflow has been tightly regulated. In these circumstances, local liquidity becomes highly responsive to changes in foreign interest rates and the exchange rate. Since domestic rates are normally regulated at levels slightly higher than the foreign rates, commercial banks and large companies can freely adjust their liquidity position by borrowing abroad. This flexibility has helped ease the pressure on foreign reserves in times of balance of payments problems.

Fourth, regulations within the banking system are also plentiful. Besides the usual monetary policy controls, there are regulations requiring new bank branches to fulfill a variety of conditions, including compulsory holdings of government bonds. This makes the market for government bonds a captive one. There is also an institutional regulation known as "agricultural credit policy," which requires commercial banks to lend a fixed proportion of their previous year's deposits (currently set at 13 percent) to agriculture. This regulation, which came into effect in 1975, is designed to enlarge the flow of private credit to agriculture.

*Labor Market Regulations*

Government regulations in the labor market are under the jurisdiction of the Ministry of Interior, to which the Labor Department belongs. Labor regulations take two basic forms: the worker protection scheme and minimum wage regulation, which is more relevant to this study.

In response to an International Labour Office appeal for workers' rights and protection, the Labor Department introduced minimum wage regulation in 1973. It was intended to guarantee workers a daily income that would be sufficient to meet their basic needs. The regulation fixes a standardized minimum daily wage for industrial workers in Bangkok and in the provinces. The figure is revised annually by representatives from the government, the employees, and the employers. From 1973 to 1987, the figures were revised fourteen times. The 1987 rate was 73 baht for Bangkok and the five nearby provinces; 67 baht for the provinces of Chonburi, Saraburi, Nakorn Rashasima, Chiengmai; and 61 baht for other provinces.

The effect of minimum wage regulations on labor market hiring has been slight, since only large companies and state enterprises adhere to them. According to a survey conducted in 1986, less than one-third of the firms in operation paid their workers the minimum level or higher. This means that fewer than half of the employed unskilled workers were paid the minimum wage. Firms paying less than the legal minimum are mostly small and medium-size firms. Obviously, the threat of unemployment leads workers to accept lower pay in order to secure employment. Only the large firms and state enterprises have formal worker organizations strong enough to police the full administration of the minimum wage regulations.

Despite the limited coverage of the minimum wage regulations, revisions to the minimum wage do have an impact, by raising the entire wage structure within the formal sector, including that of the salaried employees. An inflationary impact from such revisions would therefore seem a genuine possibility.

## Public Provision of Infrastructure

During the country's first two development plans (1961–71), the main theme of the planning process was the need for basic infrastructure. By the 1980s, the nature of public provision had changed significantly. The emphasis of public investment shifted from infrastructure to development projects. The idea was to develop strategic industries that would help strengthen the economy's ability to absorb external shocks as well as to provide a foundation for resource-based industrialization. The fertilizer project, the steel project, and the Eastern Seaboard Project were examples of such development.

The provision of infrastructure during the first two development plans was concentrated in roads, irrigation, power, and telecommunication. The expansion of the road network in 1960s, which was tacitly linked to an American-supported counterinsurgency program, had a considerable impact on agricultural development and overall economic growth. It provided farmers with direct access to external markets, which significantly increased farmgate prices for cash crops, as well as access to a vast amount of uncultivated land. The extension of the land frontier was instrumental in the agricultural growth of the 1960s.

Investment in irrigation was designed to provide a degree of water control in wet-season agriculture. It took the form of building large dams and waterways. These activities provided a source of power supply and a basis for investing in power, telecommunication, and electrification projects. Considerable effort also went into developing airports and harbors. Some of these projects were undertaken because of the security fears associated with the Vietnam War. By the middle of the 1970s Thailand's infrastructure compared favorably with that of other developing countries.

Through the provision of basic infrastructure in the 1960s, the government provided a stimulus for private investment and economic growth. The main drawback of this effort was its unequal distribution of benefits. The irrigation system, for example, was concentrated in the central plains and the lower north and lacked a proper feeder system, with the result that the main beneficiaries were large farmers in close proximity to the irrigation sites. Similar problems were observed in the distribution of power, telecommunications, and electricity.

In the Third Plan (1972–76), the pattern of public expenditure was modified slightly to give greater emphasis to the distribution problem. One reason for this shift was the move in 1974 toward representative government. More emphasis was given to providing rural areas with services, notably, electrification, rural health centers, and family planning. Between 1974 and 1976, the share of public expenditure on health, education, and agriculture rose considerably.

In the Fourth Plan (1977–81), however, public expenditure on agriculture, health, and education declined while that on industry, energy, transport, defense, and administration increased. This change was the result of a number of economic and political developments. Following the military coup of 1976, control of the government's finances was back in the hands of the military and the bureaucrats. In 1977 a special government decree significantly extended the public sector's direct access to foreign borrowings. For the first time, state enterprises were able to borrow directly from abroad, with government guarantees, in order to finance their capital investment. This decree led to a dramatic expansion in defense expenditure and in the role of state enterprises. Between 1978 and 1983, there was a steady increase in capital expenditure by the state enterprises, financed in particular by foreign borrowing. The bulk of this spending was on energy-related activities because of the need to develop alternative local sources of energy so as to reduce the economy's dependence on imported energy.

In 1977, at the time the decision was made to liberalize the public sector's foreign borrowing, there was no definitive policy on the management of public debt. Regulations on foreign debt merely limited the amount each state enterprise could borrow, but not the aggregate for the public sector. The enlarged foreign debt commitment became a serious policy problem in the early 1980s, when the economy went into a recession following a slump in primary commodity exports. The current account deficit reached 7.1 percent of GDP in 1983, and the debt-service ratio reached 23.3 percent and was still rising. This development, which was considered a threat to the country's financial stability, prompted the government to revise its foreign borrowing policy and to establish the National Debt Reform Committee. One of its new policy measures was to set annual limits on the public sector's foreign borrowing. Several of the large development projects being planned, most of which relied on foreign funds, were either scaled down or postponed owing to lack of foreign exchange.

## Public Enterprises

As in many other developing countries, public enterprises play a significant role in the Thai economy (Jones 1982). The sector has grown rapidly in recent years and its role in resource allocation has become an important concern of economic policy. Far from being confined to infrastructure, the activities of Thailand's state enterprises stretch into many areas of business, including manufacturing, transport, hotels, services, trade, and finance. The Bank of Thailand is also formally a state enterprise. At present, there are sixty-eight state enterprises, seventeen of which operate in infrastructure. Most state enterprises began as special projects (revolving funds) under central government departments with their own staffs and financial accounts, then slowly graduated to the status of state enterprises when their activities expanded.

### History

Until the end of absolute monarchy in 1932, state business ventures consisted mainly of royal trade monopolies in a small number of luxury commodities and the provision of basic utilities. This situation continued until the beginning of World War II, whereupon Thai nationalists in the government began expanding the role of state trading companies in reaction to the Chinese domination of domestic commerce. This was a move to reassert Thai control over domestic trade (Silcock 1967: 260).

After the war, public enterprises became increasingly important in other sectors of the Thai economy because of the income they could provide for military officials and civilian politicians. By 1957, a large part of the country's industrial capacity was controlled by public enterprises. The industries they dominated included tobacco, paper, sugar, gunny bags, timber, tin, metal cabinets, pharmaceuticals, batteries, tanneries, textiles, cement, spirits, glass, rubber footwear, alum, and shoe polish (World Bank 1959: 90–91).

The growth of the public enterprises had been haphazard. Not only was there little economic rationale for the choice of industries entered by the public enterprises, but they had become uncontrolled in their operation, finance, and investment behavior. Furthermore, their practice of lending public funds to one another made their accounts difficult to interpret (Kraiyudht 1993). The end result was that these enterprises became major vehicles for the purchase of political patronage. This was especially important for those Chinese businessmen whose interests were directly threatened by the public enterprises.

On taking control of the government in 1959, Field Marshal Sarit Thanarat established a government committee to investigate the country's state enterprises. The recommendations—based on its findings and on later, similar studies—were not implemented. For example, a 1965 study by the United States Agency for International Development, (USAID) on behalf of the Thai government recommended the sale of thirty state enterprises to private industry, almost all of which still remain in the public sector (Kraiyudht 1993).

Because the management of a state enterprise comes under the jurisdiction of its parent ministry, its chairman is a political appointee. Following the move toward constitutional government in 1974 and the increased number of civilian politicians assuming ministerial portfolios, the political influence in state enterprises has continued to increase. In 1986, fifty-six out of sixty-eight chairman of state enterprises were members of political parties. Through their control of state enterprises, the political parties have therefore been exerting increasing influence on economic decisions. In the past, these chairmanships were dominated largely by senior bureaucrats and military officers.

*Role in the Economy*

The recent increase in the overall importance of public enterprises within the Thai economy is shown in table 4.6. In 1970 the public enterprise sector was smaller than the central government, as measured by recurrent expenditures, capital expenditure, and revenue. By 1988, however, it was larger than the central government by all three measures.[2]

The size and growth rate of public enterprises appears quite different when one looks at employment. Thailand's public enterprises tend to be capital intensive, in comparison with the central government. They employed almost 300,000 persons in 1988, which was approximately one-quarter the number employed by the central government. The rate of increase of employment in the public enter-

## Table 4.6 Economic Importance of Public Enterprises, 1970 and 1988

*(percent)*

| Year | Recurrent expenditure/ GDP | | Capital expenditure/ GDP | | Revenue/GDP | |
|---|---|---|---|---|---|---|
| | Public enterprises | Central government | Public enterprises | Central government | Public enterprises | Central government |
| 1970 | 9.5 | 12.1 | 1.9 | 5.9 | 11.2 | 13.7 |
| 1988 | 18.9 | 15.9 | 7.7 | 2.7 | 20.8 | 16.3 |

*Source*: Bank of Thailand, *Monthly Bulletin*, various issues.

prise sector from 1970 to 1988 was 7 percent per year, which was slightly smaller than the 7.8 percent registered by the central government.

*Trading Profits/Losses and Pricing Policy*

The public's perception of these enterprises is that they incur huge losses. This is only partly correct. It is true that some important public enterprises regularly lose large sums. The main examples are in the transport sector: the Bangkok Mass Transit Authority incurs losses averaging the equivalent of roughly $30 million a year, and the State Railway of Thailand about $23 million. Nevertheless, in most years, the aggregate revenues of public enterprises exceed their aggregate expenditures. The problem with these calculations is that the expenditures of the state enterprises do not include proper allowance for a return on the public sector's capital investment in them. In any case, some of the state enterprises included in these statistics operate as profit-maximizing monopolists and generate large operating surpluses. Examples are the Thailand Tobacco Monopoly and the State Lottery Bureau.

The structure of public enterprise supervision is summarized in figure 4.2. Each enterprise has a board of control and is under the supervision of a government ministry. In general, the board has formal responsibility for setting prices, but the supervising ministry may also play a role. The more important the enterprise, the greater the role of the ministry. A few of the most important enterprises must have any changes in their prices approved by the cabinet. This makes it politically difficult to raise prices in key public enterprises. In addition to the transport sector mentioned above, this applies to the water, electricity, and telephone utilities. The cabinet also approves the price structure of all petroleum-related products. For these key public enterprises, the redistributive effects of changes in prices and the political implications of these effects dominate discussions of tariff rates. Decisions to change prices are made only rarely, and long after economic circumstances have changed. In the past, this slowness to adjust prices has accounted in large part for the losses incurred by key public enterprises. The role of the boards in setting prices has been increasing. In the face of financial problems,

**Figure 4.2.  Structure of Public Enterprise Supervision**

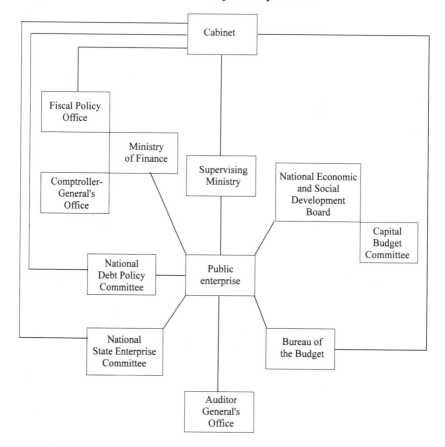

*Source:* Authors' compilation.

the Prem government placed more power over pricing within the boards of the public enterprises.

*Investment Behavior and Foreign Debt*

In 1985 capital expenditure by state enterprises accounted for more than 70 percent of total (consolidated) public sector expenditure. State enterprises' capital budgets are subject to the review and approval of the National Committee on State Enterprises, whose secretariat function is shared by the National Economic and Social Development Board, the Budget Bureau, and the Fiscal Policy Office. It is at this stage that the investment plans of state enterprises are scrutinized in detail. This practice allows the NESDB to tailor the proposed investment plans to the priorities laid down in the national development plan. Once approved, the projects seeking budgetary support in the form of a contribution from the central government receive further review by the Budget Bureau. Such support, if granted, becomes part of the central government's expenditure budget.

Public enterprises accounted for about two-thirds of the public sector's foreign debt outstanding in 1985. Servicing this debt absorbs roughly half the total debt-servicing burden of the public sector. In recent years, recognition of this problem has caused the investment plans of all public enterprises to come under close scrutiny from the NESDB. The implications of enterprises' investment plans for foreign debt servicing receive the closest examination. Not only are public enterprises now required to have foreign and domestic borrowing plans examined by the National Debt Policy Committee, but all such loans are then negotiated and signed by the Finance Ministry's Fiscal Policy Office.

**Regulation of External Public Sector Debt**

The history of Thai public debt regulations is summarized in table 4.7. Before the 1960s, Thai governments avoided external borrowing. This implied that a sound investment program would have to be canceled if it called for heavy borrowing from abroad. Beginning in the early 1960s, with the launching of the first development plan and its heavy public investment in infrastructure, the government recognized that foreign borrowing would be necessary to finance such investment.

Despite this change in policy, the government continued to favor financial conservatism, as reflected in the 1959 proclamation limiting the size of the budget deficit to within 25 percent of its expenditure. In the following year an external public debt law was setting a 5 percent ceiling on the permissible debt-service ratio, defined as the total debt service as a percentage of total exports, as measured by the Ministry of Finance, and limiting the size of foreign debt service to less than 13 percent of forecast revenue. In 1964, the ceiling on the debt-service ratio was raised to 7 percent in anticipation of heavy borrowing for public investment.

Also in 1960, the National Debt Policy Committee (NDPC) was established to monitor and regulate the foreign borrowing activities of government departments. Review by the NDPC became mandatory for public sector projects requiring foreign loans. This committee reports to the cabinet and is chaired by the finance minister. Its main responsibility is to ensure that the conduct of foreign borrowing by the public sector is within the framework set by the cabinet. Foreign loan proposals of all public sector agencies are compared and ranked in order of priority. It is here that political lobbying for foreign loan quotas is most intense.

In 1960 the NDPC consisted of five members from the Finance Ministry, the Budget Bureau, the National Economic Development Board, the Bank of Thailand, and a foreign representative. In 1964 the number was increased to nine and included the president and the general secretary of the National Economic Development Board. The British-trained economist Puey Ungphakorn, governor of the

**Table 4.7  A Chronology of Public Debt Policy, 1959–90**

| Year | Policy |
| --- | --- |
| 1959 | Government budget deficit limited to less than 25 percent of government expenditure. |
| 1960 | Ceiling on public sector debt service ratio (DSR) set at 5 percent. Foreign debt service of public sector limited to less than 13 percent of forecast revenue. |
| | National Debt Policy Committee (NDPC) set up to monitor and regulate foreign borrowing. |
| 1964 | Ceiling on DSR raised to 7 percent. |
| 1976 | Total public sector foreign borrowing limited to less than 10 percent of total government expenditure. |
| | Ministry of Finance empowered to borrow from abroad. |
| 1977 | Ceiling on DSR raised to 9 percent, of which 2 percent was reserved specifically for military borrowing. |
| | NDPC empowered to control public enterprises' foreign borrowing. |
| 1981 | Ministry of Finance empowered to negotiate foreign loans for military procurements. |
| | Ceiling on DSR of 9 percent set to include borrowing for both military and nonmilitary purposes. |
| 1984 | DSR ceiling temporarily raised to 11 percent for the period 1984–87 to accommodate refinancing program. |
| 1986 | A limit on total public sector foreign borrowing for all purposes established at 1 billion dollars per year. |
| 1990 | Limit on public sector foreign borrowing raised to 2.5 billion dollars per year. |

*Source*: Authors' compilation.

Bank of Thailand between 1959 and 1971, was closely involved in implementing the government's financial discipline plan. Dr. Puey was at times director of both the Budget Bureau and the Fiscal Policy Office of the Ministry of Finance, as well as governor of the Bank of Thailand. His influence on policy was profound and reflected his conservative attitudes regarding financial management.

The decisions of the Foreign Debt Policy Commission were not directly influenced by politicians, since most of the members were civil servants. To avoid corruption and mismanagement of the infrastructure funds, the commission encouraged foreign borrowing from sources such as the World Bank, because these funds would be closely monitored and supervised. Since 1982, the Foreign Debt Policy Commission has consisted of ten members, six of them from the Ministry of Finance. They are also empowered to regulate public enterprises' foreign borrowing. Aside from the Minister of Finance and his deputy, the members have all been civil servants, with the result that the influence of politicians and the military in manipulating foreign borrowing has been greatly reduced.

Most military procurement was in the form of military aid from the United States after Thailand signed an agreement with the U.S. government on suppressing communism. In 1954 and 1963, for example, foreign borrowing for military purposes amounted to only $0.9 million and $1.5 million, respectively. Military foreign borrowing resumed in 1975, when the U.S. military bases were withdrawn from Vietnam. Borrowing for military purposes substituted for military aid from the United States, especially in 1975 and 1976, when Vietnam occupied Cambodia. A new regulation on foreign borrowing imposed in 1976 stipulated that foreign borrowing had to be less than 10 percent of government expenditure and was to be undertaken through the Ministry of Finance, which was to act as the representative of the Thai government.

In 1977, owing to an increase in foreign borrowing for military procurement, the ceiling on the debt-service ratio from foreign borrowing for military purchases was set at 2 percent, leaving the 7 percent ceiling on the debt-service ratio for other purposes intact. Recognizing that public enterprises were responsible for the mounting foreign debt, the Foreign Debt Policy Commission was empowered to control their foreign borrowing. Between 1972 and 1977 the public and total debt-service ratio were below 3 and 13 percent, respectively. Since 1978, the ratio has increased rapidly because of foreign borrowing for military purchases and borrowing by public enterprises. From 1978 to 1982, the total ratio ranged from 14.6 to 16.6, while the public ratio was rising. Public debt was the major cause of growing external debt. After the second oil shock in 1979, Thailand sought help from the IMF for standby-arranged funds.

In 1981 the Prem government empowered the Ministry of Finance to negotiate all foreign loans for military procurement. In the following year, it decreed that the ceiling on the debt-service ratio was to remain at 9 percent, but no distinction was made between military and nonmilitary borrowing. The implication of this regulation was that military purchases financed by foreign loans would have to be considered together with other investment projects under the 9 percent limit. Since the military could negotiate loans directly, this placed them in direct conflict with the Ministry of Finance. Usually, military loans were obtained with fairly high interest rates and shorter grace periods. In 1978 the share of interest payments on public debt for military purposes was 14 percent. This share increased to 34 percent in 1979, 47 percent in 1980, and 56 percent in 1981.

In 1984 the Prem government raised the ceiling on the debt-service ratio from 9 to 11 percent for the period 1984–87 to accommodate its refinancing program. In 1986 the amount of foreign borrowing allowed in any one year was set at a maximum of $1 billion. In effect, the ceiling discourages foreign borrowing for large investment projects of heavy industries. In the early 1990s two other important regulations were passed: total debt service could not exceed 9 percent of expected export earnings, and total new borrowings in any year could not exceed $2.5 billion.

In 1986 the foreign debt of public enterprises was more than 60 percent of total public debts (table 4.8). The acceleration of the public debt in 1978 and 1979 was due to military borrowing. Although military foreign borrowing slowed after 1979, the debt of public enterprises accelerated from 41.4 percent in 1978 to 60.7 percent of total public external debt in 1980. As a result, the ratio of total outstanding foreign debt to GDP rose rapidly after 1978. At the same time, the growth of government sector and public enterprise slowed from 1981 to 1984. The refinancing scheme raised the growth rate of public debt somewhat in 1985 and 1986.

## Table 4.8  Growth Rate and Components of External Public Debt
*(percent)*

| Year | Government | | Public enterprises | | Total outstanding debt/GDP | Reserves/debt oustanding disbursed only |
|------|-----------|-------|----------|-------|----------|----------|
| | *Growth rate* | *Share* | *Growth rate* | *Share* | | |
| 1970 | 16.2 | (57.3) | −6.0 | (42.7) | (4.8) | (279.8) |
| 1971 | −3.0 | (59.3) | −10.8 | (40.7) | (4.7) | (247.5) |
| 1972 | 3.7 | (53.7) | 30.2 | (46.3) | (4.6) | (288.8) |
| 1973 | 13.8 | (49.2) | 36.4 | (50.8) | (4.2) | (332.9) |
| 1974 | −0.3 | (43.4) | 25.8 | (56.6) | (3.9) | (427.8) |
| 1975 | −0.7 | (35.0) | 41.6 | (65.0) | (4.3) | (325.7) |
| 1976 | 12.3 | (41.9) | 10.9 | (58.1) | (4.9) | (256.9) |
| 1977 | 15.5 | (34.9) | 55.4 | (65.1) | (5.8) | (197.3) |
| 1978 | 81.3 | (40.8) | 41.4 | (59.2) | (8.0) | (140.6) |
| 1979 | 55.6 | (41.8) | 49.1 | (58.2) | (10.2) | (109.7) |
| 1980 | 29.0 | (36.6) | 60.7 | (63.4) | (12.3) | (74.4) |
| 1981 | 22.8 | (35.4) | 28.5 | (64.6) | (14.8) | (53.1) |
| 1982 | 18.6 | (35.4) | 19.3 | (64.6) | (16.4) | (43.6) |
| 1983 | 15.5 | (35.8) | 3.8 | (64.2) | (17.0) | (36.5) |
| 1984 | 10.2 | (36.5) | 7.0 | (63.5) | (20.2) | (35.6) |
| 1985 | 24.3 | (37.8) | 18.4 | (63.2) | (23.1) | (30.5) |
| 1986 | 21.9 | (37.2) | 24.9 | (62.8) | (25.3) | (34.3) |

*Note*: Figures are percentage annual growth rates, except those in parentheses, which are percentage shares.

*Source*: Calculated from data from the Budget Bureau.

# Part Two

---

# Macroeconomic Adjustment
## to External Shocks

# Chapter Five

# The Shocks

The word "shock" implies that something has happened to the environment in which economic activity takes place that is, first, a surprise, and second, serious enough to require a response. If the change had been fully anticipated, then economic agents would presumably have adjusted their behavior in advance to its implications, once the change came to be expected. If the change was not serious, then it would not be important to analyze its effects.

The macroeconomic shocks experienced by Thailand during the study period were both unanticipated and serious. This chapter concentrates on those originating outside Thailand, notably, the two OPEC-induced petroleum price increases of 1973–74 and 1979–80. An attempt is also made to quantify the importance of these shocks for Thailand's aggregate economic performance. In addition, the discussion gives some attention to the impact of the terms of trade shocks on national income and on short-term and long-term economic growth. Econometric analysis demonstrates that the effect on growth was moderate.

## Balance of Payments Shocks

The external shocks affecting Thailand were measured in terms of their direct impact on the balance of payments, expressed both in U.S. dollars and as a proportion of Thailand's GNP (see tables 5.1 and 5.2, respectively). The shocks experienced since 1970 can be divided into six types according to their area of impact:

- *Nonfuel primary exports.* Here the shock was temporary, occurring in 1973–74. It is notable that the value of these exports was maintained at a relatively constant share of GNP after the shock had abated.
- *Imports of petroleum products.* This component of the balance of payments was by far the most volatile of those listed here. Changes in the

**Table 5.1 Magnitude of External Shocks Affecting Thailand's Balance of Payments, 1970–90**
(millions of U.S. dollars)

| Year | Total exports | Exports of nonfuel primary products | Total imports | Petroleum product imports | Workers' remittances | Tourism income | U.S. government | Net direct investment |
|---|---|---|---|---|---|---|---|---|
| 1970 | 686.0 | 629 | 1,269.6 | 112 | 9.8 | 104.3 | 29.5 | 42.8 |
| 1971 | 802.5 | 706 | 1,288.8 | 131 | 13.5 | 106.2 | 25.0 | 38.9 |
| 1972 | 1,045.7 | 864 | 1,472.8 | 150 | 761.1 | 130.7 | 20.1 | 68.6 |
| 1973 | 1,515.6 | 1,202 | 2,039.5 | 226 | 122.6 | 164.6 | 17.3 | 77.8 |
| 1974 | 2,405.6 | 2,006 | 3,104.7 | 617 | 222.3 | 186.8 | 11.2 | 188.3 |
| 1975 | 2,176.9 | 1,785 | 3,166.1 | 699 | 64.9 | 219.9 | 8.2 | 85.6 |
| 1976 | 2,958.9 | 2,399 | 3,502.3 | 818 | 16.2 | 195.6 | 5.2 | 79.1 |
| 1977 | 3,454.1 | 2,804 | 4,706.1 | 1,024 | 33.1 | 225.8 | 2.6 | 106.1 |
| 1978 | 4,043.8 | 3,042 | 5,405.9 | 1,124 | 18.3 | 437.3 | 5.3 | 49.7 |
| 1979 | 5,234.1 | 3,883 | 7,515.4 | 1,599 | 34.9 | 550.1 | 4.6 | 51.3 |
| 1980 | 6,447.3 | 4,578 | 9,278.6 | 2,868 | 93.9 | 867.5 | 4.5 | 186.3 |
| 1981 | 6,884.4 | 4,981 | 9,899.2 | 2,984 | 64.5 | 983.3 | 8.1 | 291.6 |
| 1982 | 6,834.9 | 4,915 | 8,405.2 | 2,642 | 89.7 | 1,038.2 | 10.1 | 188.6 |
| 1983 | 6,307.7 | 4,284 | 10,186.0 | 2,481 | 172.1 | 1,089.1 | 18.4 | 356.2 |
| 1984 | 7,340.1 | 4,780 | 10,248.9 | 2,426 | 78.5 | 1,155.6 | 22.1 | 407.1 |
| 1985 | 7,058.3 | 4,222 | 9,327.5 | 2,088 | 71.8 | 1,169.7 | 10.9 | 161.2 |
| 1986 | 8,801.6 | 4,821 | 9,341.8 | 1,230 | 88.7 | 1,419.0 | 9.5 | 261.6 |
| 1987 | 11,590.2 | 5,449 | 13,272.8 | 1,717 | 123.7 | 1,944.9 | 8.6 | 183.2 |
| 1988 | 15,786.1 | 7,597 | 19,726.1 | 1,536 | 77.0 | 3,118.2 | 13.5 | 1,102.5 |
| 1989 | 19,856.9 | 8,383 | 25,210.9 | 2,286 | 80.5 | 3,753.3 | 19.2 | 1,692.3 |
| 1990 | 22,811.8 | 8,019 | 32,548.7 | 3,064.5 | 90.5 | — | 22.0 | 2,445.3 |

Source: Bank of Thailand; World Bank, *World Debt Tables 1991.*

**Table 5.2 Magnitude of External Shocks Affecting Thailand's Balance of Payments, 1970–90**

*(percentage of GNP)*

| Year | Total exports | Exports of non-fuel primary products | Total imports | Petroleum product imports | Workers' remittances | Tourism income | U.S. government | Net direct investment |
|------|--------------|--------------------------------------|---------------|---------------------------|----------------------|----------------|-----------------|-----------------------|
| 1970 | 9.67  | 8.87  | 17.89 | 1.58 | 0.14 | 1.47 | 0.42 | 0.6  |
| 1971 | 10.89 | 9.58  | 17.49 | 1.78 | 0.18 | 1.44 | 0.34 | 0.53 |
| 1972 | 12.83 | 10.61 | 18.08 | 1.84 | 9.34 | 1.60 | 0.25 | 0.84 |
| 1973 | 14.13 | 11.20 | 19.01 | 2.11 | 1.14 | 1.53 | 0.16 | 0.73 |
| 1974 | 17.56 | 14.64 | 22.66 | 4.50 | 1.62 | 1.36 | 0.08 | 1.37 |
| 1975 | 14.63 | 12.00 | 21.27 | 4.70 | 0.44 | 1.48 | 0.06 | 0.58 |
| 1976 | 17.46 | 14.16 | 20.67 | 4.83 | 0.10 | 1.15 | 0.03 | 0.47 |
| 1977 | 17.52 | 14.22 | 23.87 | 5.19 | 0.17 | 1.15 | 0.01 | 0.54 |
| 1978 | 16.97 | 12.77 | 22.69 | 4.72 | 0.08 | 1.84 | 0.02 | 0.21 |
| 1979 | 19.34 | 14.35 | 27.77 | 5.91 | 0.13 | 2.03 | 0.02 | 0.19 |
| 1980 | 20.22 | 14.36 | 29.10 | 8.99 | 0.29 | 2.72 | 0.01 | 0.58 |
| 1981 | 20.08 | 14.53 | 28.87 | 8.70 | 0.19 | 2.87 | 0.02 | 0.85 |
| 1982 | 19.48 | 14.01 | 23.95 | 7.53 | 0.26 | 2.96 | 0.03 | 0.54 |
| 1983 | 16.06 | 10.91 | 25.93 | 6.32 | 0.44 | 2.77 | 0.05 | 0.91 |
| 1984 | 18.04 | 11.75 | 25.19 | 5.96 | 0.19 | 2.84 | 0.05 | 1.00 |
| 1985 | 19.23 | 11.50 | 25.41 | 5.69 | 0.20 | 3.19 | 0.03 | 0.44 |
| 1986 | 21.57 | 11.82 | 22.90 | 3.02 | 0.22 | 3.48 | 0.02 | 0.64 |
| 1987 | 24.22 | 11.39 | 27.74 | 3.59 | 0.26 | 4.06 | 0.02 | 0.38 |
| 1988 | 26.93 | 12.96 | 33.66 | 2.62 | 0.13 | 5.32 | 0.02 | 1.88 |
| 1989 | 29.10 | 12.28 | 36.94 | 3.35 | 0.12 | 5.50 | 0.03 | 2.48 |
| 1990 | 28.43 | 10.00 | 40.57 | 3.82 | 0.11 | —    | 0.03 | 3.05 |

*Source:* Calculated from table 5.1.

value of these imports affected all the other external shocks throughout the 1970s and 1980s. The exploitation of natural gas from 1981 onward is believed to have reduced dependence on petroleum imports through the 1980s; both for this reason and because of declining petroleum prices, imports of petroleum as a share of GNP declined through the 1980s.

- *Workers' remittances.* The changes in workers' remittances were small throughout the two decades, except for 1972 and, to a lesser extent, 1973 and 1974. This phenomenon was essentially a statistical artifact. It included large transfers of funds from Indochina—Vietnam, Cambodia, and Laos—just before the Communist victories in those countries. The Bank of Thailand treated them as "unrequited transfers for unknown purposes." They were not really workers' remittances.

- *Income from tourism.* This source of income grew steadily throughout the two decades. By the mid-1980s it was more important to the balance of payments than Thailand's total imports of petroleum products.

- *U.S. government military expenditure.* After the Communist victories in Indochina in 1975, this expenditure became unimportant, but even before this its aggregate importance was small. At its peak, in 1975, it was equivalent to only one-sixth of Thailand's petroleum import bill.

- *Net direct investment.* This investment did not become really important until after 1987, when it rose from less than one to more than two percentage points of GNP.

The shocks can also be divided by time period and the nature of the effect.

*Shock 1*, an increase in the price of primary products, occurred in 1973–74. It had a *positive* effect. As already mentioned, it was a temporary event.

*Shock 2* was sparked by the 1973–74 increase in petroleum prices, but to separate it from the first it is treated as having spanned the period 1975–78. Its effects were *negative*. This shock initially coincided with, and was somewhat masked by, the first shock. In contrast to that event, however, the oil price shock was not temporary. The increase in petroleum import costs was permanent.

*Shock 3*, which was felt during the period 1979–85, was initiated by the petroleum price increases of 1979–80 and the international interest rate increases of 1980–82. It, too, had *negative* effects.

*Shock 4*, during 1986–90, came in the form of a decline in petroleum prices in the late 1980s, the rising prices of primary commodities, and the movement of light manufacturing enterprises from Northeast Asia to Thailand. This shock had *positive* effects.

All four shocks were initiated by a change in international prices. The effects of these shocks are traced in figures 5.1 to 5.3. One effect was a long-term downward trend in the conventional terms of trade (figure 5.1). The "overall terms of trade" corresponds to the conventional concept of an index of the international prices of Thailand's merchandise exports in relation to those of its merchandise imports. When the contribution of petroleum prices alone is considered—by ex-

**Figure 5.1  Overall Terms-of-Trade Index and Petroleum Terms-of-Trade Index, 1970–90**

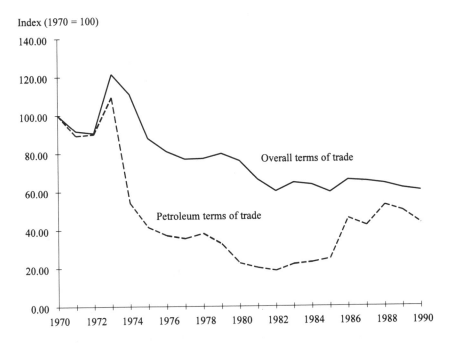

Index (1970 = 100)

*Source:* Bank of Thailand.

amining the ratio of the index of international merchandise export prices described above to an index of the international price paid by Thailand for its petroleum imports—this measure of the terms of trade experienced a dramatic and permanent change during the period of our study.

The movement in the nominal prices of Thailand's imported and exported commodities is also telling (figures 5.2 and 5.3). Between 1973 and 1976 there were significant movements in the relative prices of Thailand's imports and exports, as captured by the terms-of-trade indices, but also substantial inflation in the nominal U.S. dollar prices of both categories of commodities.

Figure 5.3 decomposes the index of Thailand's nominal import prices into its petroleum and nonpetroleum components, as follows. At time $t$, the unit value index of Thailand's import prices is given by

$$(5.1) \qquad P_t^I = \alpha_t P_t^{IO} + (1-\alpha_t)\, P_t^{IN}$$

where $P_t^{IO}$ denotes an index of oil import prices, $P_t^{IN}$ denotes an index of the prices of nonoil imports, and $\alpha_t$ is the share of petroleum in the value of total merchandise imports. All three price indices are assumed to be equal in some base year.

**Figure 5.2. Import and Export Price Indices, 1965–90**

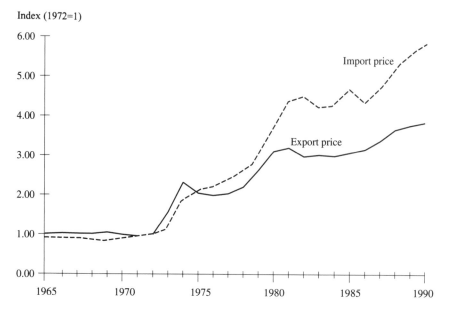

Index (1972=1)

*Source:* Bank of Thailand.

**Figure 5.3  Petroleum and Nonpetroleum Components of Import Price Index, 1970–90**

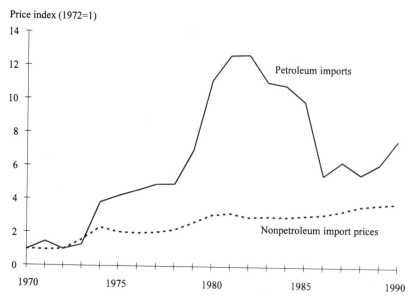

Price index (1972=1)

*Source:* Bank of Thailand.

Then the index of the prices of nonpetroleum imports can be estimated from data on $P_t^I$, $P_t^{IO}$ and $\alpha_t$ from

(5.2)
$$P_t^{IN} = \frac{1}{(1-\alpha_t)} P_t^I - \frac{\alpha_t}{(1-\alpha_t)} P_t^{IO}$$

The results of these computations are shown in figure 5.3. They confirm that the increases in import prices occurring in 1973–74 and 1979–80 were dominated, in proportional terms, by the surge in petroleum prices. But in both periods, nonpetroleum import prices rose significantly as well. Since nonpetroleum imports account for more than 80 percent of Thailand's import bill, these nonpetroleum price increases contributed significantly to the inflation that Thailand experienced in these two periods, along with most of the rest of the world.

These import price data also need to be examined in relation to the composition of Thailand's total imports, where significant changes have occurred since 1970. The country's dependence on imported petroleum products has declined markedly, at least partly because of natural gas discoveries in the Gulf of Thailand and changes in domestic petroleum pricing policy (Praipol 1993). These changes in the composition of total imports suggest that data on import prices alone should not be used to conclude whether the increase in petroleum import prices or nonpetroleum import prices, both in relation to export prices, was the more significant event. We return to this issue below.

The episodes described by shocks 1 to 4 above represent the external changes that had the largest implications for Thai national income. Of course, there were other shocks, unique to Thailand—such as the withdrawal of U.S. military aid after 1975 and the loss in foreign exchange earnings, following the withdrawal of U.S. military forces from Vietnam, connected with their "recreation" spending in Thailand—but these were less important for Thailand's balance of payments than the four shocks summarized above.

From 1972 to 1974, Thailand's petroleum and petroleum product imports, of which crude oil represented almost 90 percent by value, increased from 9 percent to 19 percent of the value of total merchandise imports. The resulting negative shock to Thailand's balance of payments was equal to about $426 million at 1973 prices, or 3.9 percent of GDP. Following the second major price increase, in 1979–80, petroleum imports increased again, this time from 21 percent of total imports in 1978 to 30 percent in 1980. This shock caused the balance of payments to deteriorate by another $640 million, or 2.4 percent of 1979 GDP.

From 1982 to 1990 the average price (in U.S. dollars) of Thailand's petroleum imports was cut in half. Over the same period the unit value of Thailand's exports rose by 12 percent. Nevertheless, the significant reduction in petroleum prices through the early and mid-1980s only partly mitigated the effects of the two oil price shocks of the 1970s. The fact was that by 1990 imported petroleum, in relation to the unit value of Thailand's exports, still cost Thailand *three times* as much per barrel as it did in 1970.

### Effects of the Shocks on National Income

Between 1971 and 1990 real income growth deviated significantly from its trend growth rate of 6.7 percent (see figure 3.1). As the following paragraphs show, this deviation clearly seems to be related to the two oil price shocks and to the high international interest rates following the second of these shocks.

Figure 5.1 reveals that Thailand experienced two major trade shocks: a moderate decline in the nonoil terms of trade, and a proportionately much larger decline in the oil terms of trade. To assess the relationship between the changes in the terms of trade and national income, we decomposed these changes into an "oil terms-of-trade" and a "nonoil terms-of-trade" component and then estimated the extent to which changes in each caused a gain or a loss in national income.

We estimated this income loss by taking the difference between the actual value of imports and the estimated counterfactual value of imports (see tables 5.3 to 5.6). The latter is based on the assumption that the terms of trade remained constant at their preshock level. The method then expresses the value of the trade shock as a sequence of lump-sum changes in national income at constant prices. This is done by constructing a sequence of counterfactual imports: estimates of what the value of imports (in constant prices) would have been in the absence of the shock. The counterfactual value of imports is estimated by multiplying the actual value of imports by the terms of trade index, with the latter set at unity in the base period, 1970. The difference between the actual and counterfactual value of imports represents the net income loss due to the terms of trade deterioration. The calculation starts from 1970 and extends to 1991. The results of our calculations are expressed in U.S. dollars, at constant 1970 prices.

The nonoil terms-of-trade effect is calculated for any year $t$ as

$$
(5.3) \qquad
\begin{aligned}
L_t^N &= Q_t^{NM}(P_t^{NM}/P_t^X) - Q_t^{NM}(P_0^{NM}/P_0^X) \\
&= Q_t^{NM}(P_t^{NM}/P_t^X) - Q_t^{NM}
\end{aligned}
$$

where $Q_t^{NM}$ = the actual real value of nonoil imports in year $t$ (valued at 1970 prices); $P_t^{NM}$ = the nonoil imports price index for year $t$ ($1970 = 100$); $P_t^X$ = the exports price index for year $t$ ($1970 = 100$); and $P_0^{NM}$, $P_0^X$ = the price indices of nonoil imports and exports in the base year of 1970. We normalize such that $P_0^{NM} = P_0^X = 1$.

The actual real value of nonoil imports is calculated in table 5.3 by deflating the current value of nonoil imports with the nonoil import price index. Thus, the term $Q_t^{NM}(P_t^{NM}/P_t^X)$ is the equivalent value of exportable goods that has to be sacrificed to obtain the current value of nonoil import in year $t$. The term $Q_t^{NM}(P_0^{NM}/P_0^X) = Q_t^{NM}$ is the counterfactual value of nonoil imports, and is equivalent to the value of exportable goods that would have been sacrificed to obtain the observed quantity of imports if the nonoil terms of trade had remained at their base-year level.

## Table 5.3 Magnitude of the Nonoil Terms-of-Trade Shocks, 1970–91

| Year | Export price index[a] (1) | Nonoil imports price index[a] (2) | Nonoil terms of trade[b] (3)[c] | Actual nonoil imports[c] (4) | Counter-factual nonoil imports[d] (5) | Nonoil terms-of-trade gain[e] (6) |
|---|---|---|---|---|---|---|
| 1970 | 100.00 | 100.00 | 100.00 | 1,157.55 | 1,157.55 | 0.00 |
| 1971 | 89.86 | 118.45 | 75.86 | 977.41 | 741.43 | 235.97 |
| 1972 | 98.70 | 118.08 | 83.59 | 1,120.28 | 936.45 | 181.83 |
| 1973 | 151.35 | 129.07 | 117.27 | 1,405.10 | 1,647.71 | 242.61 |
| 1974 | 208.92 | 188.32 | 110.94 | 1,321.02 | 1,465.54 | 144.52 |
| 1975 | 197.11 | 196.85 | 100.13 | 1,253.28 | 1,254.93 | 1.65 |
| 1976 | 191.71 | 205.92 | 93.10 | 1,303.55 | 1,213.57 | –89.97 |
| 1977 | 195.85 | 221.49 | 88.42 | 1,662.41 | 1,469.97 | 192.44 |
| 1978 | 211.74 | 244.05 | 86.76 | 1,754.50 | 1,522.17 | 232.33 |
| 1979 | 253.02 | 267.73 | 94.50 | 2,209.79 | 2,088.33 | 121.46 |
| 1980 | 299.07 | 293.17 | 102.01 | 2,186.62 | 2,230.63 | 44.01 |
| 1981 | 308.07 | 341.49 | 90.21 | 2,024.98 | 1,826.80 | 198.19 |
| 1982 | 286.23 | 354.08 | 80.84 | 1,627.65 | 1,315.75 | 311.91 |
| 1983 | 331.25 | 340.11 | 97.40 | 2,265.47 | 2,206.46 | –59.01 |
| 1984 | 287.71 | 351.68 | 81.81 | 2,224.43 | 1,819.80 | –404.63 |
| 1985 | 295.52 | 380.21 | 77.72 | 1,904.05 | 1,479.92 | –424.13 |
| 1986 | 303.78 | 396.00 | 76.71 | 2,048.44 | 1,571.39 | –477.06 |
| 1987 | 325.21 | 426.56 | 76.24 | 2,711.80 | 2,067.50 | –644.30 |
| 1988 | 352.35 | 487.84 | 72.23 | 3,731.67 | 2,695.27 | –1,036.41 |
| 1989 | 362.64 | 518.24 | 69.98 | 4,418.21 | 3,091.69 | –1,326.53 |
| 1990 | 370.23 | 533.33 | 69.42 | 5,530.83 | 3,839.43 | –1,691.40 |
| 1991 | 382.49 | 558.56 | 68.48 | 6,153.67 | 4,213.88 | –1,939.79 |

a. 1970 = 100.
b. (3) = (1) ÷ (2) x 100.
c. Millions U.S. dollars at 1970 prices.
d. (5) = (3) x (4) ÷ 100, millions of U.S. dollars at 1970 prices.
e. (6) = (5) – (4), millions of U.S. dollars at 1970 prices.
*Source*: Authors' calculations using raw data from Bank of Thailand, with the base year readjusted to 1970.

Similarly, table 5.4 estimates the extent to which changes in the oil terms-of-trade shock caused a loss of income to the country. This is called the oil terms-of-trade effect and is calculated for any year *t* according to the similar formula:

### Table 5.4  Magnitude of the Oil Terms of Trade Shocks, 1970–91

| Year | Export index imports (1970=100) (1) | Oil import price index (1970=100) (2) | Oil terms of trade (1970=100) (3) | Actual oil import (million US$) (at 1970 prices) (4) | Counter-factual oil imports (million US$) (at 1970 prices) (5) | Oil terms of trade gain (million US$) (at 1970 prices) (6) |
|---|---|---|---|---|---|---|
| 1970 | 100.00 | 100.00 | 100.00 | 112.00 | 112.00 | 0.00 |
| 1971 | 89.86 | 112.74 | 79.70 | 116.20 | 92.61 | −23.59 |
| 1972 | 98.70 | 110.60 | 89.25 | 135.63 | 121.04 | −14.58 |
| 1973 | 151.35 | 134.16 | 112.81 | 168.46 | 190.04 | 21.59 |
| 1974 | 208.92 | 436.30 | 47.88 | 141.42 | 67.72 | −73.70 |
| 1975 | 197.11 | 479.48 | 41.11 | 145.78 | 59.93 | −85.85 |
| 1976 | 191.71 | 520.18 | 36.85 | 157.25 | 57.95 | −99.30 |
| 1977 | 195.85 | 559.53 | 35.00 | 183.01 | 64.06 | 118.95 |
| 1978 | 211.74 | 553.55 | 38.25 | 203.05 | 77.67 | 125.38 |
| 1979 | 253.02 | 772.27 | 32.76 | 207.05 | 67.84 | 139.22 |
| 1980 | 299.07 | 1,306.31 | 22.89 | 219.55 | 50.26 | 169.28 |
| 1981 | 308.07 | 1,589.85 | 19.38 | 187.69 | 36.37 | 151.32 |
| 1982 | 286.23 | 1,655.24 | 17.29 | 159.61 | 27.60 | 132.01 |
| 1983 | 331.25 | 1,448.82 | 22.86 | 171.24 | 39.15 | 132.09 |
| 1984 | 287.71 | 1,400.45 | 20.54 | 173.23 | 35.59 | 137.64 |
| 1985 | 295.52 | 1,553.33 | 19.02 | 134.42 | 25.57 | 108.85 |
| 1986 | 303.78 | 851.07 | 35.69 | 144.52 | 51.59 | 92.94 |
| 1987 | 325.21 | 947.35 | 34.33 | 201.75 | 69.26 | 132.49 |
| 1988 | 352.35 | 810.48 | 43.47 | 162.14 | 70.49 | 91.65 |
| 1989 | 362.64 | 923.45 | 39.27 | 287.36 | 112.85 | 174.51 |
| 1990 | 370.23 | 1,127.40 | 32.84 | 331.80 | 108.96 | 222.84 |
| 1991 | 382.49 | 1,143.97 | 33.44 | 305.04 | 101.99 | 203.05 |

*Note*: Calculation of columns (3), (5) and (6), as in table 5.3.

*Source*: Authors' calculations using raw data from Bank of Thailand, with the base year readjusted to 1970.

$$(5.4) \qquad L_t^P = Q_t^{PM}(P_t^{PM}/P_t^X) - Q_t^{PM}(P_0^{PM}/P_0^X)$$
$$= Q_t^{PM}(P_t^{PM}/P_t^X) - Q_t^{PM}$$

where $Q_t^{PM}$ = the actual real value of oil imports in year $t$ (valued at 1970 prices); $P_t^{PM}$ = the oil imports price index for year $t$ (1970 = 100); and $P_0^{PM}$, $P_0^X$ =

the oil imports and exports price indices at the base year of 1970. Again we normalize such that $P_0^{PM} = P_0^X = 1$.

The actual real value of oil imports is the current value of oil imports deflated by the oil imports price index. The term $Q_t^{PM}(P_t^{PM}/P_t^X)$ is the equivalent value of exportable goods that has to be sacrificed to obtain the current value of oil imports in year $t$. The term $Q_t^{PM}(P_0^{PM}/P_0^X) = Q_t^{PM}$ is the counterfactual value of oil imports and is equivalent to the value of exportable goods that would have had to be sacrificed to obtain the observed volume of imports if the oil terms of trade index had remained at its level in the base year.

It must be stressed that these calculations relate to actual outcomes in relation to counterfactual outcomes. The estimated income effects of the terms-of-trade changes presented above should not be confused with the change in *total* income that actually occurred in relation to the base period. The changes in total income reflected the impacts of many factors, of which the terms of trade was only one component. Rather, the results above represent an attempt to isolate the impact that the observed changes in the terms of trade had on national income, other things being held constant. They are estimates of the difference between what occurred—as reflected in the observed data—and hypothetical estimates of what would otherwise have occurred without the terms-of-trade shock, or the counterfactual.

In constructing a counterfactual, we assumed that the volume of imports was unaffected by the shock. Obviously, this method is somewhat crude. If the shock had not occurred, the allocation of resources and of real consumer expenditures would have been different from those observed, and in this counterfactual situation national income would have been increased as a result of those reallocations. The volume of imports would presumably have been greater as a result. Insofar as our estimated counterfactual does not allow for this fact (in assuming the observed volume of imports to have been unaffected by the shock), it may thus underestimate the counterfactual value of imports and hence overestimate the value of the income loss due to the shock. Nevertheless, the error involved seems likely to be small.

Table 5.5 summarizes our estimates of the total income loss resulting from both the nonoil and oil terms-of-trade changes and their combined effect. Table 5.6 expresses these results as proportions of GDP. It should be kept in mind that the results for the later periods are less reliable than the earlier results because the counterfactual used in the calculations is based on the year 1970. This base period therefore becomes increasingly irrelevant as it recedes into the past. Thus only the results for the first three shocks are presented.

From 1971 to 1985 there was a loss of Thai national income of about $3.5 billion (in 1970 prices) as a result of the total terms-of-trade loss. This was equivalent to about 1.3 percent of total GDP over this period. Only about 40 percent of this loss was directly attributable to the effect of the oil terms-of-trade shock. This is a significant result. Other discussions of the terms-of-trade decline experienced by Thailand since the early 1970s have concentrated on the effects of the oil price

**Table 5.5  Counterfactual Effects of the Terms of Trade on National Income, 1970–91**

*(millions of U.S. dollars at 1970 prices)*

| Year | Nonoil terms of trade effect (1) | Oil terms of trade effect (2) | Total terms of trade effect (3)[a] |
|---|---|---|---|
| 1970 | 0 | 0 | 0 |
| 1971 | −236 | −24 | −260 |
| 1972 | −184 | −15 | −198 |
| 1973 | 243 | 22 | 264 |
| 1974 | 145 | −74 | 71 |
| 1975 | 2 | −86 | −84 |
| 1976 | −90 | −99 | −189 |
| 1977 | −192 | −119 | −311 |
| 1978 | −232 | −125 | −358 |
| 1979 | −121 | −139 | −261 |
| 1980 | 44 | −169 | −125 |
| 1981 | −198 | −151 | −350 |
| 1982 | −312 | −132 | −444 |
| 1983 | −59 | −132 | −191 |
| 1984 | −405 | −138 | −542 |
| 1985 | −424 | −109 | −533 |
| 1986 | −477 | −93 | −570 |
| 1987 | −644 | −132 | −777 |
| 1988 | −1,036 | −92 | −1,128 |
| 1989 | −1,327 | −175 | −1,501 |
| 1990 | −1,691 | −223 | −1,914 |
| 1991 | −1,940 | −203 | −2,143 |
| Shock 1, 1973–74 | 387 | −52 | 335 |
| Shock 2, 1975–78 | −513 | −429 | −943 |
| Shock 3, 1979–85 | −1,475 | −970 | −2,445 |
| Whole period, 1971–85 | −2,021 | −1,490 | −3,511 |

a. (3) = (1) + (2).

*Note*: The summary data at the bottom of the table shows the estimated income effects for changes in the terms of trade during each shock period.

*Source*: Calculated from tables 5.3 and 5.4.

**Table 5.6  Conterfactual Effects of the Terms of Trade on National Income, 1970–91**

*(percentage of GDP)*

| Year | Nonoil terms of trade effect (1) | Oil terms of trade effect (2) | Total terms of trade effect (3)[a] |
|---|---|---|---|
| 1970 | 0.00 | 0.00 | 0.00 |
| 1971 | –3.48 | –0.35 | –3.82 |
| 1972 | –2.60 | –0.21 | –2.81 |
| 1973 | 3.07 | 0.27 | 3.34 |
| 1974 | 1.72 | –0.87 | 0.84 |
| 1975 | 0.02 | –0.97 | –0.95 |
| 1976 | –0.93 | –1.03 | –1.96 |
| 1977 | –1.81 | –1.12 | –2.93 |
| 1978 | –2.02 | –1.09 | –3.10 |
| 1979 | –1.00 | –1.15 | –2.16 |
| 1980 | 0.35 | –1.34 | –0.99 |
| 1981 | –1.57 | –1.20 | –2.77 |
| 1982 | –2.51 | –1.06 | –3.57 |
| 1983 | –0.44 | –0.99 | –1.43 |
| 1984 | –2.91 | –0.99 | –3.90 |
| 1985 | –3.38 | –0.87 | –4.25 |
| 1986 | –3.51 | –0.68 | –4.20 |
| 1987 | –4.23 | –0.87 | –5.10 |
| 1988 | –5.92 | –0.52 | –6.45 |
| 1989 | –6.90 | –0.91 | –7.81 |
| 1990 | –7.91 | –1.04 | –8.95 |
| 1991 | –8.45 | –0.88 | –9.33 |
| Shock 1, 1973–74 | 2.40 | –0.32 | 2.08 |
| Shock 2, 1975–78 | –1.28 | –1.07 | –2.36 |
| Shock 3, 1979–85 | –1.66 | –1.09 | –2.75 |
| Whole period, 1971–85 | –0.75 | –0.55 | –1.30 |

a. (3) = (1) + (2).

*Note*: The summary data at the bottom of the table indicates the total income effect for each shock period, as reported in table 5.5, divided by the sum of GDP in the years covered by the shock.

*Source*: Calculated from tables 3.4, 5.3 and 5.4.

rises of 1973–74 and 1979–80. According to our calculations, changes in other components of the terms of trade, taken together, were more important.

Shock 1 was equivalent to a positive income windfall of 2.1 percent of GDP per year, and shocks 2 and 3 were equivalent to negative windfalls of 2.4 and 2.8 percent of GDP per year, respectively. From the data on GDP growth (see table 3.4), the average GNP growth rate for the years 1970 to 1991 inclusive was 7.3 percent. The effects of the terms-of-trade shocks would seem to be large enough to explain the full magnitude of the deviations around trend growth rates that actually occurred. For the years 1974 and 1975, the average growth rate was 4.55 percent, 2.75 percentage points below trend; and for the years 1979–85, the average rate was 5.5 percent, 1.8 percentage points below trend. These are significant changes to the external environment, but they would not seem large enough to produce macroeconomic crises unless they were handled poorly.

## Effects of the Shocks on Economic Growth

We now use an alternative analytical approach to investigate more systematically the effects of the external shocks on Thailand's growth performance. Whereas the type of analysis presented in the previous section can address only the short-run income effects of the trade shocks, this statistical analysis makes it possible to distinguish short-run from long-run growth effects.

To study long-term effects systematically, it is necessary to separate the effect of variations in the terms of trade from the effect of variations in the conventional determinants of economic growth, growth in the inputs of primary factors of production. Our analysis aims to improve upon the usual growth accounting analysis by distinguishing between the economic variables that affect national output—the inputs of capital, labor, and land—on the one hand, and changes in the country's external trading environment, on the other. The shock consists of changes in the latter variables, not the former, but the former are changing over time as well.

In the usual analysis, an attempt is made to identify a simple relationship between GDP and the terms of trade, ignoring changes in the levels of physical inputs. The impact of the shock is that it alters the economic productivity of national factors of production. It is therefore appropriate to distinguish between those changes in national output caused by variations in the levels of inputs of factors of production and those changes caused by externally induced enhancement or diminution of their productivity.

### Growth Accounting

The objective here is to determine the extent to which variations in the rate of Thai economic growth can be explained by the growth of the conventional primary factors of production—capital, labor and land—or by other factors, such as technological change or external price movements. We applied the standard techniques of growth accounting to Thai data in an attempt to answer this question.

Our estimating equation was derived by hypothesizing that the terms of trade enter the aggregate production function. Thailand's international trade involves intermediate goods and capital goods, not merely consumption goods. Thus real national output depends not only on the supplies of physical factors of production and their productivity but also on the terms on which the domestic economy is able to trade with the rest of the world. That is, for given levels of the primary factors of production, real GDP also is affected by variations in the terms of trade because these variations affect the quantities of intermediate goods (like petroleum) that can be purchased in exchange for a given quantity of domestic output. They thus affect the net output that can be produced with a given stock of primary factors.

Let the aggregate production function be

$$(5.5) \qquad Y = f(K, L, H, P^*, t)$$

where $Y$ is GDP at constant prices, $K$ is the aggregate capital shock at constant prices, $L$ is the aggregate labor force, $H$ is the total area of cultivated land, $P^*$ is the terms of trade (ratio of export prices to import prices), and $t$ denotes time.

SHORT-TERM GROWTH EFFECTS. To capture the short-term effects that changes in the terms of trade have on aggregate output we estimated the above equation in Cobb-Douglas form. We used Thai annual data for 1961–89, drawn from the World Bank's *World Tables*, except for the capital stock series, which is a new series recently released by Thailand's National Economic and Social Development Board. The data on GDP and real factor inputs used in this exercise are displayed in figure 5.4; real GDP, the real capital stock, and the labor force are all indexed to unity in the initial year of our data set, 1961. The terms-of-trade series is as described above. Constant returns to scale were imposed via the restriction that the coefficients on the variables $K$, $L$, and $H$ sum to unity. It is then possible to rearrange the estimating equation as

$$(5.6) \qquad ln(Y/H) = \alpha_0 + \alpha_K ln(K/H) + \alpha_L ln(L/H) + \beta lnP^* + \sigma t$$

The estimated parameters and relevant diagnostics (*t*-statistics in parentheses) were

$$(5.7) \quad ln(Y/H) = -0.33 + 0.27\ ln(K/H) + 0.52\ ln(L/H) + 0.12\ lnP^* + 0.036t$$
$$\qquad\qquad (-0.50)\ (1.82) \qquad\quad (2.21) \qquad\quad (2.26) \qquad\quad (7.50)$$

where $\overline{R}^2 = 0.99$, $DW$ statistic = 2.05, and log likelihood = 54.67.

The estimated coefficient on the terms-of-trade variable is positive and significantly different from zero at the 5 percent significance level. When the lagged value of this variable is included in the regression, its estimated coefficient is

**Figure 5.4. Indexes of Real GDP, Real Capital Stock, Labor Force and Land, 1961–89**

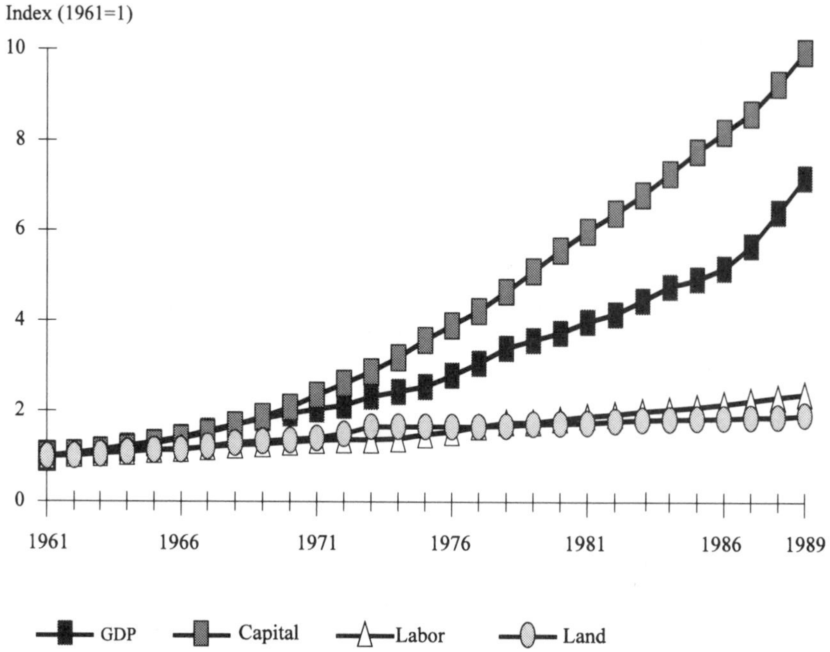

Index (1961=1)

*Source:* Table 5.7.

considerably smaller and insignificant. The estimated elasticity of current GDP with respect to the current terms of trade is 0.14. That is, a 10 percent rise (fall) in the terms of trade leads to a 1.4 percent rise (fall) in GDP. From 1970 to 1990, Thailand's terms of trade declined by 40 percentage points, from an index of 100 to an index of 60, an annual rate of decline of 2.55 percent. Our estimates imply that this decline reduced Thailand's rate of growth by an average 0.35 percent per year. Alternatively, the lump-sum reduction in GDP implied by a 40 percent decline in the terms of trade was 5.6 percent of mean GDP over this period.

Using these estimated parameters, it is now possible to study total factor productivity growth on an annual basis by applying the equation

$$(5.8) \qquad F_t = \frac{dlnY}{dt} - \alpha_K \frac{dlnK}{dt} - \alpha_L \frac{dlnL}{dt} - \alpha_H \frac{dlnH}{dt}$$

where $F_t$ denotes the estimated rate of total factor productivity growth in year $t$ and $\alpha_K$, $\alpha_L$ and $\alpha_H$ denote the estimated coefficients above, and where the implied value of $\alpha_H$ is 0.21.

These results were summarized for five periods: 1970–72, the period before shock 1; 1973–74, which captures the impact of the first shock; 1975–78, which captures the impact of the second shock; 1979–85, which captures shock 3; and

1986–89, which captures the impact of shock 4 (see table 5.7). The impacts of the two negative terms-of-trade shocks caused by the two OPEC price increases are clearly evident by comparing the results for 1975–78 (shock two) and 1979–85 (shock 3) with the other three periods—before and after the two oil price shocks, respectively. Total factor productivity (TFP) growth was apparently reduced by the two oil price shocks, but the effect was far from catastrophic. Significantly, TFP growth remained positive in spite of the shocks.

LONG-TERM GROWTH EFFECTS. The lagged value of the dependent variable may be included as a regressor in order to distinguish between short- and long-run effects. The Cochrane-Orcutt autoregression technique was again used to correct for autocorrelation.[1] The estimated equation was:

**Table 5.7  Growth Accounting, 1970–89**

| Variable | 1970–72 | Shock 1 1973–74 | Shock 2 1975–78 | Shock 3 1979–85 | Shock 4 1986–89 | Whole period 1970–89 |
|---|---|---|---|---|---|---|
| *Growth data (percent per year)* | | | | | | |
| GDP | 4.42 | 6.83 | 8.27 | 5.33 | 9.41 | 6.87 |
| Labor force | 1.97 | 0.95 | 5.80 | 2.53 | 3.28 | 3.15 |
| Capital stock | 2.37 | 2.96 | 4.66 | 6.15 | 8.26 | 5.07 |
| Land | 5.00 | 4.98 | 0.39 | 0.69 | 1.29 | 1.81 |
| Terms of trade | –5.22 | 10.35 | –9.24 | –3.61 | 0.75 | –2.58 |
| TFP | 1.71 | 4.50 | 3.62 | 3.35 | 5.16 | 3.47 |
| | | | | | | |
| *Contribution to overall growth (percent)* | | | | | | |
| Labor | 23.34 | 7.28 | 39.99 | 22.18 | 18.56 | 23.96 |
| Capital | 14.54 | 11.70 | 15.24 | 31.03 | 23.77 | 19.99 |
| Land | 23.47 | 15.13 | 0.97 | 2.70 | 2.85 | 5.49 |
| Terms of trade change | –14.00 | 17.96 | –13.25 | –8.04 | 0.94 | –4.45 |
| TFP | 38.65 | 65.89 | 43.80 | 44.09 | 54.82 | 50.56 |

*Source*: Author calculations, with data drawn from World Bank, *World Debt Tables*, various issues, and National Statistical Office, *Quarterly Bulletin of Statistics*, various issues.

$$(5.9) \quad ln(Y/H) = 0.31 + 0.09\ ln(K/H) + 0.71\ ln(L/H) + 0.16\ lnP* + 0.027t + 0.25\ ln(Y/H)_{-1}$$
$$\phantom{(5.9) \quad ln(Y/H) = }(0.47)\ (0.55)\qquad\ (2.99)\qquad\quad (2.50)\qquad\ (3.19)\quad (1.17)$$

where $\overline{R}^2 = 0.99$, the *DW* statistic = 2.13, the Durbin *h*-statistic = 0.74, and log likelihood = 54.58.

The estimated short-run elasticity of real GDP with respect to the terms of trade is 0.16, which is slightly higher than indicated above and is again significantly different from zero. The advantage of this specification is that the long-run elasticity is given by $\beta/(1-\delta)$, where $\delta$ is the lagged dependent variable. Thus the estimated long-run elasticity is 0.21. The long-term decline in the terms of trade over the twenty years from 1970 was 2.55 percent per year, which implies a long-term reduction in real GDP of 0.54 percent per year. According to these estimates, GDP growth would have been 0.54 percent higher than it was but for the terms-of-trade decline that actually occurred. From shocks 1 to 4 the terms of trade changed at annual rates of 10.35, –9.24, –3.61, and 0.75 percent, respectively (table 5.7). Combined with our estimates of the short-run and long-run elasticity of GDP with respect to the terms of trade, these imply short-run changes in GDP growth of 1.66, –1.48, –0.58, and 0.12 percentage points, respectively. The implied long-run changes are 2.15, –1.94, –0.76, and 0.16 percentage points, respectively.

## Conclusions

The most important external shocks to affect Thailand from 1970 to 1990 were the two rounds of OPEC-induced oil price increases of the 1970s. The effects of these two shocks on Thailand's balance of payments were equivalent to 4 percent of 1973 GDP and 2.4 percent of 1979 GDP, respectively. Shocks of this size seem large enough to cause serious problems but are not necessarily large enough to produce crises, unless badly managed.

We found that the size of the shocks was large enough to explain fully the deviations of Thai GDP growth around its trend. This may be taken to mean that the shocks were large, or that the shocks caused GDP to fluctuate by roughly the magnitude of the effect of the shocks on the balance of payments, and no more. That is, the shocks were not destabilizing.

Our analysis of Thailand's total factor productivity growth indicates a positive relationship between total factor productivity growth and the terms of trade (ratio of export prices to import prices). Total factor productivity was affected in the short run by terms-of-trade movements in the predicted direction, but this effect was mild and short-lived. Adjustment to these short-run effects was rapid in that the estimated long-run effects were only 1.33 times as large as the estimated short-run effects. In the long run, total factor productivity continued to increase, despite a long-term decline in Thailand's terms of trade. The estimated long-term reduction in GDP growth caused by the long-term decline in the terms of trade was 0.54 percent per year.

# Chapter Six

# Thailand's Macroeconomic Response

Thailand's aggregate economic responses to the shocks described in chapter 5 can be examined by reviewing, first, the various alternative responses that Thailand could have adopted, second, the pattern that would have been optimal and, third, Thailand's actual responses. In this chapter, Thailand's responses are examined in the light of internal and external balance, the changes in aggregate saving and investment, and the level of external debt. The analysis is conducted at an aggregate, economy-wide level and leaves the discussion of specific instruments of government policy to subsequent chapters.

### Analyzing the Adjustment Response

It is helpful to begin with a simple analytical framework. The discussion opens with a taxonomy of alternative patterns of adjustment responses that emphasizes the concepts of internal and external balance. We then present a simple intertemporal framework for analyzing the pattern of *optimal* adjustment in the face of external shocks like those experienced by Thailand. As this exercise shows, the crucial issue is whether the shock is expected to be temporary or permanent.

*Alternative Adjustment Responses*

Suppose there is a negative terms-of-trade shock. National income falls and along with it, tax revenue. Government expenditure may or may not change. Absorption may fall, but not as much as income. The current account will thus move into deficit. The government's possible responses can be summarized in terms of three simple stylized cases, which can be called the neutral response, the response aimed at restoring internal balance, and the response aimed at restoring external balance.[1]

NEUTRAL RESPONSE. Under this "nonadjustment" response, the disequilibria in internal and external balance are allowed to persist. The internal disequilibrium is such that as income falls, some domestic resources will become idle. The extent to which this consists of unemployment depends in part on the downward flexibility of real wages and the flexibility of firms' employment and output decisions.

The external disequilibrium will be given by

$$(6.1) \qquad\qquad M - X = (I^P - S^P) + (G - T)$$

where $M$ denotes gross imports, $X$ denotes gross exports, $I^P$ denotes private sector investment, $S^P$ denotes private sector saving, $G$ denotes government expenditure, and $T$ denotes government revenue. The left-hand side of this expression is the external deficit. The right-hand side states that this imbalance is equal to the sum of the private sector and public sector deficits—the two expressions in parentheses. The objective of the neutral private sector response is to save less in relation to investment as a result of the shock. The neutral public sector response will be to run a budget deficit as tax revenues fall.

RESPONSE TO RESTORE INTERNAL BALANCE. When GDP falls, the government may respond by stimulating domestic demand so as to maintain growth. The fiscal means of achieving this outcome include a tax cut, an expenditure increase, or a subsidy to petroleum imports. The result of this response will be a restoration of internal balance at the expense of worsening public sector and external deficits. The private sector outcome will be to maintain consumption and investment spending, at the expense of dissaving. The dissaving of individual agents will be financed by domestic and foreign borrowing, and the dissaving of the public sector will correspond to budgetary deficits, also financed by borrowing. In aggregate, foreign borrowing will be the ultimate source of finance.

RESPONSE TO RESTORE EXTERNAL BALANCE. In this case, when income falls, absorption must fall more than in either of the above two cases. Total investment must fall. If there is a private sector deficit, $(I^P > S^P)$, then this must be offset by a public sector surplus $(G < T)$.

*Optimal Aggregate Response*

Which of the above responses is most appropriate for a country faced with the kind of external instability Thailand has experienced? When a simple two-period theoretical model is used to explore this question, it seems that the answer will depend on whether private and public sector agents expect the shock to be temporary or permanent. The Thai experience in this regard is discussed later in the chapter.

ADJUSTMENT TO EXTERNAL SHOCKS: A SIMPLE FRAMEWORK. Figure 6.1 presents a simple two-period theoretical model of the adjustment of saving, investment, and the balance of payments in response to an external shock. The axes show aggregate national consumption and the production of a single commodity in each of two periods: period 0, the present, shown on the horizontal axis; and the future, period 1, shown on the vertical axis. The initial output in each of the two periods is shown by point A. The initial output in period 0, $y_0$, may be consumed or invested. Investment allows output in period 1 to be increased. The schedule PP describes these investment possibilities.

In a closed economy, in which borrowing from or lending to other countries is not possible, consumption and production must both occur on the PP schedule. If social preferences have the form described by indifference curve U', then consumption and production will each occur at point B. Investment in period 0 is given by $y_0 - c_0$, which is also the level of saving. This enables future consumption (period 1) to exceed output in that period (dissaving).

If an international capital market is now introduced, borrowing from or lending to other countries becomes possible. The line marked KK describes these possibilities. Its slope is $-(1 + r)$, where $r$ is the international rate of interest, in real terms. The optimal production point is now point C and consumption ideally occurs at point D, allowing a level of social welfare U", higher than U', to be attained. There is now a difference between saving and investment in period 0. Saving is given by $y_0 - c_0''$ and investment is higher at $y_0 - z_0''$. The difference between investment and saving in period 0 corresponds to $c_0'' - z_0''$. That is, it is optimal for investment to be $y_0 - z_0''$ and for this to be financed in part by domestic saving $(y_0 - c_0'')$ and in part by borrowing from abroad $(c_0'' - z_0'')$. The amount borrowed from abroad is equivalent to a current account deficit and a capital account surplus. This deficit is given by the national accounting identity

(6.2)                     $$D_t = M_t - X_t = I_t - S_t$$

where $D_t$ is the deficit, in year $t$, and $M_t$, $X_t$, $I_t$ and $S_t$ denote imports, exports, investment, and saving in year $t$, respectively.

Before using this diagram for the analysis of trade shocks, it is useful to note that a balance of payments deficit or surplus is not in itself necessarily either desirable or undesirable. In the case shown, optimal utilization of the opportunities provided by international capital markets and domestic investment opportunities requires that a current account deficit exist in period 0. There is nothing undesirable about this. Of course, the borrowings must be repaid in the future, but social welfare is raised in the process.

Obviously, the actual level of any current account deficit that might be observed in period 0 could in principle be either larger or smaller than this optimal amount. This point is important because it is common for observers of macroeconomic statistics to describe any increase of a current account deficit as a "worsening" and any reduction as an "improvement." Our analysis shows that this approach is unsatisfactory. An increase or a reduction in a current account deficit from one year to the next could be either desirable or undesirable, depending on whether it represented a move toward or away from an optimal intertemporal allocation of resources. Similarly, the analysis in figure 6.1 suggests that for a net borrower there is an optimal level of debt in the present period. A current account deficit in any year is a flow item that adds to the existing stock of debt (minus reserves). This is desirable if the present level of debt is suboptimal, and undesirable if present debt is excessive.

OPTIMAL ADJUSTMENT. The foregoing apparatus is now used to analyze the optimal adjustment to an external shock, such as an improvement in the country's terms of trade. A distinction between temporary and permanent shocks is central to the analysis. A temporary shock is taken to mean one that improves the value of production possibilities in period 0, leaving the value of period 1 potential output

**Figure 6.1. A Model of Savings, Investment, and Balance of Payments**

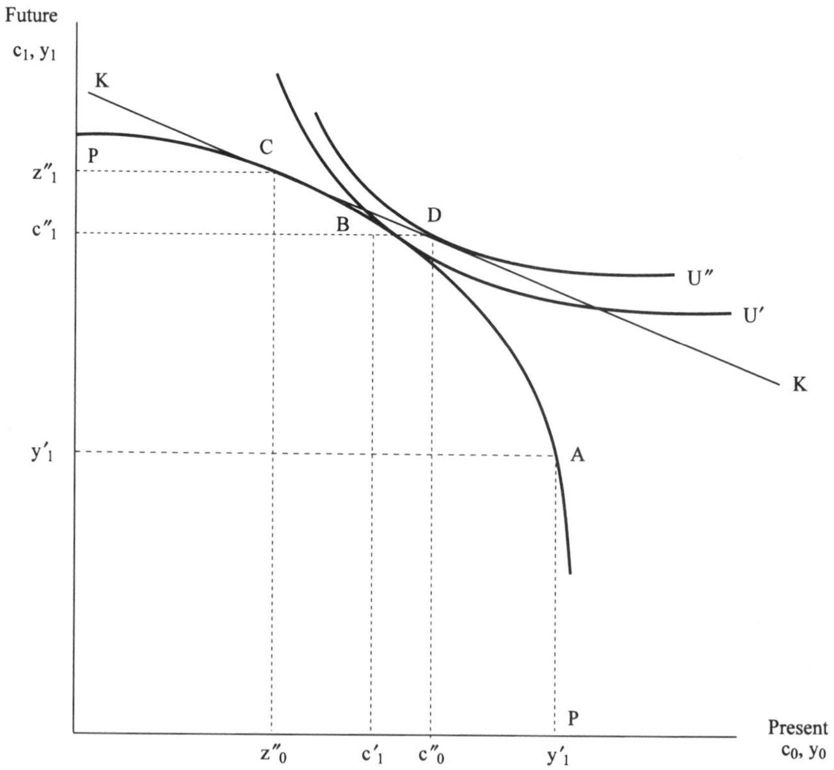

*Source:* Authors' compilation.

unchanged from before. A permanent shock will be one that raises production possibilities in both periods. The optimal response to these two types of shocks will be different.

A temporary, positive shock may be represented in figure 6.1 as a rightward movement of the endowment point, A, and the associated investment possibilities schedule, PP. Each point on the new PP schedule will have the same slope as one on the old PP schedule immediately to its left. A permanent, positive shock will correspond to a movement of point A outward along a ray from the origin, and a corresponding proportional movement of each point on the PP schedule outward from the origin. The resulting diagrams are complex, and it is sufficient here to summarize the characteristics of an optimal adjustment as they would be observed in period 0. We hold the international real interest rate $r$ constant throughout the analysis.

In response to a temporary and positive shock, the optimal level of investment would be unchanged. The intuitive reason for this outcome is that the optimal level of investment depends on the shape of the PP schedule and the international interest rate, neither of which is affected by a temporary shock. Only the position of the PP schedule changes; however, saving in period 0 rises. The intuitive reason is that present consumption is only an imperfect substitute for future consumption. Smoothing consumption over time is therefore desirable, and saving a high proportion of the temporary windfall is a way of achieving this outcome. It follows that the current account deficit, the difference between aggregate investment and saving, must decline.

A permanent shock will induce an increase in investment, because the change in the shape of the PP schedule implies improved productivity of investment. Savings will also rise, but not as much as in the case of a comparable temporary shock, that is, one that has the same effect on output in period 0, because output possibilities in period 1 are also improved and the necessity for consumption smoothing is thus reduced. The current account deficit may rise or fall, but any decline would be smaller than that observed under a comparable temporary shock.

An example of a positive trade shock in the case of a petroleum importer like Thailand would be a reduction in petroleum prices. The optimal patterns of adjustment to a negative trade shock will, of course, be the reverse of those described.

## Thailand's Aggregate Response

Using the above theoretical framework, what can be said of Thailand's aggregate adjustment response to the four shocks identified in chapter 5?

### Changes in Internal and External Balance

Data on the attainment of internal and external balance in Thailand are presented in figures 6.2 and 6.3, respectively. Figure 6.2 resembles a Phillips diagram except that

**Figure 6.2. Income Shocks and Internal Balance, 1971–90**

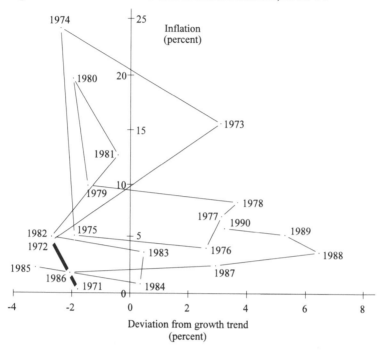

Source: Table 3.4 and authors' calculations.

the horizontal axis shows deviations from trend growth instead of rates of unemployment. As with most developing countries, Thailand's data on unemployment are unreliable, and deviations from trend GDP growth rates are the best proxy for internal balance. The vertical axis of figure 6.2 shows the annual rate of inflation and the horizontal axis shows deviations from the trend rate of growth of real GDP. Figure 6.2 is thus intended to reveal departures from internal balance. Figure 6.3 shows the ratio of the current account deficit to GDP on the vertical axis and (as with figure 6.2) deviations from the real GDP growth trend on the horizontal axis. The figure therefore plots the relationship between Thailand's external and internal balance.

As figure 6.2 indicates, from 1972 to 1974 inflation surged. The reason was the surge in nominal import and export prices, together with Thailand's fixed exchange rate. Beginning in 1974, growth rates fell below the trend rate of 6.7 percent, but when inflation abated in 1975, income growth also recovered. Growth was above the trend from 1976 to 1978 and inflation remained moderate. Shock 3 coincided with reduced growth (during 1979–81) and increased inflation, especially in 1980. The inflation quickly subsided, but growth remained below the trend until 1982. Inflation remained low in the rest of the decade, but growth rates did not recover until 1987.

The two oil price shocks triggered not only large relative price movements among Thailand's imported and exported commodities, but also substantial in-

**Figure 6.3.  Income Shocks and External Balance, 1971–90**

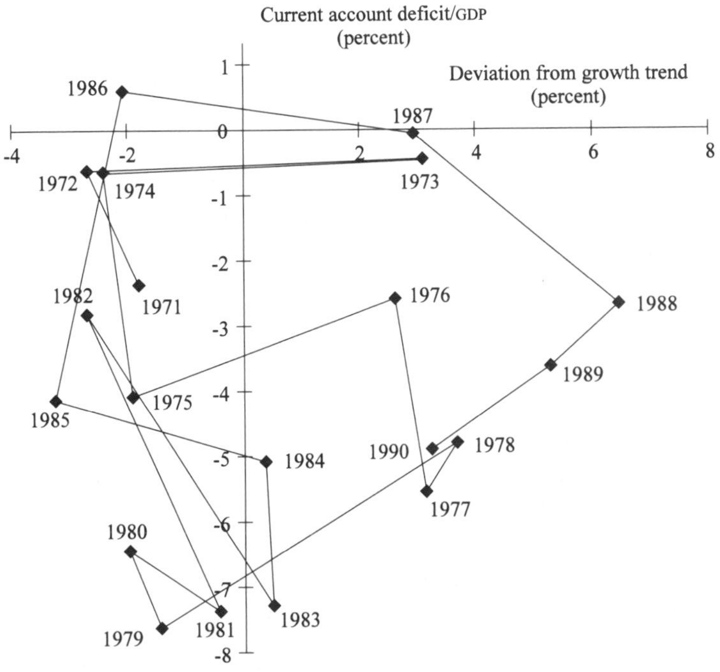

Current account deficit/GDP
(percent)

Deviation from growth trend
(percent)

*Source:* Table 3.4 and authors' calculations.

creases in their nominal prices (see figure 5.2). The nominal price of imported petroleum and of nonoil imports and exports also increased. Since the Thai exchange
rate was fixed in terms of the U.S. dollar during these periods, the external inflation was imported into Thailand (see figure 3.7 and table 3.4). Following each of
the oil price shocks, inflation surged to roughly 20 percent but then quickly abated,
in contrast to the pattern in many other developing countries. The reasons for the
temporary nature of the inflation in Thailand are examined in chapter 8.

From figure 6.3 it is apparent that the shocks disrupted Thailand's external
balance for extended periods. Both shock 2 and shock 3 led to large current account deficits, and these were allowed to persist until 1985. It seems clear that
maintaining external balance was accorded a lower priority than achieving low inflation (which was first on the agenda) or maintaining growth.

*Changes in Aggregate Saving and Investment*

Shock 1, the 1973–74 commodity price boom, was too short-lived to be analyzed
in the present framework, but the response to the shock 2 (1974–76) round of oil

**Figure 6.4. Investment-Savings Gap, 1970–90**

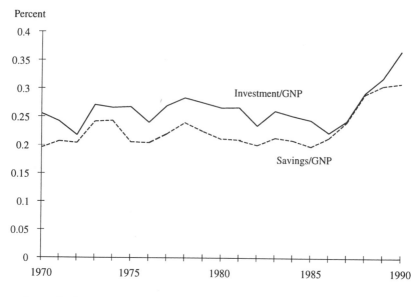

*Source:* Bank of Thailand.

price increases, is clearer. Investment was maintained, and savings fell (figure 6.4). The shock was treated as if it were temporary. Consumption and investment were maintained on the implicit assumption that the shock would not last. As income growth recovered through the late 1970s, both the investment/GDP and savings/GDP ratios increased, but in parallel. The contribution of foreign saving to the financing of total investment remained steady.

The response to the shock 3 (1979–80) round of petroleum price increases was initially similar. The shock was again treated as being temporary. From 1979 to 1985 investment rates were again maintained, with the brief exception of 1982, and saving rates fell slightly. But by 1985 the resulting external imbalance was becoming a serious concern. From 1986 onward, adjustment took two forms. First, saving rates rose and investment rates fell. Thereafter, the adjustment story is complicated by shock 4, caused by the export and investment-led boom of the late 1980s. The GDP growth rate rose sharply, and both savings and investment rates responded. The larger response of savings, however, virtually eliminated the investment-savings gap over the interval 1986 to 1989. From 1990 the current account again began showing a growing deficit.

From figure 6.4 it is clear that the main culprit behind the rising saving-investment gap of the late 1970s was the rapid increase in aggregate investment as a proportion of GDP and simultaneous stagnation in aggregate savings. Public fixed investment was responsible for this expansion in investment (figure 6.5). From 1980 to 1986, however, the main explanation for the high investment-savings gap

**Figure 6.5. Composition of Gross Domestic Investment, 1970–90**

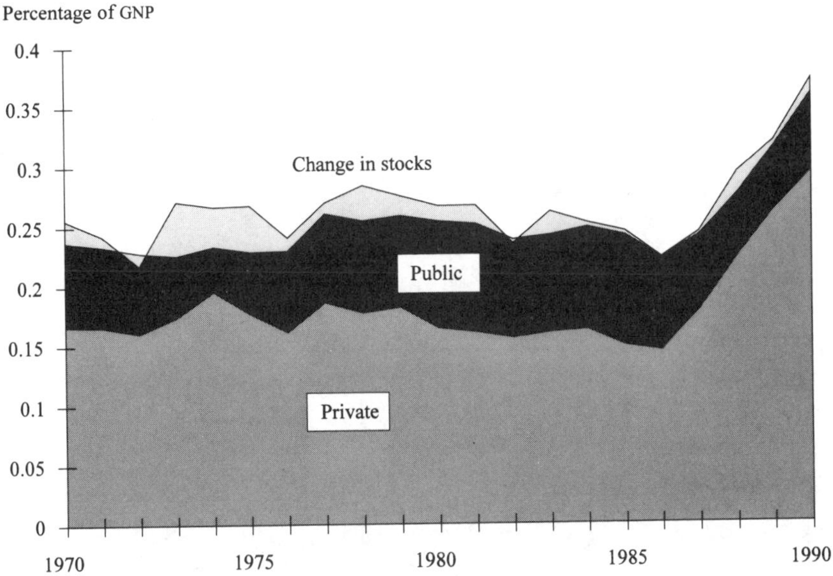

Percentage of GNP

*Source:* Bank of Thailand.

was a dramatic decline in gross national savings, which dropped from 20.7 percent of GDP in 1980 to 17.1 percent in 1985 (table 6.1). As a share of GDP, gross national savings fell by more than one-sixth.

Many experts in Thailand and foreign observers attributed the growth in the external debt over the first half of the 1980s to the behavior of the public sector deficit. Public sector savings had indeed declined (table 6.1), but far more significant was the one-third drop in household savings, which had fallen from 13.7 percent to 9.0 percent of GDP.

The decline in household savings as a share of GDP accounted for well over half of the total savings-investment gap. One possible explanation for this drop is that the slowdown in income growth was seen as a temporary phenomenon and therefore was not matched by a slowdown in consumption growth. Another, more speculative suggestion is that the contraction of rural incomes resulting from low commodity prices squeezed aggregate household savings, because rural Thais have a higher marginal propensity to save than urban dwellers. Such a squeeze could hardly be large enough, however, to explain the decline in savings that actually occurred.

Public sector savings, operating through fiscal outcomes, without doubt had a stabilizing effect (see chapter 7), but the household sector made a far greater contribution in this regard, through its saving behavior (figure 6.6). Personal savings are highly responsive to changes in growth—they are more sensitive than total in-

**Table 6.1  National Savings, 1980–85**

*(percentage of GDP, current prices)*

| Savings | 1980 | 1981 | 1982 | 1983 | 1984 | 1985 |
|---|---|---|---|---|---|---|
| Net private | 14.8 | 12.2 | 11.5 | 8.7 | 8.1 | 8.7 |
| Households | 13.7 | 11.2 | 10.9 | 7.9 | 8.3 | 9.0 |
| Corporations | 1.1 | 1.0 | 0.6 | 0.8 | –0.2 | –0.3 |
| Net public | 0.8 | 0.9 | –0.4 | 1.3 | 1.0 | 0.4 |
| General government | 0.6 | 0.6 | –0.8 | 0.5 | 0.0 | –0.3 |
| State enterprises | 0.2 | 0.3 | 0.4 | 0.8 | 1.0 | 0.7 |
| Net national | 15.6 | 13.1 | 11.1 | 10.0 | 9.1 | 9.1 |
| Depreciation | 7.4 | 7.5 | 7.8 | 8.0 | 8.0 | 8.0 |
| Statistical discrepancy | –2.0 | –3.0 | –0.5 | –2.1 | — | — |
| Gross national | 20.7 | 17.8 | 18.4 | 15.9 | 17.1 | 17.1 |

*Source*: NESDB, Bank of Thailand, and World Bank mission estimates. Reproduced from World Bank (1986).

**Figure 6.6.  Composition of Domestic Saving, 1970–90**

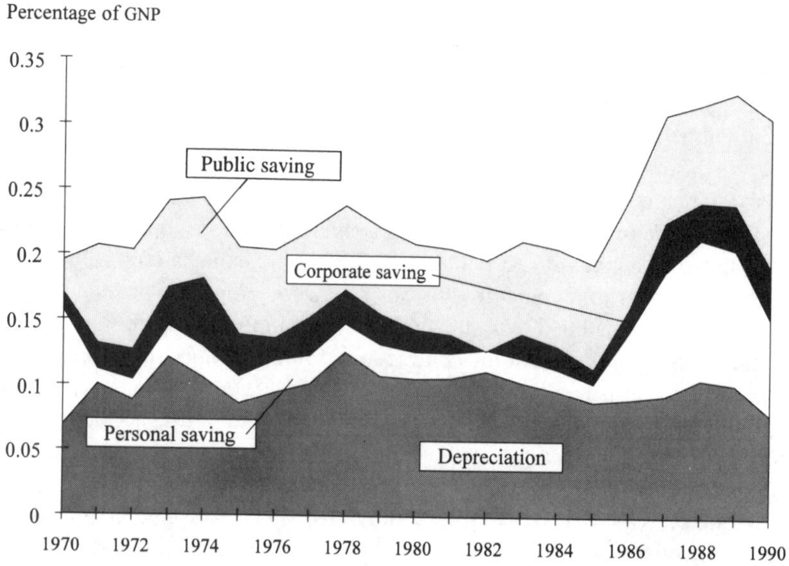

Percentage of GNP

*Source:* Bank of Thailand.

vestment or public sector savings—and this point is central to an understanding of the long-term macroeconomic stability of the Thai economy.

### Changes in External Debt

The military government that came to power in 1976 introduced some important changes in economic policy. As explained in chapter 4, restrictions on the foreign borrowing of state enterprises and the military itself were relaxed, and public expenditure expanded. The latter move caused the current account deficit to increase to 5.7 percent of GDP. From 1977 to 1985 the investment-savings gap averaged 6.4 percent of GDP, compared with an average of 2.1 percent from 1970 to 1976. By the early 1980s Thai policymakers were greatly concerned about the growth of the external debt. Table 6.2 summarizes the movement of Thailand's external debt from 1970 to 1990 and its composition.

EXTERNAL DEBT, 1980–85. Perhaps the closest that Thailand has come to a "crisis" in the past two decades was in 1982–85. The external debt situation was by then a serious public issue. The subsequent export boom relieved this pressure, but insofar as this boom seems to have owed more to external developments than to any changes Thailand itself made, the situation could just as well have been very different. The post-1985 boom might not have occurred.

Table 6.3 provides useful background data to the 1985 debt "crisis." Thailand's credit rating is one of the highest among developing countries. This, combined with prudent management of the composition of Thailand's debt, has enabled Thailand to borrow on favorable terms, as reflected in the relatively low interest rates and long maturity of Thailand's debt. In the period 1980–85, Thailand had ready access to international bond markets, a rarity among developing countries. Moreover, a high proportion of its debt was held with official rather than private institutions. Nevertheless, the size of the foreign debt had become a serious concern.

By 1985 public long-term debt was in excess of $8 billion and private debt just over $4 billion, with roughly another $4 billion in total short-term debt. The total debt stock in 1985 was $16 billion, which represented 41 percent of GDP and 146 percent of exports. The debt-service ratio (total debt service, including obligations to the IMF, divided by total exports, including factor services) had reached 26 percent, an alarming figure for Thailand's conservative financial managers.

Tables 6.4 and 6.5 show the time path of the growth of this debt. Note that in years when the public sector borrowed heavily, the growth of private borrowing was smaller, and vice versa. This relationship appears to be at least partly the result of the way in which domestic and foreign borrowing are used to finance the public sector's deficit. Whenever concern is raised about foreign borrowing, public borrowing has concentrated on domestic sources, forcing the private sector to borrow offshore to avoid the resulting high domestic interest rates. Because of this crowding-out effect, public or private foreign debt in isolation could be a misleading indicator. Total debt is more relevant.

**Table 6.2  Total Foreign Debt, 1970–90**
*(millions of U.S. dollars)*

| Year | Private | Public | Total | Interest payments |
|------|---------|--------|-------|-------------------|
| 1970 | 401 | 348 | 749 | 34 |
| 1971 | 425 | 368 | 793 | 41 |
| 1972 | 505 | 407 | 913 | 43 |
| 1973 | 461 | 459 | 920 | 56 |
| 1974 | 648 | 528 | 1,176 | 86 |
| 1975 | 736 | 623 | 1,360 | 106 |
| 1976 | 785 | 830 | 1,615 | 107 |
| 1977 | 880 | 1,151 | 2,031 | 127 |
| 1978 | 931 | 1,788 | 2,719 | 205 |
| 1979 | 1,243 | 2,713 | 3,957 | 318 |
| 1980 | 1,751 | 3,953 | 5,704 | 510 |
| 1981 | 2,099 | 5,077 | 7,175 | 697 |
| 1982 | 2,296 | 6,021 | 8,318 | 695 |
| 1983 | 2,663 | 6,865 | 9,528 | 703 |
| 1984 | 3,372 | 7,425 | 10,797 | 809 |
| 1985 | 3,370 | 9,406 | 12,776 | 880 |
| 1986 | 3,117 | 10,954 | 14,071 | 1,038 |
| 1987 | 2,837 | 12,911 | 15,748 | 1,093 |
| 1988 | 3,016 | 12,363 | 15,379 | 1,144 |
| 1989 | 4,658 | 11,743 | 16,401 | 1,064 |
| 1990 | 7,341 | 11,253 | 18,594 | 1,501 |
| *Accumulation* | | | | |
| 1974–78 | 469 | 1,329 | 1,799 | 631 |
| 1979–83 | 1,733 | 5,077 | 6,809 | 2,923 |
| 1984–90 | 4,677 | 4,387 | 9,065 | 7,529 |
| 1971–90 | 7,741 | 11,600 | 19,342 | 11,223 |

*Source*: Bank of Thailand.

## Table 6.3 Indicators of Indebtedness, 1970–85

| Indicator | 1970 | 1975 | 1980 | 1981 | 1982 | 1983 | 1984 | 1985 |
|---|---|---|---|---|---|---|---|---|
| *Stock of debt (U.S. billions of dollars)* | | | | | | | | |
| Total | 1.09 | 2.28 | 8.11 | 10.10 | 11.34 | 13.15 | 14.49 | 16.06 |
| Long-term | 0.72 | 1.36 | 5.80 | 7.22 | 8.45 | 9.66 | 10.92 | 12.21 |
| Public long-term[a] | 0.32 | 0.62 | 4.10 | 5.13 | 6.14 | 7.00 | 7.57 | 8.16 |
| Private long-term | 0.40 | 0.74 | 1.70 | 2.10 | 2.32 | 2.66 | 3.37 | 4.05 |
| Short-term[b] | 0.37 | 0.92 | 2.30 | 2.88 | 2.88 | 3.49 | 3.55 | 3.85 |
| | | | | | | | | |
| *Debt ratios (percentage)* | | | | | | | | |
| Total debt/ GDP | 16.6 | 15.5 | 24.2 | 28.0 | 30.8 | 32.6 | 34.5 | 40.6 |
| Total debt/ exports[a] | 92.9 | 76.7 | 94.6 | 109.2 | 120.5 | 142.5 | 138.6 | 146.0 |
| Public | 27.3 | 20.9 | 47.9 | 55.4 | 65.2 | 75.9 | 72.4 | 74.2 |
| Private | 34.2 | 24.9 | 19.9 | 22.7 | 24.6 | 28.8 | 32.2 | 36.9 |
| Short-term | 31.4 | 30.9 | 26.9 | 31.1 | 30.6 | 37.8 | 34.0 | 35.0 |
| | | | | | | | | |
| *Debt service/exports[c]* | | | | | | | | |
| Total debt | 17.1 | 15.1 | 17.3 | 17.4 | 13.89 | 22.9 | 24.8 | 26.1 |
| Long-term debt | 14.0 | 12.0 | 14.6 | 14.3 | 15.9 | 19.1 | 21.4 | 22.3 |
| Public | 3.4 | 2.4 | 5.1 | 6.7 | 8.3 | 10.2 | 11.9 | 11.7 |
| Private | 10.6 | 9.6 | 9.5 | 7.6 | 7.5 | 8.9 | 9.4 | 10.6 |
| Short-term[d] | 3.1 | 3.1 | 2.7 | 3.1 | 3.1 | 3.8 | 3.4 | 3.8 |
| Total debt-service ratio including IMF[e] | 17.1 | 15.1 | 17.5 | 18.3 | 19.3 | 23.3 | 25.4 | 26.3 |

a. Long-term debt is debt with over 12 months maturity.
b. World Bank staff estimates for 1970 and 1975 (official data not available).
c. Exports of goods and services.
d. Interest payments only.
e. Includes repurchase obligation to the IMF. IMF debt is not included elsewhere in the table.
*Source*: World Bank Debtor Reporting System (MLT data); B.I.S. and government data (short-term debt); IMF (repurchase obligation). 1985 data are staff estimates. Based on World Bank (1986).

**Table 6.4  External Debt, 1967–85**
*(millions of baht)*

| Year | Government | Private | Total | Debt-export ratio |
|------|-----------|---------|-------|-------------------|
| 1967 | 38 | 49 | 87 | 8.5 |
| 1968 | 45 | 71 | 116 | 11.3 |
| 1969 | 43 | 95 | 138 | 12.8 |
| 1970 | 40 | 125 | 165 | 15.1 |
| 1971 | 41 | 159 | 200 | 16.5 |
| 1972 | 45 | 140 | 185 | 12.1 |
| 1973 | 55 | 216 | 271 | 13.0 |
| 1974 | 61 | 207 | 268 | 8.7 |
| 1975 | 76 | 295 | 371 | 13.0 |
| 1976 | 87 | 299 | 386 | 10.8 |
| 1977 | 123 | 329 | 452 | 11.0 |
| 1978 | 200 | 644 | 844 | 17.0 |
| 1979 | 296 | 698 | 994 | 15.4 |
| 1980 | 442 | 859 | 1,301 | 15.7 |
| 1981 | 668 | 818 | 1,486 | 16.5 |
| 1982 | 869 | 792 | 1,661 | 18.1 |
| 1983 | 952 | 897 | 1,849 | 20.5 |
| 1984 | 1,065 | 1,032 | 2,097 | 20.4 |
| 1985 | 1,154 | 1,221 | 2,375 | 21.3 |

*Source*: Bank of Thailand

The composition of Thailand's foreign debt in 1985 was favorable (table 6.6). New commitments in 1984 were secured at an average interest rate of 8.7 percent in Thailand, compared with an average 10.1 percent for middle-income oil importers. The average maturity of Thai debt was 17.2 years with a grace period of 6.9 years, compared with 12.2 years and 4.1 years, respectively, for these oil importers. In addition, official sources accounted for 63 percent of Thailand's debt, while the average for middle-income oil importers was 39 percent. This left scope for increased private sector borrowing when necessary. The international financial community evidently perceived Thailand to be a creditworthy borrower. The attitude among Thai government officials was that Thailand underborrowed in the early 1970s but that—following the change in regulations in 1977 permitting state enterprises to borrow abroad—borrowing was excessive in the late 1970s and early 1980s.

## Table 6.5  External Public Debt, 1970–86

| Year | Public debt outstanding (millions of U.S. dollars) | Debt outstanding/ GDP[a] | Interest payments[b] | Public debt-service ratio |
|------|------|------|------|------|
| 1970 | 325.7 | 5.0 | 1.4 | 4.4 |
| 1971 | 359.6 | 5.2 | 1.5 | 3.2 |
| 1972 | 386.0 | 4.9 | 1.2 | 2.7 |
| 1973 | 441.5 | 4.2 | 1.2 | 2.5 |
| 1974 | 512.9 | 3.8 | 0.9 | 1.9 |
| 1975 | 616.1 | 4.2 | 1.2 | 2.4 |
| 1976 | 822.7 | 5.0 | 1.2 | 2.4 |
| 1977 | 1,119.2 | 5.8 | 1.4 | 2.9 |
| 1978 | 1,819.2 | 8.0 | 1.8 | 3.7 |
| 1979 | 2,827.1 | 10.6 | 2.4 | 4.8 |
| 1980 | 4,070.1 | 12.4 | 3.1 | 5.0 |
| 1981 | 5,127.1 | 14.6 | 4.3 | 6.8 |
| 1982 | 6,137.9 | 17.2 | 5.1 | 8.5 |
| 1983 | 7,000.4 | 17.9 | 5.7 | 10.2 |
| 1984 | 7,540.7 | 18.6 | 5.4 | 12.0 |
| 1985 | 9,836.7 | 26.7 | 5.9 | 14.7 |
| 1986 | 11,022.6 | 27.4 | 6.4 | 16.7 |

a. Percentage of disbursed debt outstanding only.
b. As percentage of exports of goods and services.
*Source*: World Bank, *World Debt Tables*, various issues.

EXTERNAL BORROWING AND THE PETROLEUM PRICE SHOCKS. Because Thailand's external position changed markedly after 1985, it is helpful to focus on the adjustments that occurred until then. The two questions of particular interest are whether it is possible that Thailand did not adjust to the oil price shocks, except by borrowing, and how the increase in Thailand's external debt compares with the increased petroleum import bill that the oil shocks produced.

Consider, first, the value of Thailand's actual imports of petroleum products from 1973 to 1985 and, second, what their value would have been if petroleum prices had maintained the relationship to the export unit price index of the industrialized countries that existed in 1972. Suppose that Thailand had financed this difference by external borrowing. How large would the resulting stock of debt have been by 1985? The result is an accumulated principal of approximately $15.5 billion (table 6.7). This calculation assumes that all interest is serviced but the

**Table 6.6  The Structure of External Public Debt for Selected Countries, 1984 and 1985**

| Terms and structure | Thailand | Korea | Malaysia | Philippines | Average, East Asia | Average, middle-income oil importers |
|---|---|---|---|---|---|---|
| *Terms on new commitments, 1984* | | | | | | |
| Interest rate | 8.7 | 9.7 | 9.4 | 9.0 | 9.3 | 10.1 |
| Maturity (years) | 17.2 | 11.9 | 15.4 | 14.3 | 14.4 | 12.2 |
| Grace period (years) | 6.9 | 4.4 | 9.1 | 4.0 | 5.5 | 4.1 |
| *Structure of outstanding debt, January 1985* | | | | | | |
| Percentage from official sources | 63.0 | 39.3 | 21.9 | 47.8 | 44.6 | 39.2 |
| Percentage at floating rates | 29.4 | 46.8 | 61.6 | 41.0 | 39.6 | 46.9 |

*Source:* Word Bank, *World Debt Tables 1985 and 1986*; and World Bank (1986).

principal accumulates. The actual increase in Thailand's total stock of external debt from 1972 to 1985 was the remarkably similar amount of $14.5 billion, which is 94 percent of our hypothetical increase in debt.

Furthermore, Thailand's international reserves, measured in terms of months of import coverage, were depleted between the early 1970s and 1985. In 1972 reserves were equivalent to 7.9 months of merchandise imports, compared with 2.4 months in 1985. The difference in 1985 was worth roughly $4.1 billion. Thus the depletion of reserves plus the increase in the external debt of $18.6 billion—more than accounts for the increased cost of Thailand's petroleum imports since the first oil shock. The former exceeds the latter by 20 percent.

It is likely that Thailand's domestic adjustments caused the actual quantities of petroleum imports to be lower than they might have been, but these aggregate statistical calculations are surprisingly consistent with the hypothesis that the petroleum price increase was financed by a combination of external borrowing and a depletion of reserves. These calculations suggest that by 1985 Thailand's domestic macroeconomic adjustment to the oil price shocks had been deferred.

## Table 6.7  Foreign Exchange Cost of Petroleum Price Increases, 1972–85

*(U.S. millions of dollars)*

| Year | Actual petroleum imports (1) | Petroleum price (1972 = 100) (2) | Export unit value[a] (1972=100) (3) | Proportional price increase[b] (4) | Annual cost increase[c] (5) | Cumulative cost increase (6) |
|------|------|------|------|------|------|------|
| 1972 | 135   | 100   | 100 | 0     | 0     | n.a.   |
| 1973 | 209   | 134   | 119 | 0.108 | 23    | 23     |
| 1974 | 588   | 470   | 149 | 0.683 | 402   | 425    |
| 1975 | 708   | 468   | 168 | 0.642 | 455   | 880    |
| 1976 | 830   | 467   | 191 | 0.591 | 491   | 1,371  |
| 1977 | 1,041 | 503   | 206 | 0.591 | 615   | 1,986  |
| 1978 | 1,118 | 516   | 233 | 0.549 | 614   | 2,600  |
| 1979 | 1,592 | 689   | 269 | 0.610 | 972   | 3,572  |
| 1980 | 2,859 | 1,164 | 303 | 0.740 | 2,116 | 5,688  |
| 1981 | 2,974 | 1,320 | 291 | 0.779 | 2,318 | 8,006  |
| 1982 | 2,624 | 1,359 | 281 | 0.794 | 2,081 | 10,087 |
| 1983 | 2,466 | 1,190 | 272 | 0.772 | 1,902 | 11,989 |
| 1984 | 2,410 | 1,156 | 264 | 0.771 | 1,859 | 13,848 |
| 1985 | 2,090 | 1,159 | 264 | 0.772 | 1,613 | 15,461 |

a. Index of industrial countries.
b. $(4) = [(2) - (3)] \div (2)$.
c. $(5) = (4) \times (1)$.
Source: World Bank (1980, 1986); and IMF, *International Financial Statistics*, various issues.

*Adjustment of Petroleum Imports*

The 1973–74 oil price shock exposed Thailand's vulnerability to fluctuations in international petroleum prices. Although it seemed obvious to all that reduced import dependence was desirable, domestic political conflicts delayed the changes in domestic pricing policy that were required to achieve this end. The prices of virtually all Thailand's major commercial energy products are controlled by the government. These include all petroleum products, natural gas, electricity, and lignite (a mineral product used primarily to generate industrial energy). Petroleum products are especially sensitive in this regard. Kerosene is used by the rural poor for cooking and lighting. Fuel oil is used industrially and, critically, in the generation of electricity, itself a major item in the urban cost of living.

In 1970 imported petroleum, principally crude oil, accounted for more than 80 percent of the total consumption of petroleum products in Thailand and 60 percent of total energy use (Praipol 1993: 297). But the increase in the international price of crude oil occurring with the first oil shock was not passed on to domestic consumers. The combination of import taxes and excise taxes on petroleum that had previously been a major source of government revenue was scaled down to stabilize domestic retail prices. As a result, domestic prices were not adjusted significantly in real terms throughout the aftermath of the first oil shock. The shock was implicitly treated as a temporary event. The second oil price shock of 1979–80 showed that this assumption was no longer tenable.

When the domestic prices of petroleum products and electricity were raised in 1980, the reaction was so strong that it brought down the Kriangsak government. The Prem government that succeeded it promptly reversed these price reforms. The oil fund that had been established by the government in 1974 to tax the windfall profits of petroleum companies on old stock at the time of the first oil shock went into deficit because it became an administrative instrument for financing subsidies on the consumption of petroleum products. In the early 1980s all petroleum products were subsidized in this way except for gasoline (Praipol 1993). The heaviest subsidies were on kerosene, fuel oil, and LPG. The subsidies on fuel oil delayed the move on the part of industrial users to natural gas and the subsidies on LPG encouraged costly refits of commercial vehicles to facilitate its use in place of gasoline.

Through the mid-1980s, natural gas finds in the Gulf of Thailand reduced Thailand's dependence on imported petroleum. In particular, the Electricity Generating Authority of Thailand moved increasingly away from heavily subsidized

**Figure 6.7. Petroleum Imports at Current and Constant Prices, 1970–90**

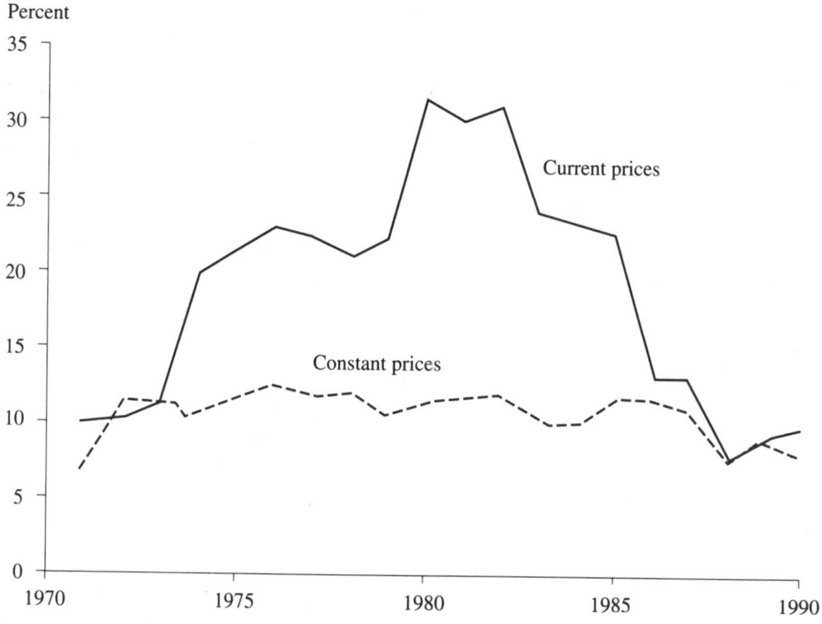

*Source:* Bank of Thailand and IMF.

fuel oil and toward natural gas. By 1990 imported petroleum had declined to 40 percent of total petroleum product use (including natural gas), in comparison with 80 percent in 1970. But Thailand's import dependence had not declined as much as these data might suggest because total petroleum use had increased rapidly in the interim (see figure 6.7, which shows petroleum products as a share of total imports in both current and constant 1972 prices). Indeed, these calculations reveal that, at constant prices, petroleum as a share of total imports changed little over the entire twenty-year period. The dramatic changes in petroleum products as a share of imports (at current prices) was due almost entirely to movements in the international prices of petroleum products in relation to other imports and owed almost nothing to quantity adjustments.

Moreover, almost twenty years after the first oil price shock, petroleum imports had resumed roughly their 1972 share of total imports, measured at both current and constant prices (figure 6.7). It follows that by the end of this period the ratio of petroleum import prices to import prices in general had returned to roughly their 1972 level. But Thailand's terms of trade had declined by more than 20 percent (see table 3.4). Although the increase in petroleum prices in relation to other import prices had vanished, export prices in relation to imports had declined significantly.

## Conclusions

Thailand's aggregate adjustment to its terms-of-trade shocks was quite different from what the theoretical literature would describe as optimal adjustment. Our analysis suggests that optimal adjustment depends on whether the shocks are seen as temporary or permanent phenomena. In the case of a negative shock, if it is temporary, then it may be optimal to borrow abroad to smooth consumption during the life of the shock. If it is permanant, aggregate absorption will have to be adjusted, and the full value of the income loss should not be borrowed. Analysis of Thailand's actual borrowing in relation to the magnitude of the two OPEC oil price shocks shows that the value of additional external borrowing almost exactly matched the value of the loss in the terms of trade due to the shocks. That is, Thailand behaved as if the shocks were strictly temporary. It is difficult to describe this as optimal adjustment.

Previous studies of Thailand's adjustment to the petroleum price shocks have made much of the decline in Thailand's dependence on imported petroleum. Since the two oil price shocks of the 1970s and early 1980s, Thailand's imports of petroleum products have indeed declined as a proportion of total imports. Nevertheless, this outcome was almost entirely a result of changes in the international prices of petroleum products in relation to other imports. When the data are examined at constant prices, there is little change in the share of petroleum products in total imports. Quantity adjustments played almost no role. Again, this could not reasonably be described as optimal adjustment.

Balance of payments shocks of the type considered in chapter 5 had the potential to produce severe macroeconomic problems. Although problems occurred, they could not be considered crises. But since macroeconomic crises did occur in other countries affected by these and similar shocks, it is helpful to review the circumstances that *could* have produced crises in Thailand's case.

MID-TO-LATE 1970s. By 1974–75, Thailand had experienced the following external shocks: a deterioration in the terms of trade caused by the first oil shock (initially cushioned by an export commodity price boom, which had vanished by 1975); the withdrawal of U.S. military grants; and the withdrawal of U.S. bases and associated spending by U.S. military personnel.

Remittances from Thai workers abroad, increased tourism, and the growth of manufactured exports then became important, but not until the late 1970s. In the meantime, Thailand was experiencing a serious problem because the government decided to defer adjustment and to borrow internationally. In the mid-1970s Thailand and the foreign commercial banks, then flush with petrodollars, discovered one another. To facilitate foreign borrowing, the Thanin government in 1976–77 eased the restrictions on foreign borrowing by the public sector (see chapters 2 and 4).

Was this an irrational move? In the mid-1970s the stock of Thai foreign debt was fairly low and the country could sustain a higher level. From the foreign banks' point of view, Thailand had been a reliable debtor in the past and seemed to have good economic prospects. Moreover, in the mid-1970s few observers, including economists, recognized that the international oil price increases would be permanent. Nor did they anticipate the increases in international interest rates in the late 1970s and early 1980s. Given the information available at the time, Thailand's borrowing strategy could not be described as reckless, or even as unwise, but it was clearly somewhat uncontrolled.

In addition, in the mid-1970s Thailand was experiencing severe domestic political problems. Politically, this was one of the most turbulent periods of Thailand's modern history. The democratic governments of Kukrit Pramoj and Seni Pramoj were on shaky ground. They had come to power in 1973 through a popular revolt against the Thanom military government, but the military remained hostile and politically strong. The democratic period was to end with a military coup in 1976, and the new government was itself replaced by a yet another military coup in the following year. In this political environment, deferred adjustment was obviously the preferred strategy of the politicians. International interest rates were low, and a borrowing constraint was not binding because of Thailand's credit rating. The pressure to defer adjustment by borrowing internationally could not be resisted, and this strategy was to prevail until the early 1980s.

EARLY-TO-MID 1980s. Thailand's substantial debt burden was the consequence of the adjustments made in the 1970s and early 1980s. But national savings had declined alarmingly in the early 1980s at the very time that repayment of the debt was becoming a problem. The resulting balance of payments deficit was clearly unsustainable. The public sector was also unsustainably in deficit. In particular, the government's tax base was narrow, evasion was widespread, and the antiquated public revenue system seemed generally incapable of raising the increased revenue the government now required. These problems are not yet fully resolved today, but by the early 1990s they had abated considerably. Strong policy measures had been taken (including some fiscal reform), foreign borrowing was curtailed, and several large-scale public investments were either abandoned or scaled down.

# Chapter Seven

# The Role of Fiscal Policy

At a theoretical level, fiscal policy is more likely to be effective under a fixed exchange rate regime than under a flexible exchange rate. The opposite applies to monetary policy. Fiscal policy therefore seems a good candidate for a significant stabilizing or destabilizing role in the Thai context, as has indeed been suggested in the literature on Thailand's adjustment experience (Robinson, Yangho, and Ranjit 1991). Whether the manner in which Thailand's fiscal aggregates responded to external shocks exacerbated or ameliorated the short-term macroeconomic effects of those shocks is the subject of this chapter.

## Fiscal Adjustment: 1970–90

As noted in chapter 4, Thailand's consolidated public sector consists of the central government, local government, and the public enterprises. The fiscal position of the consolidated public sector is dominated by that of the central government (table 7.1). The deficits of public enterprises have on average been smaller than those of the central government and have tended to move with them. Local government deficits are insignificant. This chapter concentrates primarily on the central government. Unless otherwise stated, terms such as "public sector expenditure," "public sector revenue," and "public sector deficit" thus refer to the fiscal positions of the central government.[1]

### A Brief History of Fiscal Adjustments

Throughout the 1960s and into the early 1970s, Thailand's public sector deficits was small. The Thai economy expanded steadily, as did revenue. The goal of fiscal policy was to modify the indirect tax system with a view to promoting exports and

**Table 7.1  Selected Fiscal Indicators, 1970–90**
*(ratio to GDP)*

| Year | Central government | | | Public enterprise deficit | Consolidated public sector deficit |
|---|---|---|---|---|---|
| | Expenditure | Revenue | Deficit | | |
| 1970 | 18.32 | 13.11 | 5.22 | 0.22 | 5.52 |
| 1971 | 18.24 | 12.85 | 5.39 | 0.26 | 5.71 |
| 1972 | 17.63 | 12.37 | 5.26 | 0.29 | 5.75 |
| 1973 | 14.88 | 11.81 | 3.07 | 0.59 | 3.71 |
| 1974 | 13.07 | 13.80 | –0.73 | 0.43 | –0.25 |
| 1970–74 | 16.43 | 12.79 | 3.64 | 0.36 | 4.09 |
| 1975 | 15.49 | 13.31 | 2.18 | 0.62 | 2.85 |
| 1976 | 17.76 | 12.73 | 5.02 | 1.24 | 6.30 |
| 1977 | 18.01 | 13.55 | 4.46 | 1.03 | 5.53 |
| 1978 | 18.83 | 13.57 | 5.26 | 1.78 | 7.12 |
| 1979 | 19.54 | 14.24 | 5.30 | 1.40 | 6.63 |
| 1980 | 21.27 | 14.94 | 6.33 | 2.62 | 8.99 |
| 1975–80 | 18.48 | 13.72 | 4.76 | 1.45 | 6.24 |
| 1981 | 21.70 | 14.61 | 7.09 | 2.55 | 9.60 |
| 1982 | 21.53 | 13.91 | 7.62 | 2.01 | 9.53 |
| 1983 | 21.12 | 15.38 | 5.74 | 1.51 | 7.20 |
| 1984 | 21.80 | 14.46 | 7.34 | 0.93 | 8.24 |
| 1985 | 23.15 | 14.57 | 8.58 | 1.69 | 10.24 |
| 1981–85 | 14.59 | 7.27 | 1.74 | 8.96 | 21.86 |
| 1986 | 20.84 | 14.28 | 6.57 | 0.95 | 7.46 |
| 1987 | 18.25 | 15.09 | 3.16 | 0.47 | 3.45 |
| 1988 | 16.56 | 16.79 | –0.23 | 0.71 | 0.46 |
| 1989 | 21.63 | 18.42 | 3.21 | 0.26 | 3.86 |
| 1990 | 24.78 | 20.07 | 4.71 | –0.07 | 4.94 |
| 1986–90 | 20.41 | 16.93 | 3.48 | 0.46 | 4.03 |

*Source*: National Economic and Social Development Board, *National Income of Thailand*, various issues.

supporting import-substitution industrialization. Public expenditure, which was concentrated mostly on infrastructure, expanded moderately. This pattern was to change significantly after the 1973–74 oil price shock. For most of the period since 1970, the Thai public sector has been in deficit, running at an average of 3 to 4 percent of GDP. The exceptions were 1974 and the boom years after 1988, which

**Figure 7.1. Government Expenditures and Revenues, 1970–91**

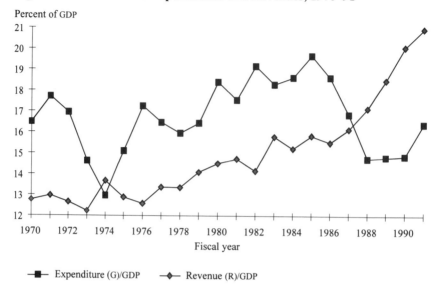

*Source:* NESDB, *National Income of Thailand,* various issues.

brought budgetary surpluses. From an examination of the size of government expenditures in relation to revenues since 1970, expressed as proportions of GDP (figure 7.1), and in relation to GDP growth and inflation (figure 7.2), it appears that the years of budgetary surplus (largest deficits) coincide roughly with years of most rapid (slowest) income growth. A more systematic test of this proposition appears below.

Between 1970 and 1974 the ratio of public expenditures to GDP declined from 18 percent to 13 percent. Public revenue as a percentage of GDP also declined, though at a slower rate than expenditure, and thus the ratio of the deficit to GDP declined as well. The world commodity boom of 1973, together with the subsequent oil price shock, raised revenues. High prices of commodity exports and high domestic inflation caused tax revenues to increase substantially (by 28 percent in 1973 and 48 percent in 1974). But high domestic inflation thwarted the plan to expand public expenditure, holding the expansion to the levels of 7 and 11 percent in 1973 and 1974, respectively.[2]

These changes resulted in a public sector surplus in fiscal 1973–74 and substantially improved the financial position of the public sector. The government took this opportunity to reduce indirect tax rates so as to lessen their inflationary effect on production costs and incomes. From 1973 to 1976, a series of tax reduction schemes was implemented to alleviate the burden of inflation and to offset the slowdown in GDP growth. Notwithstanding the tax-cut policy, tax revenue as a proportion of GDP rose by two percentage points in 1974, thereby producing a budgetary surplus at the same time that Thailand was experiencing its most rapid consumer price inflation since the 1940s.

**Figure 7.2a. Public Sector Deficit and Real GDP Growth Rate, 1970–90**

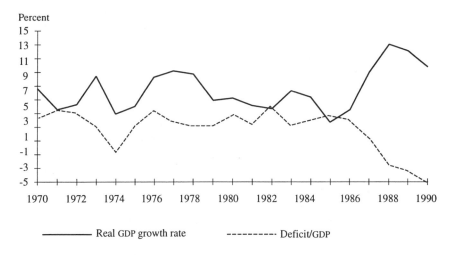

Real GDP growth rate          ---------- Deficit/GDP

**Figure 7.2b. Public Sector Deficit and Rate of Inflation, 1970–90**

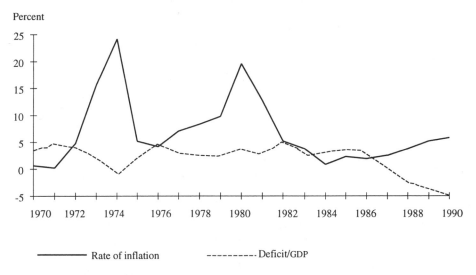

Rate of inflation          ---------- Deficit/GDP

*Source:* Tables 3.4 and 7.1.

After 1975 public sector expenditure increased significantly, particularly in the areas of defense and administration, which in 1976 and 1977 saw the average annual rate increase by 29 and 13 percent, respectively. Capital expenditure by the state enterprises increased even faster, at annual rates of 21 percent in fiscal 1975, 35 percent in fiscal 1976, 61 percent in fiscal 1977, and 59 percent in fiscal 1978.

As mentioned in previous chapters, these increases in consolidated public sector expenditure were facilitated by regulatory changes that increased the defense loan allocation and authorized the Ministry of Finance to give financial guarantees on foreign borrowing by state enterprises. In aggregate, between fiscal 1975 and 1978 public expenditure rose at an average annual rate of 24 percent, while revenue rose 19 percent. In fiscal 1978, the public sector's cash deficit was 16 million baht, or 3.3 percent of 1978 GDP. The foreign indebtedness of the public sector had increased from $87 million in 1976 to $200 million in 1978.

In 1975 the government decided to use an overt fiscal stimulus in an effort to counteract the slowdown in income growth resulting from the first oil shock. Public investment increased in 1975 and 1976, while domestic consumption demand was stimulated by tax reductions. By 1976 the deficit had expanded and GDP growth had returned to its preshock levels. A series of tax increases was then implemented in 1977 and 1979. The change in fiscal stance slowed the growth of the public deficit, despite the continued rise in public expenditure: from 13 percent of GDP in 1974 to 21 percent in 1980. From 1975 to 1980, the deficit-to-GDP ratio rose an average 4.8 percent a year, up from an average 3.6 percent over the period 1970–74.

The public finance problems that followed the second oil price shock of 1979–80 were more serious than those produced by the 1973–74 shock. In the second case, the shock was followed in 1981–82 by a slump in primary commodity prices, which subsequently led Thailand into a recession and significantly reduced tax revenue. Furthermore, international real interest rates rose significantly in the early 1980s, and together with the expanded public debt from the late 1970s they served to increase the public sector's debt-servicing burden. The oil price shock caused domestic inflation to increase dramatically: it peaked at 25 percent during one-quarter of 1980, with an average rate for the year of 20 percent. By the anti-inflationary standards of Thailand's economic managers, these rates of inflation were unacceptably high.

The Ministry of Finance responded to the second oil shock by increasing the already high rates of subsidy contained in public enterprise prices and public utility charges. The subsidies were expected to help control inflation, even though their impact on the price level was a once-only event. That is, their impact on the rate of consumer price inflation could be sustained beyond the initial year of impact only if they were continually increased. The new subsidies greatly increased the transfers from the central government to the state enterprises. Between fiscal 1979 and 1982, the expenditure of the state enterprises continued to expand at a rate slightly higher than that of the central government, 21 percent for state enterprises and 19 percent for the central government.

From 1981 to 1985 the government's fiscal stance continued to be expansionary, as reflected in a rising deficit, which reached 66 billion baht in fiscal 1982, or 7.9 percent of GDP. The highest level was 9 percent of GDP in 1985, up from an average of 4 percent in the 1970s. The enlarged public sector deficits of the early 1980s led to a serious balance of payments problem. It was clear that the public sector deficits had to be reduced.

Accordingly, the period between 1980 and 1986 was marked by repeated cuts in planned expenditure and a series of tax reforms to boost revenue. But all this did little to close the deficit gap. There is no doubt that the government wished to reduce the fiscal deficit, but this objective was not achieved. Seemingly, the slowdown in GDP growth was the main factor making revenue mobilization difficult. Public expenditure continued to grow faster than revenue, and the deficit widened correspondingly. The growth in consolidated public sector expenditure continued to be dominated by debt repayments, capital expenditure of state enterprises, defense, and administration.

From 1987 on, Thailand's fiscal position changed radically. Restraints on spending, partly a product of the fiscal concerns of the early to mid-1980s–and more particularly, the increased tax capacity caused by the abrupt acceleration of real GDP growth in the late 1980s–resulted in a strong fiscal position, allaying many of the deep concerns of only a few years before.

To determine whether the behavior of Thailand's fiscal aggregates was stabilizing or destabilizing, it is necessary to examine the statistical relationships between the main fiscal aggregates and variations both in aggregate income and in the price level. Table 7.2 shows the correlation between real public expenditure, real public revenue, and the real public sector deficit, on the one hand, and the current and lagged values of GDP growth rates and rates of inflation, on the other, for the period 1970–90. It is clear that the size of the budgetary deficit is negatively related to GDP growth.

The above evidence suggests that Thai fiscal aggregates have behaved in a stabilizing manner. The next question to consider is whether this behavior was the result of discretionary policy decisions, made in response to short-term fluctuations in real income, or an automatic outcome of the structure of the Thai expenditure and revenue systems.

### Discretionary or Automatic Fiscal Stabilizers?

Thailand's fiscal history over the past two decades suggests that the short-term intentions of the fiscal authorities to expand or contract the public sector deficit may have had only marginal effects on fiscal outcomes. Exogenous forces, determining

**Table 7.2  Correlation between Fiscal Variables, Income Growth, and Inflation**

| Change | GDP growth (current period) | GDP growth (previous period) | Inflation (current period) | Inflation (previous period) |
|---|---|---|---|---|
| Total expenditure/GDP | 0.32 | 0.56 | 0.009 | 0.03 |
| Total revenue/GDP | 0.69 | 0.68 | –0.09 | –0.20 |
| Total deficit/GDP | –0.70 | –0.54 | 0.13 | 0.29 |

*Note*: Data cover the period 1970–90.
*Source*: Authors' calculations from data in tables 3.4 and 7.1.

income growth and short-term changes in rates of inflation, appear to have had a much greater short-run impact on fiscal aggregates.

In the industrialized countries, both discretionary adjustments in government fiscal policy and autonomous adjustments in fiscal outcomes are considered potentially important sources of stabilization (see, for example, Dornbusch and Fischer 1992). The operation of the discretionary component depends on the way government policy responds to external shocks. Autonomous adjustments, the outcome of automatic stabilizers, operate through the structure of the tax and revenue systems themselves, and not through short-term discretionary changes in government policy.

Textbook descriptions of automatic stabilizers emphasize the role of personal income taxes on the revenue side and welfare payments on the expenditure side. In the economies that make up the Organisation for Economic Co-operation and Development (OECD), personal income tax revenues are the dominant sources of revenue. These revenues rise as real incomes or rates of inflation rise, but in a greater proportion than the increase in nominal income because of the progressive income tax schedules. In contrast, welfare and social security expenditures rise as incomes fall because income relief is required most in times of recession.

The result is that the public sector deficit declines during periods of rapid growth, as tax revenues rise and welfare expenditures decline as proportions of GDP. The public deficit rises in periods of recession as income tax revenues decline and welfare payments rise. As a consequence of these processes, the countercyclical behavior of the government's fiscal deficit plays a stabilizing role, reducing the impact of externally induced fluctuations in national income.

Automatic stabilizers are seldom mentioned in the context of developing countries. This is not so surprising in one sense. If personal income taxes on the revenue side and welfare payments on the expenditure side were truly the important variables to look for, one would not expect automatic stabilizers to be significant at all for developing countries such as Thailand. Personal income taxes are only a small source of revenue in such countries, and, most of them, like Thailand, have no public social security systems. Thus it would seem that automatic stabilizers are unlikely to play an important role in developing countries.

The present chapter will demonstrate that for Thailand, the reverse is true: automatic stabilizers are important on both the expenditure and the revenue sides of the public sector accounts. Indeed, they are far more important sources of short-run stabilization than discretionary changes in fiscal policy.

To some extent at least, it is must be expected that tax revenues and expenditures will be responsive to short-term changes in economic activity and that some degree of automatic stabilization will result. If the government's forecasts of income growth and inflation are inaccurate—and they must inevitably involve some errors—then the actual levels of spending and taxation revenue will presumably be somewhat different from their planned levels. As a result, the planned level of deficit will be different from the actual level. An unexpected expansion (slowdown) of economic activity presumably causes fiscal planners to underestimate (overestimate) future revenues.

Because planned expenditure of the Thai government is constrained by fore-cast revenue, through the operation of the 1959 Budgetary Law (see below), the size of the actual budget deficit will then be anticyclical. In boom years, the planned level of deficit would tend to exceed the level that is finally experienced, if it is assumed that the boom was not fully anticipated by the planners. Similarly, during a slump, the planned level of deficit will be less than the actual deficit. This mechanism would produce a stabilizing feature from the revenue side of the budget. But how important is this effect in relation to discretionary policy changes?

It is possible to study the behavior of fiscal intentions in relation to fiscal out-comes because the planned levels of revenue and expenditure are declared in the government's annual budget documents in advance of fiscal outcomes. The magni-tude of the planned deficit reflects discretionary fiscal policy, which reacts to changing macroeconomic policy variables such as deviation from the trend growth rate, the inflation rate, and the ratio of the current account deficit to GDP. The pur-pose here is not to study the way fiscal intentions are formed, but to compare fiscal intentions with fiscal outcomes and to relate both to income growth and inflation. We define the unplanned deficit as the difference between the planned and actual deficit. The unplanned revenue, unplanned expenditure, and unplanned deficit can be thought of as a result of the responsiveness of automatic fiscal stabilizers.

Figure 7.3 shows the relationship between the planned and unplanned deficits, expressed as percentages of GDP. The underlying data are summarized in table 7.3. The government planned to run a budget deficit in each year between 1970 and 1990, except for 1989. The surpluses that occurred in 1974, 1988, and 1990 were

**Figure 7.3. Actual, Planned, and Unplanned Deficits, 1970–90**

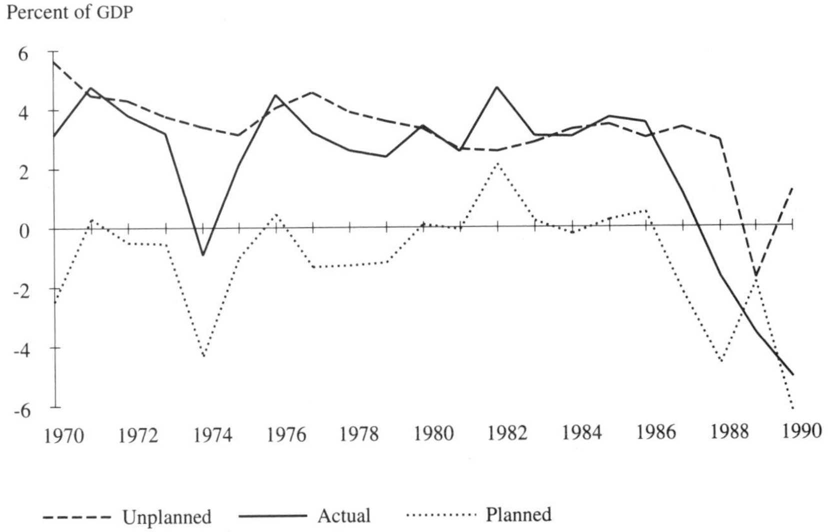

*Source*: Table 7.3 and authors' calculations.

the result of unexpected increases in revenue. The planned deficit, which reflects the discretionary intention of the government, apparently varied less than the unplanned deficit (table 7.4). The variability of the unplanned fiscal deficit/GDP ratio and the unplanned fiscal impulse exceed that of the corresponding planned variables. Stabilization can now be examined over the short and intermediate terms.

### Short-Run Stabilization

The first point to note is the relationship between year-to-year variations in fiscal policy and year-to-year fluctuations in income, inflation, and the external balance. Expansionary fiscal policy is taken to mean that the ratio of the deficit to GDP is

**Table 7.3  Central Government Budget: Planned versus Actual Level, 1970–90**

*(millions of baht)*

| Fiscal | Expenditure | | Revenue | | Deficits/expenditure | |
|--------|-------------|---|---------|---|----------------------|---|
| year | $Planned(G_p)^a$ | $Actual(G_a)^b$ | $Planned(R_p)^a$ | $Actual(R_a)^b$ | $[(G_p-R_p)/G_p]$ | $[(G_a-R_a)/G_a]$ |
| 1970 | 27,300 | 23,617 | 19,020 | 17,909 | 0.30 | 0.24 |
| 1971 | 28,645 | 26,978 | 21,800 | 19,088 | 0.24 | 0.29 |
| 1972 | 29,000 | 28,905 | 21,700 | 21,165 | 0.24 | 0.29 |
| 1973 | 31,600 | 30,937 | 23,300 | 25,344 | 0.26 | 0.18 |
| 1974 | 36,000 | 34,629 | 26,520 | 37,921 | 0.26 | −0.10 |
| 1975 | 48,000 | 43,541 | 38,500 | 38,229 | 0.20 | 0.12 |
| 1976 | 62,650 | 53,686 | 48,675 | 42,731 | 0.22 | 0.20 |
| 1977 | 68,790 | 63,470 | 50,470 | 51,710 | 0.27 | 0.19 |
| 1978 | 81,000 | 74,716 | 62,000 | 62,022 | 0.23 | 0.17 |
| 1979 | 92,000 | 86,157 | 72,000 | 75,109 | 0.22 | 0.13 |
| 1980 | 114,557 | 114,287 | 92,680 | 92,147 | 0.19 | 0.19 |
| 1981 | 140,000 | 129,941 | 120,000 | 110,329 | 0.14 | 0.15 |
| 1982 | 161,000 | 152,168 | 140,000 | 113,810 | 0.13 | 0.25 |
| 1983 | 177,000 | 165,100 | 151,000 | 136,448 | 0.15 | 0.17 |
| 1984 | 192,000 | 177,402 | 160,000 | 147,847 | 0.17 | 0.17 |
| 1985 | 213,000 | 197,468 | 178,000 | 159,196 | 0.16 | 0.19 |
| 1986 | 218,000 | 204,016 | 185,000 | 166,254 | 0.15 | 0.19 |
| 1987 | 227,500 | 207,817 | 185,500 | 192,484 | 0.18 | 0.07 |
| 1988 | 243,500 | 220,655 | 199,500 | 245,646 | 0.18 | −0.11 |
| 1989 | 285,500 | 266,310 | 262,500 | 316,370 | 0.08 | −0.19 |
| 1990 | 335,000 | 308,320 | 310,000 | 403,030 | 0.07 | −0.31 |

a. Based on Thailand, Ministry of Finance, *Thailand's Budget in Brief,* various issues.
b. Based on Bank of Thailand, *Monthly Bulletin,* tables 23 and 24.

**Table 7.4  Statistical Properties of Fiscal Variables, 1970–90**
*(percent)*

| Variable | Mean | Minimum | Maximum | Variance | Coefficient of variation |
|---|---|---|---|---|---|
| Revenue/GDP | 14.71 | 12.00 | 20.00 | 4.01 | 0.14 |
| Expenditure/GDP | 16.74 | 13.00 | 19.70 | 3.10 | 0.11 |
| Deficit/GDP | 2.06 | −5.20 | 5.00 | 7.86 | 1.36 |
| Current expenditure/GDP | 13.66 | 11.17 | 15.87 | 2.41 | 0.11 |
| Capital expenditure/GDP | 3.64 | 2.68 | 4.59 | 0.39 | 0.17 |
| Actual fiscal deficit/GDP | 2.07 | −5.08 | 4.76 | 7.14 | 1.29 |
| Planned fiscal deficit/GDP | 3.22 | −1.74 | 5.62 | 2.07 | 0.45 |
| Unplanned fiscal deficit/GDP | −1.15 | −6.30 | 2.13 | 3.91 | −1.73 |
| Actual fiscal impulse | −0.41 | −4.12 | 3.05 | 3.34 | −4.45 |
| Planned fiscal impulse | −0.22 | −4.66 | 2.96 | 1.81 | −6.11 |
| Unplanned fiscal impulse | −0.19 | −4.44 | 3.30 | 4.70 | −11.38 |

*Source*: Authors' calculations from data in tables 3.4 and 7.3.

larger than in the previous year. Fiscal impulse is defined as the change in the ratio of the deficit to GDP, and an expansionary fiscal policy will thus mean a positive fiscal impulse. The unplanned fiscal impulse is defined as the difference between the actual and planned fiscal impulse. The relationship between fiscal impulses and important macroeconomic variables can be explored from the information provided in table 7.5.

FISCAL STIMULUS AND AGGREGATE INCOME. In table 7.5 the variable "growth deviation" denotes the difference between the actual and trend real GDP growth rates. A positive value of this variable indicates strong economic growth, and a negative value a slowdown. Years are classified into three groups according to economic growth performance: low, medium, and high.

The behavior of these variables is clearer from figure 7.4. Deviations from the trend growth rate (normalized GDP growth rate) are negatively correlated with the actual fiscal impulse (figure 7.4, panel a). Fiscal impulse was stronger during pe-

**Table 7.5  Policy Goals and Budget Deficit, 1970–90**
*(percent)*

| Year | Growth deviation[a] | Inflation (CPI) | CAD[b]/ GDP | Budget deficit (percent of GDP) | | |
|------|------|------|------|------|------|------|
| | | | | Actual | Planned | Unplanned |
| 1970 | −1.31 | −0.09 | 3.53 | 3.13 | 5.62 | −2.49 |
| 1971 | −2.84 | 0.44 | 2.37 | 4.76 | 4.46 | 0.30 |
| 1972 | −3.73 | 4.82 | 0.62 | 3.79 | 4.29 | −0.51 |
| 1973 | 2.06 | 15.56 | 0.45 | 3.19 | 3.74 | −0.54 |
| 1974 | −3.45 | 24.33 | 0.64 | −0.93 | 3.40 | −4.32 |
| 1975 | −2.95 | 5.30 | 4.08 | 2.12 | 3.13 | −1.02 |
| 1976 | 1.58 | 3.78 | 2.59 | 4.48 | 4.03 | 0.45 |
| 1977 | 2.10 | 7.60 | 5.55 | 3.20 | 4.54 | −1.33 |
| 1978 | 2.64 | 7.90 | 4.80 | 2.60 | 3.89 | −1.29 |
| 1979 | −2.49 | 9.91 | 7.62 | 2.38 | 3.58 | −1.19 |
| 1980 | −3.02 | 19.67 | 6.44 | 3.42 | 3.32 | 0.09 |
| 1981 | 1.47 | 12.70 | 7.37 | 2.55 | 2.63 | −0.08 |
| 1982 | −3.74 | 5.23 | 2.82 | 4.69 | 2.56 | 2.13 |
| 1983 | −0.55 | 3.75 | 7.28 | 3.07 | 2.86 | 0.21 |
| 1984 | −0.67 | 0.85 | 5.08 | 3.05 | 3.29 | −0.24 |
| 1985 | −4.29 | 2.43 | 4.13 | 3.69 | 3.45 | 0.24 |
| 1986 | −2.88 | 1.85 | −0.59 | 3.51 | 3.01 | 0.50 |
| 1987 | 1.67 | 2.50 | 0.74 | 1.14 | 3.35 | −2.21 |
| 1988 | 5.42 | 3.80 | 2.69 | −1.69 | 2.92 | −4.61 |
| 1989 | 4.25 | 5.36 | 3.63 | −3.60 | −1.74 | −1.86 |
| 1990 | 2.20 | 5.98 | 9.05 | −5.08 | 1.22 | −6.30 |

a. Deviation from real GDP growth trend (6.7 percent).
b. CAD = Current account deficit
*Source*: National Economic and Social Development Board, *National Income of Thailand,* various issues; Thailand, Ministry of Finance, *Thailand's Budget in Brief,* various issues; Bank of Thailand, *Monthly Bulletin,* tables 23 and 24.

riods when the real growth rate fell below its trend path and weaker during economic expansion. A decomposition of the actual impulse into its planned and unplanned components reveals that the planned level of fiscal impulse (figure 7.4, panel b) does not exhibit an anticyclical pattern as strong as the unplanned fiscal impulse (figure 7.4, panel c). A striking negative correlation can be observed between unplanned fiscal impulse and growth deviation. The key to this inverse re-

**Figure 7.4.** GDP **Growth Compared with Actual, Planned, and Unplanned Fiscal Impulse, 1971–90**

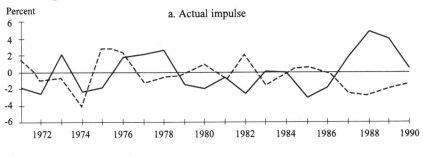

a. Actual impulse

Normalized real GDP growth rate      ----- Actual fiscal impulse

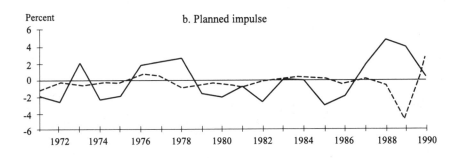

b. Planned impulse

Normalized real GDP growth rate      ----- Planned fiscal impulse

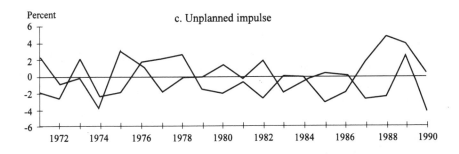

c. Unplanned impulse

Normalized real GDP growth rate      ----- Unplanned fiscal impulse

*Source:* Tables 3.4 and 7.3, and authors' calculations.

lationship is clearly that tax revenues are more responsive than expenditures to changes in aggregate income (see table 7.2).

The correlation between these variables is shown in table 7.6. Although it is obviously difficult to draw reliable inferences from short sample periods, the results suggest that to the extent that short-term stabilization with respect to income occurred, it was due entirely to the role of automatic stabilizers. Planned fiscal impulses were weakly destabilizing with respect to current income. Clearly, to understand Thailand's fiscal stabilization with respect to income, it is vital to consider the operation of automatic stabilizers.[3]

FISCAL STIMULUS AND THE PRICE LEVEL. The behavior of the actual fiscal impulse during inflationary periods can be observed in figure 7.5. Again, there is a negative correlation between the two variables, almost as strong as that between growth deviation and fiscal impulse (table 7.6). During inflationary periods with strong economic growth, tax revenues increased, capital expenditures declined, and the actual fiscal stance became less expansionary. If inflation is associated with an economic slowdown, as it was in the case of the two oil price shocks, tax revenue collection will not increase sufficiently to reduce the fiscal impulse. This reduces the negative correlation between the fiscal impulse and inflation.

FISCAL STIMULUS AND EXTERNAL BALANCE. It has been argued that in Thailand the public deficit drives the current account deficit. According to the monetary approach to the balance of payments, excessive growth in the money supply creates an increased demand for imports as an outlet for the excess money supply. In the absorption approach, if aggregate demand or domestic absorption rises faster than output, net exports will be negative. Thus, if a public deficit stimulates aggregate demand, the current account will deteriorate if the income elasticity of demand for imports is high. Furthermore, if the public deficit produces pressure on the price level, net exports will decline because of the deterioration of price competitiveness.

**Table 7.6  Correlation between Planned and Unplanned Fiscal Variables, Income Growth, and Inflation, 1970–88**

| Fiscal impulse | GDP growth (current period) | GDP growth (previous period) | Inflation (current period) | Inflation (previous period) |
|---|---|---|---|---|
| Actual | −0.35 | −0.38 | −0.32 | 0.27 |
| Planned | 0.18 | −0.09 | −0.25 | −0.38 |
| Unplanned | −0.39 | −0.37 | −0.24 | 0.37 |

*Source*: Authors' calculations from data in tables 3.4 and 7.5.

**Figure 7.5.  Inflation Rate Compared with Actual, Planned, and Unplanned Fiscal Impulse, 1971–90**

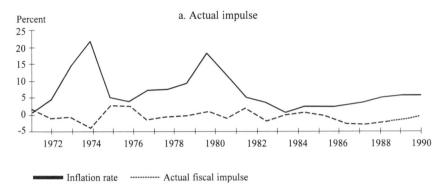

a. Actual impulse

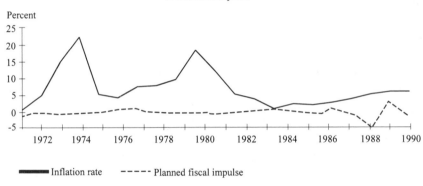

b. Planned impulse

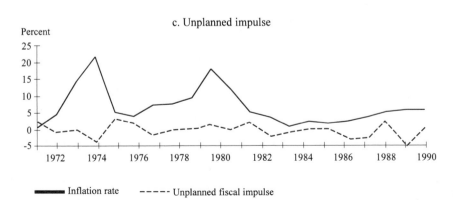

c. Unplanned impulse

*Source:* Tables 3.4 and 7.3, and authors' calculations.

In Thailand's case, the income elasticity of demand for imports is high, and the current account deficit typically expands during economic booms. If the public deficit was driving these events, one would expect to observe a positive relationship between fiscal impulse and the current account deficit. The relationship between the unplanned fiscal impulse and current account deficit as a percentage of GDP is illustrated in figure 7.6.

Between 1970 and 1977, the relationship between fiscal deficits and external deficits was positive. The data for this period are consistent with fiscal deficits driving short-term outcomes on the current account. That is, that growth was led by public sector demand. After 1977, however, the relationship was clearly negative, owing to the fact that strong economic growth also generates higher tax revenue from business and sales taxes. Furthermore, increased imports also resulted in high tariff revenue. Since the strong economic growth was due to export and investment growth rather than fiscal stimulus, the unplanned fiscal impulse moved inversely with the current account deficit. The fiscal impulse variable is affected by other macrovariables that also affect the current account deficit simultaneously.

Again, it is evident that fiscal impulse does not increase the current account deficit. It provides a stabilizing feature with respect to external balance, since it tends to be weak when the current account deficit is large and stimulates aggregate demand during periods of current account surplus.

**Figure 7.6. Current Account Deficit and Unplanned Fiscal Impulse, 1971–91**

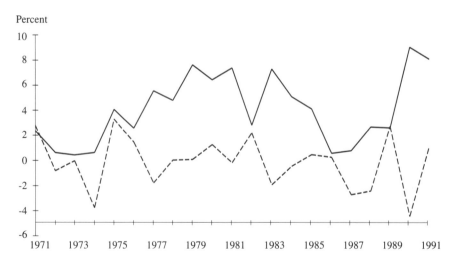

Percent

— Current account deficit/GDP     ---- Unplanned fiscal impulse

*Source:* Table 7.5 and authors' calculations.

**Table 7.7 Estimates of the Reaction Functions of Fiscal Policy Variables, 1972–90**

| Reaction function | $(Y_t - Y_t^*) \div Y_{t-1}$ | $dln(P)$ | $CAD/GDP$ | $R^2$ | $DW$ |
|---|---|---|---|---|---|
| $D_a/GDP$ | −0.30 | −0.10 | −0.08 | 0.80 | 2.10 |
|  | (4.80) | (2.10) | (0.71) |  |  |
| $D_p/GDP$ | −0.14 | −0.004 | 0.03 | 0.37 | 2.10 |
|  | (2.90) | (0.13) | (0.28) |  |  |
| $D_u/GDP$ | −0.19 | −0.08 | −0.12 | 0.48 | 2.10 |
|  | (3.10) | (1.50) | (0.84) |  |  |
| $G_u/GDP$ | −0.004 | 0.076 | −0.06 | 0.40 | 1.70 |
|  | (0.33) | (4.00) | (1.40) |  |  |
| $R_u/GDP$ | 0.14 | 0.16 | 0.20 | 0.41 | 2.10 |
|  | (2.20) | (2.60) | (0.40) |  |  |

*Note*: t-statistics are shown in parentheses. $Y^*$ = trend income level growing at 6.7 percent; $D$ = budget deficit; $G$ = government expenditure; $R$ = government revenue; and $D_u = D_a - D_p$.
*Subscripts*: $a$ = actual; $p$ = planned; and $u$ = unplanned.
*Source*: Authors' calculatons from data in tables 3.4, 7.3, and 7.5.

The regression results in table 7.7 relate the magnitudes of actual, planned, and unplanned fiscal aggregates to deviations from trend growth, inflation, and the ratio of the current account deficit to GDP. The results confirm that automatic fiscal stabilizers played an important role in Thailand. The coefficients of the ratio of the unplanned deficit to GDP are negative with respect to all explanatory variables, although not all are statistically significant in this equation. An unexpected boom causes an unplanned rise in revenue and a decline in the public deficit. The automatic stabilizing effect operates more strongly through the revenue side than through variations in expenditure.

Inflation also causes a rise in unplanned revenue and expenditure, but its impact on revenue is stronger, and it causes the actual deficit to decline. The coefficients of the current account/GDP ratio (CAD/GDP) are not significant in any of these equations; at most, there may be a weak negative relationship between the ratio of the unplanned deficit to GDP and the current account deficit. Our interpretation—namely, that the period falls into two discrete parts, in which the relationship between these two variables is reversed—is consistent with this result.

*Intermediate-Run Stabilization*

Two intermediate-run issues are of interest here. To what extent did planned deficits drive the fiscal adjustments in the mid- to late 1970s, on the one hand, and the early 1980s, on the other?

As figure 7.1 indicates, the rising fiscal deficits that followed the first oil price shock were led by unplanned deficits, which began to rise after 1974 as a consequence of slowed income growth and accelerated inflation. Planned deficits also rose from 1975 to 1977, reinforcing the unplanned component. As income growth recovered from 1977 to 1979, planned deficits remained high, but unplanned deficits declined, dominating the actual fiscal outcome, which was a decline in the actual deficit from 1976 to 1979. Nevertheless, the intention of planning over this period, as reflected in the planned deficits, was consistent with the outcome: the public sector deficit was higher than it had been before the oil price shock.

The period of the early 1980s is more controversial. The question is, when did Thailand begin to adjust to the growing external imbalance? From 1987 on, Thailand was enjoying an economic boom led at least in part—we would argue in the main—by external events. If adjustment was not demonstrably in place by then, some doubt must remain as to whether Thailand adjusted significantly at all. If not, then it might reasonably be thought that Thailand was simply lucky. It could then be said that Thailand had borrowed its way out of the need to adjust to the terms of trade decline of the 1970s and early 1980s and that it was saved from the long-term consequences of this nonadjustment by an externally led boom beginning, fortuitously, about 1986 or 1987.

From 1981 to 1984 planned public sector deficits were without doubt significantly below their levels of the late 1970s (figure 7.3), but actual deficits were above their levels of the late 1970s. In the early 1980s the fiscal authorities were attempting a steady fiscal adjustment, but their efforts were clearly defeated by the operation of automatic fiscal stabilizers, responding to the slowed income growth of the first half of the 1980s, and the inflation of the early 1980s. It would be correct to say that in the early 1980s the intention of fiscal policy was to adjust to the growing external imbalance, but here as elsewhere it is essential to distinguish between the intention of policy and its actual outcome. The evidence provides little support for the claim that fiscal adjustment, defined to mean fiscal outcomes rather than fiscal intentions, began significantly before 1986 or 1987.

Thus it seems that the fiscal expansion of the early to mid-1970s stimulated growth but that the short-term and intermediate-term fiscal outcomes observed thereafter were primarily a *consequence* of growth, caused by other more powerful economic forces, rather than a cause of it.[4]

## Sources of Stabilization

If the actual fiscal adjustments have been stabilizing, and automatic stabilizers were the principal mechanism through which this occurred, what, then, is the source of these stabilizers? Do they originate on the revenue or the expenditure side of the budget, and from which of their components?

THE DETERMINATION OF PUBLIC EXPENDITURE AND REVENUE. The Thai budgetary process requires expenditures to be planned a year in advance of actual outlays. As already mentioned, budgetary regulations restrict the size of planned expenditures as a proportion of planned revenues. This system seems likely to produce a relationship between actual expenditures in the current period and previous period revenues. The latter are known at the time expenditures must be planned and actual revenues in year $t-1$ are the principal basis for determining planned revenues in year $t$.

We used a log-linear regression analysis based on data from 1970 to 1990 to investigate this relationship. The estimated elasticities of real expenditures with respect to real previous period revenues are summarized in table 7.8. The positive elasticity of response indicates that as planned (previous period) revenues rise in real terms, expenditures also rise; but the elasticity of less than unity suggests that expenditures rise in a smaller proportion than the increase in revenues. That is, as incomes rise, the deficit contracts. We wish to go beyond this analysis, however, because the estimated relationship only partly explains the behavior of expenditures and, of course, it does not explain the behavior of revenues.

To study the responsiveness of government expenditure and revenue to changes in income and the price level, we regressed real expenditures and real revenues on real GDP and the nominal GDP deflator (table 7.9). Our estimate of the elasticity of total tax revenue with respect to real GDP is 1.4, which falls within the range found in earlier studies, but at its upper end (table 7.10). This estimate is also significantly greater (at the 5 percent level of significance) than our estimate of the income elasticity of total real expenditures (0.5). The implication is that as incomes rise, the gap between aggregate expenditure and aggregate revenue narrows. The real fiscal stimulus declines.

**Table 7.8  Public Expenditure Elasticities and Tax Buoyancy, 1970–90**

| | *Elasticity* | |
|---|---|---|
| *Expenditure* | *Previous period revenue* | *GDP deflator* |
| Current | 0.82 | 0.29 |
| | (3.68) | (0.94) |
| Capital | 0.36 | −2.53 |
| | (0.59) | (−2.37) |
| Total public | 0.75 | −0.86 |
| | (5.79) | (2.25) |

*Note*: Numbers in parentheses are *t*-statistics.
*Source*: Calculated from Bank of Thailand, *Monthly Bulletin*, various issues, tables 23 and 24.

## Table 7.9 Elasticities of Real Public Expenditures and Revenues with Respect to Real GDP and GDP Deflator, 1970–90

| Real aggregate | Elasticity | |
| --- | --- | --- |
| | Real GDP | GDP deflator |
| Revenue | 1.40 | −0.16 |
| | (12.5) | (1.8) |
| Expenditure | 0.48 | −0.86 |
| | (1.02) | (2.25) |

*Note*: Numbers in parentheses are *t*-statistics.
*Source*: Calculated from Bank of Thailand, *Monthly Bulletin*, various issues, tables 23 and 24.

A similar point applies to the effects of inflation. Inflation seems to have no effect on public revenues in real terms, but it has an important negative impact on public expenditures, as indicated by the significance of the GDP deflator. The estimated magnitude of the elasticity (−0.86) indicates that as the price level rises nominal expenditure remains almost constant.[5] These findings suggest that the behavior of Thailand's fiscal aggregates contributes to price stability. When the price level rises, the government does not insist on acquiring the intended level of expenditures, in real terms. As a result, during an economic boom that places upward pressure on the price level, there is less inflationary pressure from the public sector.

## Table 7.10  Summary of Previous Tax Elasticity Estimates

| Researcher | Period of estimation | Tax elasticities | | | |
| --- | --- | --- | --- | --- | --- |
| | | Total | Personal income | Corporate income | Business |
| World Bank (1974) | 1963–73 | 1.4 | 1.2 | 1.1 | 1.2 |
| World Bank (1978) | 1970–77 | 1.3 | — | — | — |
| World Bank (1983) | 1963–81 | 1.0 | 1.4 | 1.3 | 1.0 |
| IMF (n.d) | 1975–78 | 1.1 | 1.3 | 1.2 | 1.2 |
| IMF (n.d) | 1978–81 | 0.9 | 1.4 | 0.8 | 0.8 |
| IMF (n.d) | 1975–81 | 0.9 | 1.3 | 1.0 | 0.9 |
| Chanchai (1983) | 1972–82 | 1.0 | 1.1 | 1.3 | 1.1 |
| Chompleon and others (1982) | 1961–79 | 1.0 | 1.3 | 1.7 | 1.2 |
| Ministry of Finance (1984) | 1974–83 | 1.0 | 1.9 | 0.9 | 0.9 |
| Yuttaphon (1984) | 1974–83 | 1.0 | 1.8 | 1.0 | 0.9 |

*Source*: Rungsan Thanapornan (1985), cited in Medhi and others (1988), table 2.10.

In summary, our results confirm that the Thai fiscal system has a stabilizing feature with respect to both real income and the price level. First, although expenditures are insensitive to collected revenues, the latter are sensitive to fluctuations in aggregate economic activity. Thus, during boom years revenues rise faster than expenditures, and in recessions the reverse occurs. Second, inflation reduces real expenditures, but it leaves aggregate real tax revenues virtually unchanged. Thus when inflation accelerates, the real magnitude of the budgetary deficit declines (the budgetary surplus increases) and further inflationary pressure subsides. The sources of these mechanisms can be found among the components of aggregate expenditure and revenues.

THE COMPOSITION OF EXPENDITURE. From 1970 on, current expenditures—on salaries, the use of consumable materials, and other recurrent costs associated with government activity—accounted for an average of about 78 percent of total government expenditure (see table 4.2). Capital expenditures, those associated with increasing the public sector capital stock, averaged about 22 percent of total expenditures. But these proportions varied considerably, as did the share of total expenditure in GDP, which fluctuated between 15 and 20 percent of GDP. There was some variation in both current and capital expenditure, but capital expenditure was the more volatile of the two (see table 7.4).

The central government's spending increased most rapidly during the expansionary period between 1975 and 1980, when it grew at the rate of 23 percent per year in real terms (table 7.11). The smallest increase occurred during the deceleration period of 1986 to 1990, when it expanded at an average rate of 7 percent. The share of capital expenditure in total expenditures decreased over time, from 26 percent during 1971–74 to only 14 percent during 1986–90. Thus the role of the central government in providing infrastructure diminished substantially during the 1980s.

The budget share allocated to defense averaged 19 percent, but the rate of change of defense expenditure fluctuated widely. During years of fiscal expansion, it grew at an average rate of 22 percent, but this rate was cut to only 2.7 percent during the tight fiscal years of 1986 to 1989. The top priority of the budget is social services—such as hospitals, schools, and police. Although the share of administration gradually declined over time, the importance of the expenditure on economic services fell more significantly: from 24 percent in the early 1970s to only 14.6 percent in the late 1980s. The slowdown in public expenditure on infrastructure was the result of the attempt to restrain the rise in public spending. Its effect was to reduce the size of public capital stock in relation to national output.

Apparently, when an expenditure cut is desired, it is more expedient to cut capital expenditure than current expenditure. It has been easier to postpone large public investment projects than to delay increases in civil servants' salaries during inflation. Although the government has been able to freeze the wages of public employees from time to time—as it did from 1982 to 1989—the controllability of

**Table 7.11  Changing Structure of Government Expenditure, 1971–90**
*(percentage change, period average)*

| Expenditure | 1971–74 | 1975–80 | 1981–85 | 1986–90 |
|---|---|---|---|---|
| Total | 8.9 | 23.1 | 10.6 | 7.4 |
| *Economic classification* | | | | |
| Current | 13.9 | 21.9 | 12.2 | 8.0 |
| Average share | (74) | (76) | (82) | (86) |
| Capital | –5.0 | 28.9 | 4.9 | 4.1 |
| Average share | (26) | (24) | (18) | (14) |
| *Major functional classification* | | | | |
| Economic services | –2.0 | 24.7 | 6.1 | 7.7 |
| Average share | (24) | (22) | (17) | (15) |
| Social services | 12.4 | 22.7 | 11.0 | 8.1 |
| Average share | (28) | (30) | (30) | (30) |
| Defense | 13.6 | 22.8 | 12.4 | 2.7 |
| Average share | (19) | (19) | (20) | (19) |
| General administration | 11.4 | 22.4 | 8.7 | 8.7 |
| Average share | (14) | (13) | (13) | (13) |
| Unallocatable items | 15.7 | 26.4 | 15.5 | 10.0 |
| Average share | (14) | (14) | (20) | (23) |

*Source*: Comptroller-General's Department; Bank of Thailand.

public consumption spending is ordinarily subject to political influences and inflationary expectations.

The above arguments suggest that the fiscal spending structure, or the allocation of government expenditure between consumption and investment, depends on
the overall fiscal policy stance. If the budget was contractionary, public investment
spending would rise proportionately less than public consumption, and vice versa.
In figure 7.7, it is clear that the ratio of public investment to public consumption
is correlated with the ratio of the public deficit to GDP. From 1970 to 1974, when
fiscal policy was tight, the ratio of investment to consumption within public expenditure declined sharply. When easier fiscal policies were implemented, between 1975 and 1985, the investment-to-consumption ratio rose rapidly.

The ratio of public and private investment to GDP exhibits a striking inverse
relationship (figure 7.8), which suggests that public investment may exercise a stabilizing role with respect to aggregate investment by maintaining a high and stable
proportion of total capital formation in relation to income.[6] Table 7.12 summarizes

**Figure 7.7.  Fiscal Structure and Public Deficit, 1970–91**

Percent

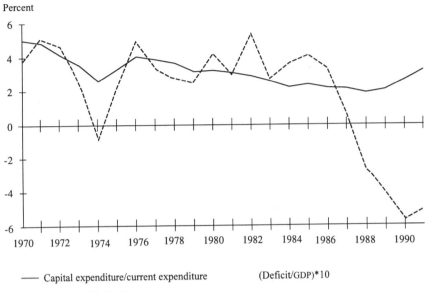

——— Capital expenditure/current expenditure          (Deficit/GDP)*10

*Source:* Bank of Thailand.

**Figure 7.8.  Public and Private Capital Accumulation, 1970–91**

Ratio to GDP

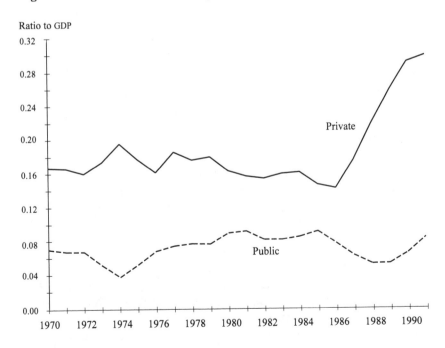

*Source:* NESDB, *National Income of Thailand,* various issues.

**Table 7.12  Growth, Inflation and Capital Formation, 1971–90**
*(percent)*

| Year | Real GDP growth | Inflation (CPI) | Rate of change of real invesment | |
|------|------|------|------|------|
| | | | *Private* | *Public* |
| 1971 | 4.96 | 0.25 | 1.45 | −2.09 |
| 1972 | 4.07 | 5.05 | −0.43 | 4.46 |
| 1974 | 4.35 | 24.37 | 6.41 | −30.32 |
| 1975 | 4.85 | 5.36 | −8.85 | 42.90 |
| 1980 | 4.78 | 19.76 | −2.59 | 18.88 |
| 1982 | 4.06 | 5.24 | 1.38 | −8.54 |
| 1985 | 3.51 | 2.42 | −11.19 | 7.57 |
| 1986 | 4.92 | 1.81 | 0.51 | −11.58 |
| Low growth | 4.44 | 8.03 | −1.41 | 2.66 |
| 1979 | 5.31 | 9.87 | 5.13 | 1.13 |
| 1981 | 6.33 | 12.70 | 3.71 | 6.35 |
| 1983 | 7.25 | 3.71 | 13.45 | 11.50 |
| 1984 | 7.13 | 0.89 | 10.62 | 11.65 |
| Medium growth | 6.51 | 6.79 | 8.24 | 7.66 |
| 1973 | 9.86 | 15.38 | 21.52 | −17.49 |
| 1976 | 9.88 | 4.13 | 3.87 | 45.14 |
| 1977 | 9.90 | 7.48 | 26.30 | 18.21 |
| 1978 | 10.44 | 7.95 | 7.38 | 21.10 |
| 1987 | 9.47 | 2.55 | 29.22 | −13.07 |
| 1988 | 13.22 | 3.84 | 32.01 | −9.39 |
| 1989 | 12.05 | 5.36 | 32.07 | 13.17 |
| 1990 | 10.00 | 5.98 | 24.24 | 35.59 |
| High growth | 10.60 | 6.58 | 22.08 | 11.66 |

*Source*: National Economic and Social Develpment Board, *National Income of Thailand*, various issues.

the data on this point, dividing years into low, medium, and high growth groups. When a private investment boom occurred in 1974, public investment declined. Although private investment remained sluggish from 1979 to 1985 after the second oil price shock, public investment expanded. Again, during the private investment boom of 1987 to 1990, the ratio of public investment to GDP declined significantly.

From table 7.8 it is apparent that public investment expenditure is highly sensitive to inflation. The stabilizing effect of public expenditure behavior with respect to the price level clearly derives from the behavior of public investment spending rather than public consumption. The large negative value of our estimate of the elasticity of real public investment expenditure with respect to the GDP deflator (–2.53, which is significantly different from zero at the 5 percent level of significance) implies that increased inflation causes nominal, and not merely real, public expenditure on capital goods to decline when inflation rises. But the elasticity of current expenditure was not significantly different from zero, as indicated by the low value of its *t*-statistic.

The economic process underlying this result is that public investment projects can be delayed in real terms if the nominal cost of capital is rising. Capital expenditures are not fixed in real terms. Actual expenditure will be lower than the planned level, even in nominal terms, if the allocated budget cannot cover the rising cost of capital. If the budgeted funds are insufficient to purchase a particular expenditure item, they will not be spent at all in that fiscal year.

It might be hypothesized that the inverse relationship between public and private investment was the result of a crowding out of public investment, which raised interest rates and discouraged private investment. As will be shown later, however, borrowing from the nonbank private sector constituted a small portion of deficit financing. A large part of the deficit was money financed and thereby created a favorable condition for private investors since there was no upward pressure on the interest rate. That relationship appears to arise from the sensitivity of public investment spending to inflation in the prices of capital goods, principally those used in the construction industry. Private investment is highly volatile. When it increases, pressure is placed on the prices of capital goods and materials used in construction. This has a powerful negative effect on public investment.

THE EFFECTIVENESS OF LEGAL EXPENDITURE LIMITS. The 1959 Budgetary Law stipulated that the excess of planned spending over planned revenue should not exceed 20 percent of the level of planned spending. The law thus implied that the planned government budget deficit was not to exceed 25 percent of the planned revenue.[7] In 1973 the limit on spending was relaxed somewhat when it was announced that the deficit was not to exceed 20 percent of planned expenditure plus 8 percent of the principal repayments of the public debt.

The effectiveness of the budgetary law in restraining the growth of public expenditure can be seen in figure 7.9. The maximum amount of public spending is calculated by multiplying the level of planned revenue by 1.25 and adding 8 percent of the level of expenditures allocated to principal repayments of public debt. The figure shows ratios of planned expenditure $(G_e)$ and actual expenditure $(G_a)$ to the maximum expenditure permitted by the budgetary law $(G_m)$. Since the actual level of spending was always below the planned level, $G_e/G_m$ was less than $G_a/G_m$. Except during 1972–74, the actual level of expenditures was well below the maximum permitted level.

## Figure 7.9. Effectiveness of Budgetary Law, 1973–88

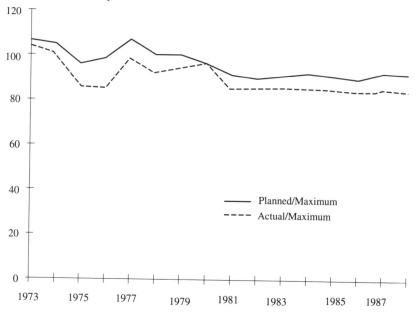

Percent of maximum expenditure

*Source:* Table 7.3 and authors' calculations.

ADJUSTMENT OF GOVERNMENT REVENUES. Since 1970 the government has been able to increase its taxing capacity gradually, as illustrated in table 7.1, thereby raising the ratio of tax revenue to GDP. It was not only the fiscal stance that was changed in response to the long-term effect of external shocks. The structure of taxation was also altered. Direct taxation became increasingly important (see table 4.1). The share of income taxes in total taxation rose from an average 13 percent in the period 1971–74 to 22 percent in the period 1986–90. Personal income and corporation taxes were equally important, at about 10 percent of total tax revenue. The share of sales taxes also rose from 19 to 28 percent over the same period, while the share of business tax in total taxation remained at roughly 20 to 22 percent.

The share of import duties in total tax revenue declined from 29 percent in the early 1970s to 22 percent in the late 1980s. Since the share of export taxes in total revenue was insignificant, the importance of foreign trade taxes declined. This implies that the feedback effect of external shocks to the government's fiscal position has diminished over time. In some developing countries whose main sources of revenue are taxes on foreign trade, an abrupt change in the external terms of trade has strong repercussions on the government's fiscal position. This is less true in Thailand.

An examination of the statistical relationship between the components of total real tax revenues, on one hand, and aggregate real income and the GDP deflator, on the other, indicate that the buoyancy of corporate income taxes, import duties, and business taxes increased significantly in the 1980s (table 7.13). Although the buoyancy of personal income tax revenues declined slightly, possibly because of the reduction in the income tax rate, it remained large.

The increase in tax buoyancy, as measured by time-series data, was partly the result of long-term structural changes within the Thai economy. The shift in the composition of output away from agriculture and toward the manufacturing and formal services sectors brought a rising proportion of economic activity within the tax base. The rise in the share of imports in total demand also led to rising tax revenues because imports are taxed on average more heavily than domestically produced goods. Moreover, during an economic boom, imports rise proportionately more than GDP because the income elasticity of demand for imports exceeds unity. The rise in imports generates import duties. The expansion of the tax base to cover activities that are sensitive to business cycles, together with more efficient tax collection, also played a role.

THE CHANGING MEANS OF DEFICIT FINANCE. The methods of deficit financing changed significantly between 1970 and 1990. The government increasingly relied on borrowing from domestic rather than foreign sources (table 7.14). Financing by the use of treasury cash balance also declined during the same period.

The share of foreign borrowing in deficit financing was again exceptionally high, at 36 percent of the total deficit during the economic slump of 1985, a year in which

**Table 7.13  Tax Buoyancy, 1970–90**

*(percent)*

| Tax and duties | 1970–79 | | 1980–90 | | 1970–90 | |
|---|---|---|---|---|---|---|
| | *Real GDP* | *GDP deflator* | *Real GDP* | *GDP deflator* | *Real GDP* | *GDP deflator* |
| Personal income | 2.7 | –1.1 | 2.2 | –2.6 | 2.0 | –0.39 |
| | (6.0) | (3.2) | (2.0) | (0.89) | (5.1) | (0.82) |
| Corporate income | 0.51 | 1.6 | 1.78 | 2.9 | 1.4 | 1.3 |
| | (0.95) | (3.8) | (2.03) | (1.6) | (2.7) | (2.3) |
| Import | 1.64 | –0.73 | 2.26 | –1.32 | 2.1 | –1.1 |
| | (4.8) | (2.7) | (3.5) | (0.96) | (14.8) | (7.3) |
| Business | 0.81 | 0.37 | 2.86 | 0.02 | 1.6 | –0.24 |
| | (1.65) | (0.96) | (4.7) | (0.24) | (5.8) | (0.8) |
| Sales | 0.18 | 0.26 | 0.81 | 0.98 | 1.45 | –0.78 |
| | (0.15) | (0.27) | (0.98) | (0.56) | (4.4) | (2.2) |

*Note:* Numbers in parentheses are *t*-statistics.
*Source:* Calculated from Bank of Thailand, *Monthly Bulletin*, various issues, tables 23 and 24.

### Table 7.14  Financing the Public Deficit, 1970–90
*(percent of total deficit)*

| Year | Net domestic borrowing | Net foreign borrowings | Net other liabilities of Treasury | Use of Treasury cash balances |
|------|------|------|------|------|
| 1970 | 73.9 | 0.1 | 4.1 | 21.9 |
| 1971 | 74.3 | 0.6 | 12.0 | 13.1 |
| 1972 | 113.4 | −1.0 | 6.1 | −8.6 |
| 1973 | 85.3 | 2.4 | 36.0 | −23.8 |
| 1974 | −67.5 | 0.5 | 76.9 | −109.9 |
| 1970–74 | 55.9 | 0.5 | 27.0 | −21.5 |
| 1975 | 37.8 | −1.5 | 31.1 | 32.5 |
| 1976 | 69.0 | −0.2 | 19.9 | 11.4 |
| 1977 | 88.0 | 1.7 | 4.7 | 5.6 |
| 1978 | 109.3 | −4.9 | 3.2 | −7.6 |
| 1979 | 98.0 | −7.1 | 1.6 | 7.5 |
| 1980 | 102.5 | −4.2 | 4.8 | −3.1 |
| 1975–80 | 84.1 | −2.7 | 10.9 | 7.7 |
| 1981 | 104.5 | −9.5 | 4.3 | 0.1 |
| 1982 | 105.9 | 1.9 | −6.5 | −1.3 |
| 1983 | 111.2 | 4.1 | −17.1 | 1.8 |
| 1984 | 108.2 | −2.2 | −7.1 | 1.2 |
| 1985 | 81.1 | 36.4 | −15.7 | −1.8 |
| 1981–85 | 102.2 | 6.1 | −8.4 | 0.0 |
| 1986 | 147.2 | −18.9 | −23.3 | −4.9 |
| 1987 | 120.1 | −36.9 | −3.8 | 20.6 |
| 1988 | −79.9 | −12.6 | 1.3 | 8.9 |
| 1989 | −17.1 | −9.5 | −7.1 | −66.4 |
| 1990 | −11.1 | −36.6 | −1.4 | −50.8 |
| 1986–90 | 31.8 | −22.9 | −6.9 | −18.5 |

*Source*: Computed from Bank of Thailand, *Monthly Bulletin*, table 25.

private investment declined by 11 percent in real terms. The large increase in foreign borrowing in 1985 enabled public investment to expand 8 percent and thus compensate for the shortfall in private investment. It is clear that the government has, in general, endeavored to avoid foreign borrowing except when it has been clearly necessary. Note, too, that foreign borrowing is subject to the legally imposed ceiling on the debt-service ratio (figure 7.10). Although the ceiling was adjusted in some years, its significance in restraining public sector foreign debt cannot be denied.

Not only did the size of domestic borrowing to finance the deficit increase, its composition also changed. Reliance on inflationary means of deficit financing, such as borrowing from the Bank of Thailand, was reduced substantially from its high levels of the early 1970s (figure 7.11). In the period 1970–74, borrowing from the Bank of Thailand was 78 percent of total net domestic borrowing. It fell to only 25 percent during the period 1986–88. From 1970–74 to 1986–88, the government's borrowing from commercial banks increased from 16 to 29 percent of its total borrowing, and its borrowing from government savings banks increased from 3 to 40 percent of total borrowing.

Through the 1980s, not only the size of the budget deficit declined, but the dependence on inflationary means of financing it, that is, borrowing from the Bank of Thailand, was also reduced. The changing pattern of deficit financing clearly contributed to long-term price stability.

### Conclusions

The short-run behavior of the public sector's fiscal system leads to a significant stabilization effect, which operates with respect to fluctuations in both income and

**Figure 7.10. Ceiling on Debt Service Ratio, 1970–88**

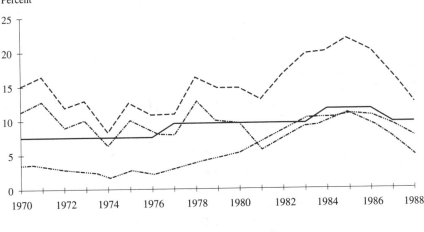

*Source:* Bank of Thailand.

**Figure 7.11.  Financing the Public Deficit, Domestic Sources, 1970–88**

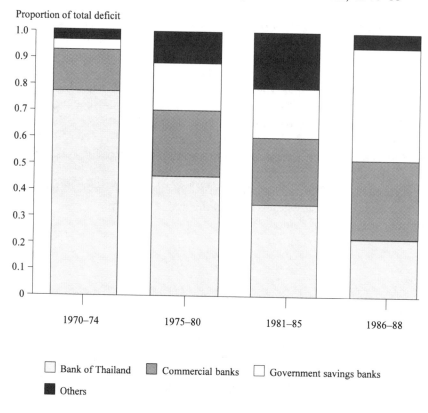

Bank of Thailand     Commercial banks     Government savings banks

Others

the price level. That effect does not arise from discretionary policy changes, however, but from the unplanned component of the observed fiscal outcomes.

The economic literature on automatic stabilization refers to the stabilizing role of income taxes and welfare payments through the social security system. When incomes rise, direct income taxes rise more than proportionately, and welfare payments fall. Thus, the size of the budget deficit falls. When incomes fall, the deficit rises. But these are characteristics of developed economies, not of developing economies like Thailand's.

The public finance literature would not lead one to look for automatic stabilization in Thailand's fiscal system. In 1990 personal income taxes accounted for only 10 percent of Thailand's total revenue. Company income taxes made up another 14 percent. Indirect taxes—import duties, business taxes, and sale taxes—were each far more important than these income taxes. Together, they accounted for 69 percent of 1990 revenues. But they are a source of the stabilization on the revenue side. On the expenditure side, Thailand has no social security system at all, but its rigid, bureaucratically driven budgetary process is a source of stabilization. Clearly, automatic stabilizers can be important for developing as well as developed economies, but the mechanisms through which they operate can be very different.

Short-run discretionary changes in fiscal policy do not seem to have been stabilizing. If stabilizing fiscal policy is interpreted in this way, then it would be wrong to attribute Thailand's record of economic stability to this source. But policy clearly had a crucial effect in a deeper and longer-term sense. Most obviously, short-term discretionary behavior was not significantly destabilizing. It could have been otherwise, and the instability experienced by so many other developing countries may well reflect a significant difference in this respect.

Equally important, the structural features of the Thai revenue and expenditure systems that produce the automatic stabilizing outcomes are themselves the products of past policies. On the revenue side, this point is so obvious that it does not require elaboration, but on the expenditure side two features of the Thai public expenditure system should be emphasized.

First, the determination of public investment expenditure has a built-in anti-inflationary feature. When rapid inflation occurs in the prices of capital goods required for public sector capital formation, public sector purchases of these materials contract markedly in real terms. Construction materials are a prime example. The result is a significant negative correlation between private sector investment and public sector investment spending. The expenditure regulations that produce this outcome are of course the products of past policy decisions and reflect the anti-inflation bias which pervades the Thai policy environment.

Second, legal limits on planned expenditures date back to laws introduced during the Sarit government of the late 1950s and early 1960s. The important point is not that this caused short-run discretionary fiscal policy to be stabilizing—apparently, it did not. But it did contribute to fiscal discipline by limiting the overall magnitude of planned fiscal deficits and so, in effect, constrained the capacity of fiscal policy to be destabilizing, both in the short and the long term.

From 1970 to 1990 the structure of Thailand's deficit financing shifted increasingly away from foreign borrowing and toward domestic borrowing. Moreover, the composition of domestic borrowing shifted away from inflationary sources, such as borrowing from the Bank of Thailand, and toward domestic sources that do not imply monetary creation. Nevertheless, the share of borrowing from the Bank of Thailand in total deficit financing remained substantial over the entire twenty-year period. It follows that fiscal discipline was an indispensable component of long-term inflation control. The monetary policy components are discussed in chapter 8.

# Chapter Eight

# The Role of Monetary Policy

The record of Thailand's monetary institutions has been impressive. Controlling inflation has been the principal mandate of the central bank, the Bank of Thailand, and it has accomplished this to an extent matched by few others.[1] Inflation has been subdued largely through long-term monetary restraint, which has made it possible to achieve a stable exchange rate combined with adequate levels of international reserves and only moderate growth of the external debt.

Another of the bank's mandates is to promote the short-term stabilization of income growth and external balance. According to the Bank itself (Bank of Thailand 1992), a discretionary, countercyclical monetary policy directed to this end has been successfully implemented. Whether this interpretation of Thailand's monetary experience is supported by the evidence is the central question explored in this chapter.

The discussion focuses on four main topics: the autonomy or otherwise of Thailand's monetary policies, in the presence of its fixed exchange rate policy; the components of Thailand's monetary base and the degree to which the Bank of Thailand can be said to control them; the manner in which the major instruments of monetary policy have been manipulated by the Thai monetary authorities in response to external shocks; and the effectiveness of these interventions in stabilizing income growth and inflation in the short run.

Thailand has followed a fixed exchange rate policy for several decades. The baht has been pegged in relation to the U.S. dollar since the 1950s except for a few, moderately sized devaluations in the early 1980s (discussed in chapter 9). But the fixed exchange rate implies that the monetary authorities cannot fully control Thailand's money supply. Under a fixed exchange rate, Thailand's monetary base would be affected by the balance of payments as a result of the Bank of Thailand's intervention in the foreign exchange market. To maintain a fixed exchange rate, the bank must stand ready to buy or sell unlimited quantities of foreign exchange at that rate, and these transactions will affect the domestic money supply in a way that the bank cannot control.

Conventional wisdom therefore dictates that, provided the capital account is open, attempts to combine a fixed exchange rate with a discretionary monetary policy will fail. The claim that Thailand has successfully combined these two therefore appears dubious at best. Yet the evidence supports the view that weakly countercyclical discretionary monetary policies have indeed been pursued successfully in Thailand. Regulations that restrict free capital movements have enabled the monetary authorities to pursue some degree of monetary independence in the short run, as is evident from significant divergences between domestic and foreign interest rates in the short run. Moreover, these divergences can be related to changes in monetary policy.

To some extent, therefore, the Thai monetary authorities can be said to possess a degree of short-run autonomy. The effectiveness of their monetary policies is aided by the stable relationship between money supply and the monetary base, but limited by offsetting capital flows. The main tools of monetary policy appear to be changes in the central bank lending rate, direct regulation of interest rates, direct regulation of volumes of credit, interventions in the bond repurchase market, and direct controls on capital flows. These monetary instruments appear to have been applied in a manner that has, on balance, been countercyclical.

Economic stabilization is but one of the Bank of Thailand's objectives. It is also concerned with such development objectives as rural development, export promotion, and maintaining the stability of financial institutions. Sometimes, those development goals are inconsistent with price stability, since they require the Bank to provide credits for regional and sectoral development, for export promotion, and for maintaining the liquidity of ailing financial institutions. The Bank must compromise between these conflicting goals in determining the appropriate level of credit growth.

The analysis of monetary policy in this chapter concentrates on the period 1970–90. But changes in Thailand's regulatory environment since 1990 will greatly change the future operation of Thai monetary policy. This issue is also given some attention in the chapter.

## Autonomy of Monetary Policy

With a fixed exchange rate and an open capital account, Thailand should, in theory, not be able to operate an independent monetary policy. According to the Mundell-Fleming hypothesis, under a fixed exchange rate policy, a monetary contraction, by raising domestic interest rates, would induce a capital inflow and force interest rates downward again. Monetary expansion would do the reverse. If applicable, this hypothesis would imply that domestic interest rates would move together with international rates and be outside the control of the Thai monetary authorities. As this chapter explains, the key to the apparent contradiction is that the Thai capital account has not been fully open.

*Regulations Restricting Free Capital Movements*

There are four reasons for a lack of openness in the period 1970–90: interest rate ceilings, direct capital controls, controls on the foreign exchange position of commercial banks, and the withholding tax on foreign borrowing.

INTEREST RATE CEILINGS. Regulatory ceilings on domestic interest rates, both lending and borrowing rates, prevented the domestic interest rate increases that would otherwise have induced capital inflows when the domestic money supply was contracted. These interest rate ceilings were adjusted only slightly during shocks. From 1970 to 1981, the rates on commercial bank deposits were equal to the ceiling rates, and from 1982 to 1985 the actual time deposit rates of interest paid by commercial banks remained 0.5 percent below the ceiling.

DIRECT CAPITAL CONTROLS. Bank of Thailand permission has been required to move capital out of Thailand, and this policy has been policed vigorously. During periods of monetary expansion, this policy enabled the monetary authorities to prevent the outward flow of capital that would otherwise deprive them of the capacity to expand the domestic money supply when desired. All outgoing payments were subject to approval. Until 1990, exporters were required to submit foreign exchange currency to banks within seven days after receiving payments from abroad.[2]

Until 1990 Thai citizens were not permitted to hold foreign exchange deposits or to purchase foreign currencies for investment overseas. Thus they were unable to take much advantage of differentials between domestic and foreign rates of interest. Individuals were not permitted to take out of Thailand domestic currency exceeding 500 baht (equivalent to about $20) or foreign currency exceeding $1,000. In 1993 these limits were 50,000 baht (equivalent to about $2,000) and $10,000 of foreign currency. The degree of substitution between domestic and foreign assets was far from perfect; similarly, foreign liabilities were imperfect substitutes for loans obtained from domestic banks, since domestic deficit units could not gain access to foreign capital markets. The government also imposed a limit on the volume of the foreign debt of public enterprises.

CONTROLS ON FOREIGN EXCHANGE POSITIONS OF COMMERCIAL BANKS. Since 1984, the net foreign exchange positions of commercial banks have also been subject to regulation. Following the 1984 devaluation, the net future and current position of each commercial bank—whether positive or negative—could not exceed $5 million in either direction or 20 percent of the net worth of the bank, whichever was smaller. In April 1990 the ceiling on the net position of commercial banks was raised to 25 percent of capital funds.

WITHHOLDING TAX ON FOREIGN BORROWING. A withholding tax is applied to foreign borrowing at rates that are varied by the Minister of Finance to encourage or discourage foreign capital inflows. This instrument creates a tax wedge between the domestic and foreign costs of capital. When the government wanted to reduce capital inflows, the withholding tax rate was usually set at 10 percent of the interest payments. It was exempted when the government considered the domestic money market too tight. Exemption was sometimes granted for loans with long maturity periods, such as one to three years, to attract long-term capital funds. As table 8.1 shows, the withholding tax rate has been varied significantly from time to time. The adjustments have been directed at influencing capital flows for stabilization purposes.

The above regulations have restricted free capital movements. Thus even if the exchange rate is fixed, scope may remain for using monetary policy in a discretionary manner. If the restrictions on capital mobility are sufficient to make this outcome possible, domestic and foreign interest rates should be imperfectly correlated. More important, divergent movements between these two sets of interest rates should be traceable to changes in Thailand's discretionary domestic monetary policies.

*Interest Rate Divergence*

Figures 8.1 and 8.2 provide some background on the long-term relationships between Thai and foreign interest rates. Figure 8.1 shows the annual average money market rates of interest in Thailand, the United States, and the three-month London interbank offer rate (LIBOR). The U.S. and LIBOR rates move closely together. The Thai rate clearly follows them over the long term, but short-term movements do not always do so.

**Table 8.1  Withholding Tax Rate on Foreign Borrowing**

| Period | Duration (months) | Tax rate | Maturity conditions for exemption |
|---|---|---|---|
| May 1979–September 1980 | 16 | — | — |
| October 1980–September 1981 | 9 | 10 | 12 months |
| August 1981–December 1982 | 16 | — | — |
| January 1983–June 1983 | 6 | 10 | 12 months |
| July 1983–June 1984 | 11 | 10 | 24 months |
| July 1984–February 1989 | 55 | 10 | — |
| March 89–February 90 | 11 | 10 | 36 months |
| March 90–December 90 | 10 | 10 | — |

*Note*: Withholding tax was exempted for loans with stipulated maturity.
*Source*: Bank of Thailand.

**Figure 8.1. Thailand and International Money Market Interest Rates, 1970–90**

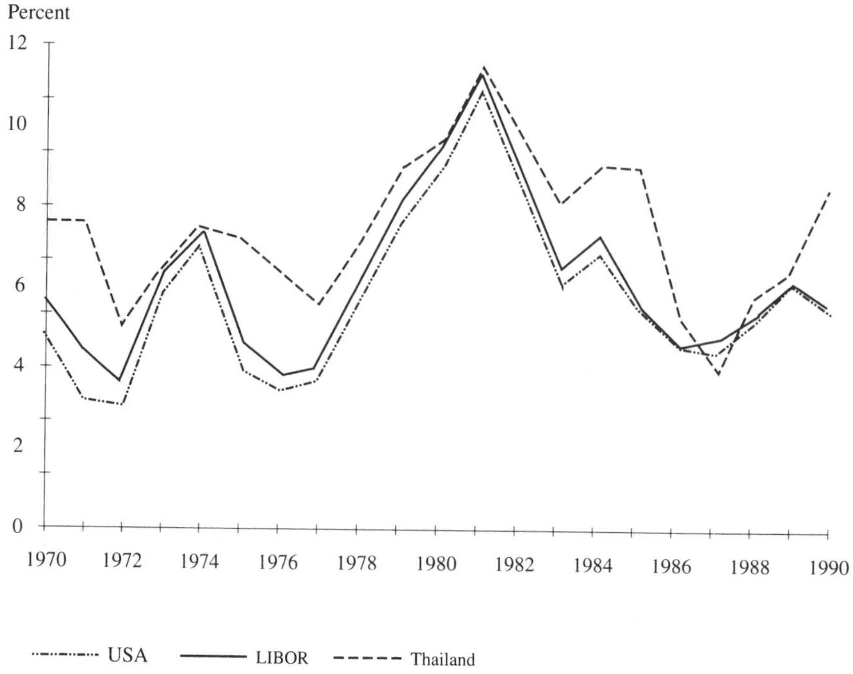

Percent

............... USA ──────── LIBOR ----- Thailand

*Source:* Bank of Thailand and IMF, *International Financial Statistics,* various issues.

Figure 8.2 shows annual average domestic deposit and lending rates in Thailand and the United States. Four points are notable here:

- Broad similarities are again evident in trends over the long term, but short-term deviations between the movement of Thai and U.S. rates clearly occur.
- Thai interest rates tend to exceed U.S. rates. This is especially true for lending rates. Thai lending rates exceeded U.S. lending rates throughout the two decades and exceeded them by four to five percentage points for all years except 1981, when the two converged. This difference seems to be greater than expectations of baht devaluation could explain. Thai deposit rates were about two percentage points above U.S. rates except in the 1978–82 period, when U.S. rates were one to two percentage points higher than the corresponding Thai rates.
- The average difference between lending and deposit rates in Thailand is about six percentage points. In the United States it is about two percentage points. The difference may reflect a lack of competition in the Thai financial system, a consequence of the barriers to entry in the banking system discussed in chapter 3 and the well-known collusive behavior of the large Thai commercial banks. The wider interest spreads in Thailand can be at-

**Figure 8.2. Thailand and the United States, Lending and Deposit Interest Rates, 1970–90**

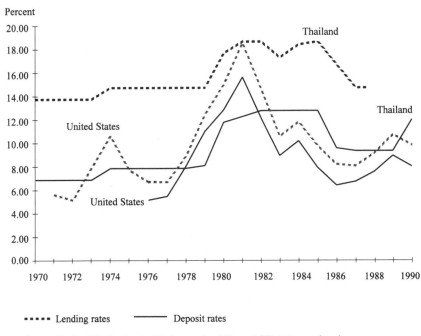

Percent

----- Lending rates          ——— Deposit rates

*Source:* Bank of Thailand and IMF, *International Financial Statistics,* various issues.

tributed in part to the high intermediation costs implied by some regulations on commercial banks' portfolios, such as credit allocation controls.
- Thai rates are less volatile than their U.S. counterparts. The margin between Thai and U.S. lending rates declines when U.S. rates rise and declines when they fall. This feature is observed even more strongly with
deposit rates. These facts suggest that Thai interest rates are more flexible
downward than upward, as a result of the interest rate ceilings.

In the long run, then, Thailand's domestic interest rate does not deviate significantly from the world rate of interest; but in the short run it can deviate significantly from the world rate. These results suggest that although capital mobility
may be close to perfect in the long run, this may be may be far from the truth in
the short run.

*Deviations from Interest Rate Parity*

The hypothesis of perfect capital mobility can be tested by examining the interest
rate parity relationship. In a world of perfect capital mobility with risk-neutral in-
vestor-speculators, interest rate parity should hold. The difference between do-

mestic and foreign interest rates would simply reflect the expected devaluation. In this case, since the foreign interest rate is exogenously given, and if the government cannot control the devaluation expectations of the public, the monetary authority would be unable to influence the domestic interest rate.

If the expected devaluation can be measured by the forward premium price of foreign exchange $(F)$, and this rate adjusts to the difference between the domestic $(R_d)$ and foreign $(R_f)$ interest rates, then

$$(8.1) \qquad\qquad F = R_d - R_f$$

which implies that in equilibrium there is no profit to be made from arbitrage. The relationship described in equation (8.1) is known as nominal covered interest parity. If the hypothesis of perfect capital mobility was correct, we would expect the difference between $F$ and $R_d - R_f$ to remain close to zero.

In our empirical analysis we use quarterly data from the beginning of 1980 to the end of 1989. The one-month forward premium of the U.S. dollar, measured in baht, is used as a proxy for the expected exchange rate devaluation. The London Eurodollar rate of interest is used as the foreign interest rate, and the interbank rate is used as the domestic interest rate. Figure 8.3, which shows the difference $(R_d - R_f) - F$, expressed as a percentage of $F$, reveals systematic deviations from covered interest parity in the 1980s. The negative deviations from 1980 to 1985 indicate that the interest rate differential was less than the forward premium. The positive

**Figure 8.3. Deviations from Covered Interest Rate Parity, 1980–90**

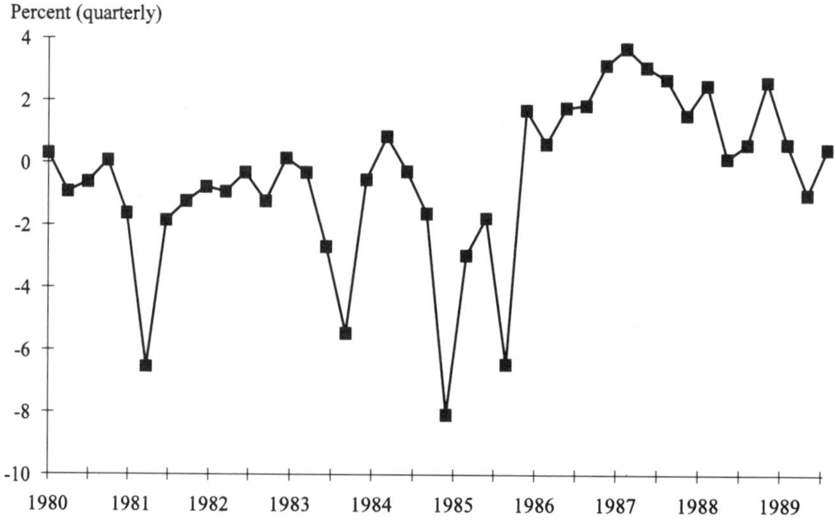

Percent (quarterly)

*Source:* Bank of Thailand and IMF, *International Financial Statistics,* various issues.

deviations after 1986, however, suggest that devaluation expectation was well below the interest rate differentials.

Transaction costs and risk-averse behavior may be the reasons for deviations from interest parity. Political risks arising from different tax structures or capital controls may also contribute to the deviations (Aliber 1973). Evidence on the distortionary effects that capital controls can have on interest rate parity comes from both Japan (Otani and Tiwari 1981) and Germany (Dooley and Isard 1980).

Even with the possibility of offsetting capital inflows and even under a fixed exchange rate, governments can in practice have a degree of monetary independence, because of various insulation mechanisms and their ability to sterilize externally induced changes in money supply (Llewellyn 1980). These insulating factors will cause a deviation of the domestic interest rate from the foreign interest rate. If the central bank induces a deceleration of monetary growth by slowing down the expansion of the monetary base, the domestic interest rate will tend to rise above the foreign interest rate. However, a withholding tax on foreign borrowing can be imposed to prevent capital inflows, in effect reducing the interest rate differential.

One such insulating factor is the forward premium exchange rate, which normally adjusts with the interest rate differential. It does so because as foreign borrowing rises to exploit the interest differential and this foreign capital is converted into baht, speculators purchase foreign exchange forward to cover themselves against the possibility of a baht devaluation. The danger of a devaluation is that it would raise the future cost (in baht) of purchasing the foreign exchange required to repay the foreign loans. But as the demand for these forward contracts rises, their price rises as well. The concern here is how quickly the forward premium rises in response to this increased demand. The profitability of covered arbitrage will be reduced if the forward rate adjusts instantaneously with the interest differential.

Forward covered positions are used for short-term borrowing and trade credit. It is possible that short-term capital flows will be inelastic with respect to changes in interest differentials, since the forward premium becomes an insulating mechanism. Figure 8.4 shows the relationship between the forward premium exchange rate and the interest rate differentials, but this time these two variables are graphed against one another. Although the relationship is not one to one, as indicated by some observations that deviate from the 45-degree line in the figure, the forward rate clearly adjusted positively to the interest rate differentials. This implies that the profitability of international arbitrage is reduced substantially when covered positions are taken into account.[3]

We can explore this issue further by estimating the relationship between the forward premium and the nominal interest rate differential discussed earlier in relation to equation (8.1). The Ordinary Least Squares (OLS) result, corrected for first-order autocorrelation, is

(8.2) $$F = 0.31 + 0.88 \ (R_d - R_f)$$
$$(0.59) \ (6.01)$$

$$\overline{R}^2 = 0.61, DW = 1.99, \rho = 0.42 \ (2.67), n = 39$$

**Figure 8.4. Interest Rate Differential and Forward Premium Rate, 1980–90**

Forward premium rate (quarterly)

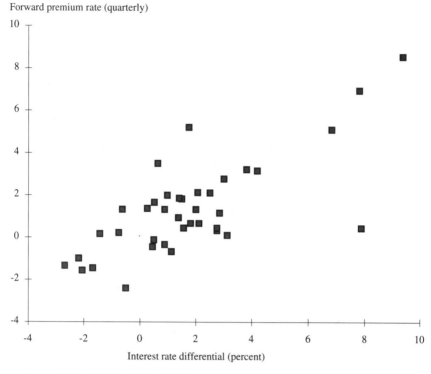

Interest rate differential (percent)

*Source:* Bank of Thailand, *Monthly Bulletin,* various issues, and authors' calculations.

where figures in parentheses are *t*-statistics, $\overline{R}^2$ is the coefficient of determination adjusted for degrees of freedom, *DW* is the Durbin-Watson statistic, r is the first-order autoregressive coefficient, and *n* is the number of observations.

Regression (8.2) essentially tests for nominal covered interest rate parity. It indicates that the forward rate adjusts in the same direction as the interest rate differentials but does not adjust fully to the change in the interest rate differential. Capital mobility is still far from perfect, since the coefficient of the explanatory variable is less than unity. The linear relationship in regression (8.2) imposes the assumption that the coefficients of $R_d$ and $R_f$ are equal but with opposite signs. We can further relax this assumption, with the result

$$(8.3) \qquad F = -3.13 + 0.95\, R_d - 0.62\, R_f$$
$$\qquad\qquad (3.99)\ (8.97)\quad\ (5.19)$$

$$\overline{R}^2 = 0.70;\ DW = 1.82;\ n = 40\ (1980\text{QI to }1989\text{QIV})$$
(*t*-statistics in parentheses).

The forward premium rate adjusts more to changes in the domestic interest rate than to changes in foreign rates. If monetary contraction leads to an increase in domestic lending rate, the forward premium would rise by the same proportion, thus mitigating the effects of offsetting capital inflows, since the cost of covered interest arbitrage also increases.

If one assumes that there is no long-run money illusion, one could argue that real covered interest rate parity should hold. In testing the hypothesis of real interest rate equality, we introduce the rate of change of the domestic price level $(p_d{}^*)$ and the rate of change of the foreign price level $(p_f{}^*)$. If real interest rate parity holds, the real return on money, taking into account the foreign exchange risk, should be equalized between countries.

$$(8.4) \qquad F = R_d - p_d{}^* - ( R_f - p_f{}^*).$$

This implies that in terms of the nominal interest rate differential,

$$(8.5) \qquad R_d - R_f = F + (p_d{}^* - p_f{}^*).$$

This equation can be used for testing the hypothesis of perfect capital mobility by examining the estimated parameters in the relationship:

$$(8.6) \qquad R_d - R_f = a + b \, [F + (p_d{}^* - p_f{}^*)].$$

If capital mobility is perfect, $a = 0$ and $b = 1$. In other words, perfect capital mobility will eliminate the covered interest rate differentials measured in real terms. Data on the forward rate between the baht and the U.S. dollar are not available before 1980. We thus employed quarterly data from 1980 to 1989, inclusive, in regressing the interest rate differential on a constant term and the difference between the forward rate and the difference between the inflation rates in Thailand and the rest of the world.[4] We obtained the following result from OLS estimation, corrected for first-order autocorrelation:

$$(8.7) \qquad R_d - R_f = 1.19 + 0.13 \, [F + (p_d{}^* - p_f{}^*)]$$
$$(2.16) \ (2.74)$$

$$\bar{R}^2 = 0.34; \, DW = 1.97; \, \rho = 0.45 \, (2.98); \, n = 38.$$

The constant term is significantly different from zero, while the slope coefficient of the forward rate and inflation differentials is significantly different from unity. Thus the hypothesis of perfect capital mobility is rejected. It could be argued that the forward premium rate may not represent the true value of the expected change in the exchange rate. According to a test of the joint hypothesis that speculators are risk-neutral and their expectations are rational, the forward premium exchange rate may be a poor predictor of future change in the exchange rate (Cumby and Obstfeld 1984).

Thus one may wish to assume perfect foresight in the sense that the public can correctly anticipate a future change in the exchange rate. The forward premium rate ($F$) can then be replaced by the actual percentage change in the exchange rate ($E$). We obtained the following result, again corrected for first-order autocorrelation:

$$(8.8) \qquad R_d - R_f = 1.40 + 0.05 \, [E + (p_d{}^* - p_f{}^*)]$$
$$\phantom{(8.8) \qquad} (2.24) \ (1.19)$$

$$\bar{R}^2 = 0.23; \, DW = 2.03; \, \rho = 0.48 \, (3.23); \, n = 38.$$

It is clear that the constant term is significantly different from zero and the estimated slope parameter (0.05) is close to zero, rather than unity. The real interest rate parity hypothesis does not hold, even if perfect foresight is assumed.

The above evidence clearly indicates that in the case of Thailand the degree of capital mobility is less than perfect. Comparable results were obtained by Monadjemi (1990): using a similar approach, he found that the degree of capital mobility of five OECD countries was far from perfect. Using an indirect testing method, Feldstein and Horioka (1980) similarly found that the ratio of domestic investment to income can be explained mainly by the ratio of domestic saving to income. Therefore, capital mobility was not high enough to destroy the relationship between the two ratios.

Evidently capital inflows do not adjust rapidly and massively to interest rate differentials. When the central bank attempts to raise domestic interest rates by monetary contraction, the interest rate differential will widen, thus inducing capital inflows to exploit the profit opportunity. The responsiveness of the forward premium will, however, partly choke off the exploitation of these interest differentials.

The explanatory power of regressions (8.2) to (8.8) is not particularly high, suggesting that there may be omitted variables that could help explain the systematic interest rate differential. The next question to consider is to what extent these interest rate differentials respond to changes in monetary policies.

## Interest Differentials and Monetary Growth

Just because the domestic rate of interest can differ from the foreign rate, does this mean that the central bank is able to manipulate the domestic rate of interest for stabilization purposes? Figure 8.5 shows the relationship between (a) the deviation between the domestic interest rate and the foreign interest rate, expressed as the difference between the domestic interbank rate and the Eurodollar interest rate in London, and (b) monetary growth, expressed as a three-year moving average of

**Figure 8.5. Autonomy of Monetary Policy, 1973–90**

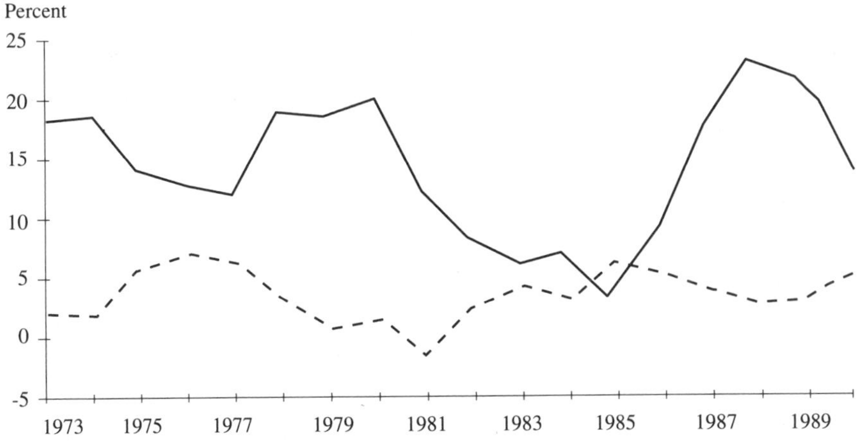

Percent

——— Rd-Rf   - - - - gM1-3 yr moving average

*Source:* Bank of Thailand, *Monthly Bulletin,* various issues.

the growth rate of $M_1$. The money market rate is employed since, unlike the lending deposits rates, it was not subject to the interest rate ceilings.

From figure 8.5, the domestic rate of interest was always higher than the foreign rate, except in 1981. The differential $(R_d - R_f)$ was more than 5 percent between 1975 and 1977, and again in 1985. To what extent were the differentials due to domestic conditions? Since the domestic rate of interest adjusts with some lags when money supply changes, a three-year moving average of monetary growth is used in figure 8.5, which reveals a striking inverse relationship between the interest rate differential and monetary growth. An acceleration in monetary growth produces a lower domestic rate of interest in relation to the foreign rate, and vice versa. The largest interest spreads—between 1975 and 1977 and in 1985—occurred when monetary growth declined substantially. After 1985, the interest spread declined, when monetary growth rose rapidly.

To confirm this finding statistically, we used quarterly data from 1970(QIII) and 1989 (QIV) to explain the interest rate differentials. We obtain the following OLS result, again corrected for first-order autocorrelation:

(8.9)    $$R_d - R_f = 5.69 - 0.099\,M^* + 0.535\,R_c + seasonal$$
$$dummies$$

(1.52) (2.31)      (2.3)

$$\overline{R}^2 = 0.44;\ DW = 2.18;\ n = 77$$

where $M*$ is the three-quarter moving average growth rate of money supply ($M_1$) and $R_c$ is the ceiling on the lending rate.

The results suggest that an increase in the growth of money supply reduces the interest rate differential. Thus, provided the money supply can be controlled, monetary policy could in principle be employed to induce a short-run deviation of the domestic interest rate from the level of the foreign interest rate. In addition, regression (8.9) suggests that the ceiling rate, a policy instrument of the Bank of Thailand, can be used to influence the adjustment of the domestic rate in response to changing conditions.

### Liberalization and the Determination of Domestic Interest Rates

Despite the impediments to full capital mobility, the effect that foreign interest rates have on domestic Thai interest rates cannot be denied. This effect is obvious from figures 8.1 and 8.2. Because of imperfect capital mobility during the study period, the monetary authorities still possessed some control over domestic interest rates. But with the relaxation of controls over the capital account after the second quarter of 1990, the domestic interest rate is expected to become more sensitive to changes in foreign interest rates. This proposition can be tested by exploring the relationship between the interbank and the Eurodollar interest rates. Monetary policy would become less effective in controlling the domestic interest rate if the interbank rate ($R_n$) became more responsive to the Eurodollar rate of interest ($R_f$).

$$(8.10) \quad R_b = -39.6 + 0.25\, R_f + 0.35\, L_d + 0.87\, R_c - 14.5\, D + 1.78\, (D \times R_f)$$
$$\qquad\qquad (5.4)\ (1.8)\qquad (4.1)\qquad (4.6)\qquad (3.7)\qquad (3.8)$$

$\overline{R}^2 = 0.82$; DW = 2.3.
D = 0 (1980QII – 1990QII)
$\phantom{D}$ = 1 (1990QIII–1991QIV)

The interbank rate reflects the interaction between the short-term demand and supply of bank funds. Its movement is determined by the domestic money market conditions proxied by the loan-deposit ratio ($L_d$) as well as the foreign interest rate. The ceiling on the end of period interest rate ($R_c$) is included in the explanation of the interbank rate, since it provides information on the stance of the monetary authorities. This information is important in an industry that has an oligopolistic structure and where price competition is consequently lacking.

The product of the dummy variable and the Eurodollar rate is highly significant and positive, as expected, which indicates that after the relaxation of capital controls, the domestic interest rate, represented by the interbank rate, became more sensitive to changes in the foreign interest rate. Nevertheless, although foreign interest rates have become more powerful in determining the course of the domestic interest rate, domestic conditions still matter.

*Monetary Growth and GDP Growth*

The autonomy of monetary policy requires the existence of efficient monetary policy instruments. We have seen that the Thai monetary authority can create a short-run deviation from the world rate of interest. However, the domestic interest rate is only an intermediate target. We wish to know whether monetary policy can achieve stabilization with respect to its ultimate targets, such as real output and inflation, at least in the short run.

Real business cycle theorists would argue that changes in the money supply have no impact on real output, either in the short run or the long run, while monetarists claim that monetary policy can affect real GDP only in the short run. The new classical economists assert that monetary policy can affect output if the policy is unanticipated. If markets clear and economic agents are rational, anticipated policies would have no effect, even in the short run. Neo-Keynesians would contend that money still matters because of wage and price rigidities caused by contractual arrangements in the labor market.

To shed light on whether money matters in Thailand, given the Thai institutional mechanisms and the underlying mode of expectations formation, we examine the relationship between growth rates of the monetary base and real output. The effectiveness of monetary policy would be enhanced by the existence of stable relationships between nominal GDP and the money supply, and between money supply and the monetary base.

**Figure 8.6. Monetary Base and Real Output, 1972–90**

Deviation from trend growth rate (percent)

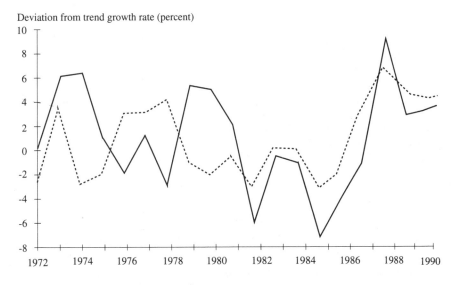

————— Monetary base (lagged one period)   ·········· GDP growth rate

*Source:* Bank of Thailand, *Monthly Bulletin,* various issues.

We first calculate the trend growth paths of output and the monetary base from a simple regression with a linear time trend. We obtain the detrended series of growth rates of these variables by taking the difference between the actual growth rates and the trend growth rates derived from the estimated equations. The relationship between output growth and monetary base growth, after removing the trend components, is shown in figure 8.6. The deviation of base money from its growth path is lagged one year to ensure that the base money variable is not a coincident indicator for real output growth. This ensures that the direction of causation, if any, is from the monetary base to income growth and not the reverse.

It seems that monetary base growth precedes real output growth. A period of monetary expansion is followed by a surge in real output growth. When monetary growth decelerates, however, the growth rate of real output also declines. The outstanding exceptions to this relationship have occurred during periods of negative external shocks. These are evident in the years 1974–76 and 1979–81. At such times, even if the growth rate of the monetary base accelerates, real output does not. That is, the relationship between monetary growth and real output growth is perturbed by negative real shocks. Clearly, after 1981, in the absence of such external shocks, the monetary base and real output became more closely related.

**Table 8.2  Monetary Volatility, 1973–90**
*(percent)*

| Item | Period | Average growth rate | Coefficient of variation[a] |
|---|---|---|---|
| Money Supply (M1) | 1973–78 | 14.07 | 0.39 |
| | 1979–85 | 6.82 | 0.86 |
| | 1986–90 | 17.97 | 0.29 |
| Monetary base | 1973–78 | 13.62 | 0.23 |
| | 1979–85 | 10.53 | 0.35 |
| | 1986–90 | 16.56 | 0.22 |

| Item | Period | Average value | Coefficient of variation |
|---|---|---|---|
| Money multiplier | 1973–78 | 1.24 | 0.02 |
| | 1979–85 | 1.15 | 0.08 |
| | 1986–90 | 1.10 | 0.02 |
| Credit multiplier | 1973–76 | 2.91 | 0.17 |
| | 1979–85 | 4.85 | 0.18 |
| | 1986–90 | 6.65 | 0.09 |
| Velocity of money | 1973–78 | 8.38 | 0.06 |
| | 1979–85 | 10.34 | 0.09 |
| | 1986–90 | 10.33 | 0.04 |

a. The coefficient of variation is the ratio of the standard deviation to the mean value.
*Source*: Calculated from Bank of Thailand, *Monthly Bulletin*, various issues.

The stability of the relationship between money supply and the monetary base is dictated by the stability of the money multiplier. As table 8.2 indicates, the coefficients of variation of the money multiplier, as well as the credit multiplier, declined from the period 1979–85 to the period 1986–90. Both the money supply and bank credit volume exhibit a more stable relationship with the monetary base after 1985.

A stable relationship between monetary base and money supply is not sufficient to guarantee the effectiveness of monetary policy. The final link between the ultimate target (output) and the intermediate target (money supply) must also exist. The velocity of money ($M_1$), shown in figure 8.7, remained stable between 1970 and 1990. Narrow money changed hands, on average, between eight and ten times within a year. The coefficient of variation of velocity also indicates that it fluctuated on average 4 percent per year from its mean value during the period 1986–89, compared with 9 percent during the period 1979–85. The velocity of money calculated from $M_2$ exhibits a greater variation than the velocity of $M_1$, because $M_2$ consists of both $M_1$ and quasi money. The demand for the latter is dictated mainly by wealth accumulation motivated by real interest rates and real income, rather than by transactions motives.

We conclude that changes in the monetary base led to deviations from the trend growth path of the monetary growth rate, which in turn produced an effect on output.

**Figure 8.7.  The Velocity of Money, 1970–90**

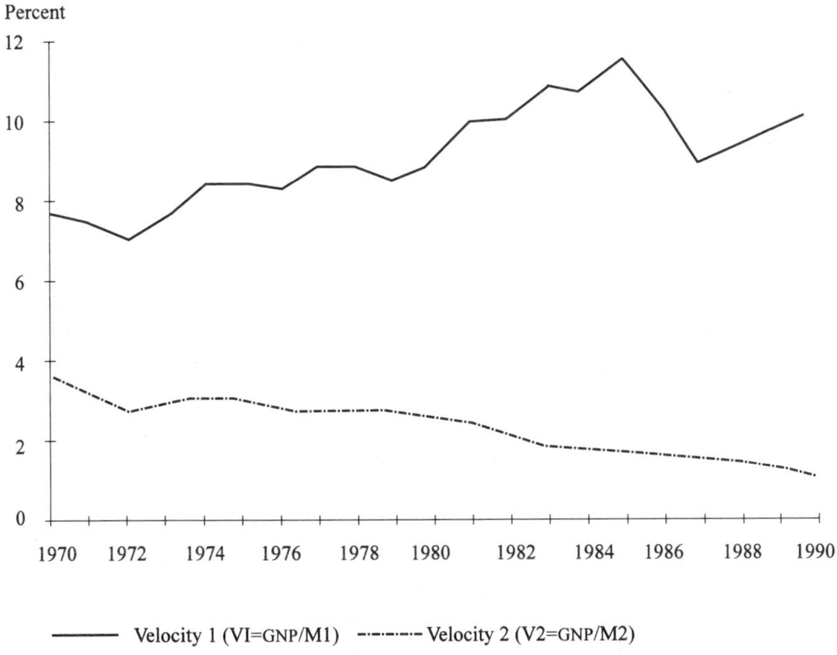

Percent

- Velocity 1 (VI=GNP/M1)   -------- Velocity 2 (V2=GNP/M2)

*Source:* Table 3.4 and Bank of Thailand, *Monthly Bulletin,* various issues.

## Control of the Monetary Base

We have argued that a stable and predictable relationship exists between the size of the monetary base and the intermediate and ultimate targets—interest rates and GDP growth. But does the Bank of Thailand really control the level of monetary base? This issue is important because it is clear that one component of the monetary base is outside the control of the Bank of Thailand—net foreign assets. It is possible that the Bank of Thailand can raise the domestic interest rate but only for a short time. The widened spread between domestic and foreign interest rates will induce capital inflows, thereby increasing the net foreign assets. If the Bank of Thailand must defend the existing level of the exchange rate, the increased monetary base would thwart the Bank of Thailand's attempt to raise domestic interest rates. Whether the impact of offsetting capital flows is strong depends on the structure of capital flows as well as the degree to which capital flows respond to changes in interest rates.

### Composition of the Monetary Base

Table 8.3 shows the decomposition of the change in the monetary base into net foreign assets (NFA) and net domestic credit (NDC). The latter consists of net claims on government (NCG), net claims on financial institutions (NCF), and net other liabilities (NOL) of the Bank of Thailand. Thus

(8.11)                    $B = \text{NFA} + \text{NDC}$

and

(8.12)                    $\text{NDC} = \text{NCG} + \text{NCF} + \text{NOL}.$

The claims of the central bank on financial institutions is a controllable item in the sources of the monetary base. To the extent that the central bank is able to act independently of the government, claims on the government is also a controllable item. These two components are the domestic assets of the central bank; they can be thought of as the part of monetary base over which the central bank has some control. Under the system of a (relatively) fixed exchange rate, in which the central bank has to intervene in the foreign exchange market to maintain the stability of the exchange rate, the net foreign assets component of the monetary base is an uncontrollable item. If the foreign assets constitute a high proportion of the monetary base, the ability of the central bank to control the money supply will be further limited. In other words, the effectiveness of monetary policy will be reduced if the central bank wishes to maintain exchange rate stability.

**Table 8.3  Foreign and Domestic Components of Monetary Base, 1971–90**
*(percent)*

| Year | dB/B | dNFA/B | dNCG/B | dNCF/B | dNOL/B | dNDC/B |
|------|------|--------|--------|--------|--------|--------|
| 1971 | 10.97 | –3.73 | 24.34 | 2.44 | –12.09 | 14.70 |
| 1972 | 17.76 | 20.60 | 3.18 | 1.53 | –7.55 | –2.84 |
| 1973 | 18.15 | 24.02 | –1.71 | 8.67 | –12.82 | –5.87 |
| 1974 | 13.04 | 47.49 | –23.40 | 5.41 | –16.46 | –34.45 |
| Average 1972–74 | 16.32 | 30.70 | –7.31 | 5.20 | –12.27 | –14.38 |
| 1975 | 10.71 | –6.21 | 11.51 | 12.85 | –7.11 | 16.92 |
| 1976 | 13.56 | 0.07 | 59.88 | –4.59 | 147.07 | 13.49 |
| 1977 | 9.32 | 2.37 | 16.98 | 0.65 | 15.49 | 6.95 |
| 1978 | 16.96 | 28.26 | 28.62 | 8.82 | 41.36 | –11.30 |
| 1979 | 16.63 | 22.44 | 20.40 | 21.74 | 47.52 | –5.82 |
| Average 1976–79 | 14.12 | 13.29 | 31.47 | 6.66 | 62.86 | 0.83 |
| 1980 | 14.03 | –2.36 | 33.28 | 4.85 | 18.45 | 16.38 |
| 1981 | 6.57 | –21.38 | 18.61 | 4.62 | –2.08 | 27.96 |
| 1982 | 11.95 | –2.38 | 27.95 | 2.20 | 13.72 | 14.33 |
| 1983 | 10.47 | –9.77 | 17.84 | 2.83 | 2.47 | 20.24 |
| Average 1980–83 | 10.75 | –8.97 | 24.42 | 3.63 | 8.14 | 19.73 |
| 1984 | 5.58 | 17.97 | –6.37 | 5.63 | 12.05 | –12.39 |
| 1985 | 8.49 | 2.12 | 16.67 | 7.73 | 12.11 | 6.38 |
| 1986 | 11.31 | 23.76 | –5.47 | 12.18 | 13.86 | –12.45 |
| 1987 | 21.10 | 36.84 | –9.07 | 7.04 | 16.45 | –15.74 |
| 1988 | 14.87 | 48.21 | –33.70 | 14.78 | 4.13 | –33.34 |
| 1989 | 16.92 | 74.76 | 24.02 | –11.34 | 6.08 | –57.84 |
| 1990 | 15.67 | 27.17 | –61.77 | –22.32 | 13.84 | –11.50 |
| Average 1984–90 | 13.42 | 32.98 | –10.81 | 1.96 | 11.22 | –19.55 |

*Note*:
   $d$ = First difference operator, $dB = B - B(-1)$.
   $B$ = Monetary base.
   NFA = Net Foreign Assets.
   NCG = Net Claims on Government.
   NCF = Net Claims on Financial Institutions.
   NOL = Net Other Liabilities.
   NDC = Net Domestic Credit ($B$-NFA).
*Source*: Computed from Bank of Thailand, *Monthly Bulletin*, various issues, table 3.

*The Structure of Capital Flows*

Over the past two decades, Thailand's current account was usually in deficit, while, correspondingly, the capital movements account was in surplus.[5] Thailand was able to sustain rapid economic growth by maintaining a high ratio of investment to GDP. The investment-savings gap is financed by net capital inflows. Long-term capital flows are usually larger than the short-term flows. In some years, the value of the long-term net flows alone overwhelmed the current account deficit (figure 8.8). Long-term capital inflows are more stable than short-term inflows, and the investment-savings gap is financed primarily by the former.

Long-term private flows accounted for 40 percent of total capital flows. The largest component is the long-term borrowing from the government enterprises. The long-term borrowing of private enterprises is 10 percent of total capital flows. Direct investment and long-term private flows represent an average of 9 and 21 percent of the monetary base, respectively. Direct foreign investment was responsible for a large surplus in the capital account in 1974 and from 1987 to 1990. Its average share in total capital flows between 1970 and 1990 was 26 percent. Table 8.4 indicates that the share of direct investment in total capital flows is relatively stable. Portfolio investment from abroad is included as part of long-term private flows. During the development stage of the capital market in Thailand, portfolio invest-

**Figure 8.8.  Net Capital Inflows, 1970–90**

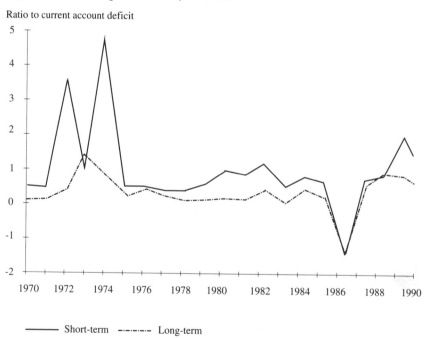

Ratio to current account deficit

Short-term   ------- Long-term

*Source:* Bank of Thailand, *Monthly Bulletin,* various issues.

**Table 8.4  Components of Capital Movements, 1970–90**

| Component | Average share | | As percent of monetary base | |
|---|---|---|---|---|
| | Mean | SD/Mean | Mean | SD/Mean |
| Direct investment | 25.6 | 0.64 | 8.49 | 0.71 |
| Long-term private flows | 39.42 | 0.57 | 20.63 | 0.92 |
| Long-term government entrepreneurship | 20.37 | 0.94 | 10.10 | 1.1 0 |
| Long-term private entrepreneurship | 9.73 | 2.66 | 7.19 | 1.4 0 |
| Portfolio investment | 8.71 | 1.59 | 3.12 | 1.74 |
| Short-term private flows | 22.88 | 0.8 | 8.84 | 0.85 |
| Short-term loan | 0.56 | 23.77 | 1.40 | 3.32 |
| Trade credit | 8.14 | 1.91 | 1.95 | 2.56 |
| Other | 14.18 | 1.43 | 5.49 | 1.01 |
| Central government | 12.1 | 1.83 | 5.91 | 1.28 |

*Note*: SD denotes standard deviation.
*Source*: Computed from Bank of Thailand, *Monthly Bulletin*, tables 3 and 39.

ment was relatively stable and remained only 3 percent of the monetary base.[6] It was only in 1986 that the Thai capital market was able to attract a considerable amount of foreign portfolio investment. The large surplus in the balance of payments in 1987 and 1989 stemmed partly from a surge in portfolio investment.

The most variable component of total capital movements is short-term loans of private enterprises, which accounted for an average of only 1.4 percent of the monetary base. Its share in total capital movement was small in relation to trade credit and other short-term capital movements. The latter two components have a larger share than short-term loans, but their fluctuations were much smaller. Total short-term private capital flows accounted for 23 percent of total movements. They also showed a small degree of variation and represented 8.8 percent of the monetary base. If short-term capital flows are large in relation to the monetary base, it will become very difficult for the central bank to sterilize the impact of offsetting capital flows.

## The Offsetting Capital Flows Hypothesis and the Feasibility of Sterilization

As table 8.3 makes clear, the net foreign assets component of the monetary base fluctuated more than other components. The offsetting capital flows hypothesis implies that the change in the policy-induced domestic component of the monetary base will be offset by (uncontrollable) capital outflows. If discretionary monetary policy induces offsetting capital flows by causing the domestic interest rate to deviate from the world market interest rate, this response must stem mainly from the interest-responsive components of capital flows. Thus to assess the validity of the offsetting capital flows hypothesis it is necessary to examine the sensitivity of different components of capital flows to interest rates.

From table 8.3, a negative correlation between changes in NFA and NCG is apparent (the correlation coefficient is –0.48). This relationship could be explained by the central bank's sterilization of capital flows, which implies that the increase (reduction) in NFA was the cause, via the sterilization response, of the reduction (increase) in NCG. The mechanism is that when a capital inflow occurs, and the central bank is thus obliged to purchase foreign currency (NFA rises), the increase in the monetary base is offset by the sale of government bonds (NCG falls).

But sterilization may not be feasible. If massive capital flows result from small interest rate differentials, the central bank may not possess the resources required to sterilize their effects on the domestic monetary base. In a world of imperfect capital mobility, it might be feasible for the central bank to prevent the domestic interest rate from converging rapidly to the foreign interest rate by sterilizing the effect of offsetting capital inflows or by using capital controls. If domestic and foreign assets are imperfect substitutes, the elasticity of capital flows with respect to interest rate differentials may be small. The elasticity of capital flows with respect to domestic and foreign interest rates thus determines the feasibility of sterilization measures.

We employed quarterly data from 1970 to 1989 to calculate the interest elasticity of short-term and long-term capital flows. This was done by regressing the values of capital flows on the interest rate differentials. For short-term flows (STF), the total values of imports and exports ($X + M$) as well as the forward premium rate ($F$) are included as regressors. Since the government's regulations did not permit the maturity of forward contracts to exceed six months, the variable $F$ was not included in the equation for long-term flows (LTF), but the level of GDP is included. In both cases, previous quarter capital flows are included to capture lagged adjustment effects. The results are

(8.13)  $STF = -940.2 + 207.8(R_d - R_f) + 0.199\,(X + M) - 294.5F + 0.449STF_{-1}$
           (3.02)  (2.08)          (5.93)                (3.18)  (4.58)
        $\bar{R}^2 = 0.78, h = 0.087$

(8.14)  $LTF = -248.6(R_d - R_f) + 0.021GDP + 0.49LTF_{-1}$
              (0.84)          (4.59)        (4.61)
        $\bar{R}^2 = 0.66, h = -1.83$

where $h$ is Durbin's $h$-statistic and other diagnostics are as before.

The results reveal that although short-term flows respond to interest rate differentials, long-term flows do not. An increase in the level of economic activity, as represented by international trade and GDP, stimulates capital inflows. A rise in the forward premium rate reduces the flows of short-term capital. Both short-run and long-run flows exhibit lagged adjustment patterns, as indicated by the significance of the lagged dependent variables.

The estimated coefficients from (8.13) and (8.14) were used to calculate the short-run and long-run sensitivity of capital flows with respect to their corresponding determinants, and the results are reported in table 8.5. The elasticities of both short-term and long-term net capital inflows with respect to interest rate differential are small, which indicates that international capital mobility is relatively low. Short-term capital flows respond more rapidly to changing trade values. Thus, as noted earlier, short-term capital inflows are able to offset the current account deficit. Although in the short run the growth rate of GDP is higher than the growth rate of net long-term capital inflows, in the long run the elasticity of long-term flows with respect to GDP is greater than unity.

Control of the monetary base involves fiscal as well as purely monetary issues. A clear example occurred in the late 1980s. Figure 8.9 shows changes in the level of the monetary base (DBASE) from 1971 to 1991 and its components: net foreign assets (DNFA), claims on financial institutions (DCF), and net claims on government (DNCG). While net foreign assets increased substantially from 1986 to 1991, the monetary base did not rise correspondingly. The reduction in the net claims on government and the slowdown in the claims on financial institutions offset the rapid increase in net foreign assets. Because of the surplus in the government budget, the increased capital inflows did not result in excessive growth in the monetary base. These issues thus have bearing on the discussion of fiscal policy in chapter 7. Had the government run a budget deficit, the level of monetary base would have risen to levels that would have threatened price stability.

**Table 8.5  Interest Rate Elasticity of Net Capital Flow, Quarterly Data, 1970 II to 1989 IV**

|  | Short-term flow | | Long-term flow | |
|---|---|---|---|---|
|  | Short run | Long run | Short run | Long run |
| Interest rate differential | 0.177 | 0.322 | $-0.069^{a}$ | $-0.135^{a}$ |
|  | Trade volume | | Domestic output | |
|  | Short run | Long run | Short run | Long run |
| Economic activity | 1.084 | 1.970 | 0.673 | 1.323 |

a. The estimated coefficient insignificant at 5 percent level.
*Source*: Authors' calculations from data in Bank of Thailand, *Monthly Bulletin*, various issues.

**Figure 8.9. Change in Monetary Base Components, 1971–91**

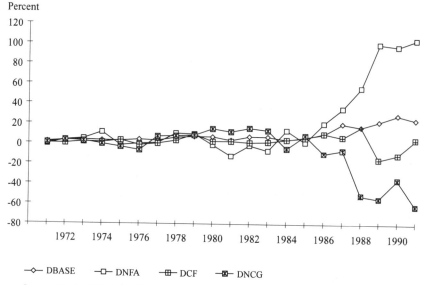

*Source:* Bank of Thailand, *Monthly Bulletin,* various issues, and authors' calculations.

## Instruments of Monetary Policy

It appears that there has been some scope for exercising discretionary monetary policy in Thailand, although that scope has been present in the short run only and has been limited by the existence of offsetting capital flows. Consider now the manner in which monetary policy has been employed over the two decades to 1990, particularly the way it conditioned Thailand's responses to external shocks. Two important instruments of monetary policy are adjustments to the bank rate and adjustments to interest rate controls.

### Adjustments of the Bank Rate

The main instrument of monetary policy is the central bank lending rate. Various monetary aggregates, including the monetary base, are used as intermediate targets. Table 8.6 provides a historical description of the changing nature of Thailand's monetary policy, based on movements of the bank rate and changes in the monetary growth rate.

Between 1970 and 1990 monetary policy changed its direction six times. The longest expansions lasted about three years (1970–72 and 1975–77), while the longest contraction lasted four years, (1978–81). The periods of expansion and contraction distinguished in table 8.6 were identified by changes in the Bank of Thailand lending rate. Comparison with table 3.4 reveals that these changes coin-

**Table 8.6  Direction of Monetary Policy and Average Key Economic Indicators, 1971–89**

*(percent)*

| Year | Direction | Real GDP growth rate | Inflation | Deviation of actual income from trend income | Current account deficit/ GDP | Monetary base growth rate | Government budget deficit/GDP |
|------|-----------|------|------|------|------|------|------|
| 1971–72 | + | 4.52 | 2.63 | –0.86 | 2.16 | 14.37 | 4.65 |
| 1973–74 | – | 7.11 | 19.93 | –0.55 | 2.09 | 15.60 | 0.63 |
| 1975–77 | + | 8.04 | 5.56 | –1.06 | 4.36 | 11.20 | 2.98 |
| 1978–81 | – | 6.72 | 12.55 | 2.80 | 6.95 | 13.55 | 2.79 |
| 1982–83 | + | 5.66 | 4.49 | –1.34 | 5.66 | 11.21 | 3.80 |
| 1984 | – | 7.13 | 0.85 | –0.87 | 5.51 | 5.58 | 3.49 |
| 1985–87 | + | 5.97 | 2.25 | –4.31 | 1.91 | 13.63 | 2.60 |
| 1988–90 | – | 12.38 | 5.06 | 5.58 | 4.94 | 16.79 | –3.77 |

a. A plus sign (+) indicates expansion, a minus sign (–) indicates contraction. Directions of monetary policy are evaluated from the direction of change in the bank rate and the growth rate of monetary base.

*Source*: (As for table 7.1).

cided closely with changes in the real quantity of narrow money ($M_1$). Table 8.6 also reveals that periods of monetary expansion (contraction) coincided broadly with periods of fiscal expansion (contraction).[7]

Net domestic credit consists of two main components: the claims on government and the claims on financial institutions. The former is dictated by the borrowing requirements of the government, which depends on the size of the deficit. The latter depends on the borrowing requirements of commercial banks, which depends on the cost of borrowing from the central bank relative to other sources. The bank rate, or the rate that the central bank charges commercial banks, can be used to affect the claims on the financial institutions (NCF) component of the monetary base and to influence capital flows.

The Bank of Thailand influences the short-term market rate of interest by adjusting the bank rate and by intervening in the repurchase market. The latter consists of buying and selling government bonds, but it is a less important instrument than adjustments to the bank rate. Bank rate adjustments occurred most frequently during the period of foreign interest volatility from 1980 to 1982.

Table 8.7 provides a more detailed summary of the adjustments in the bank rate between 1979 and 1990. Adjustments were especially frequent between 1979 and 1982, during which time monetary policy reflected the desire to increase net domestic credit in an effort to revive the recessive economy. The Bank of Thailand did not adjust the bank rate between 1987 and 1988, since the other component of net domestic credit (the claims on government) was already declining owing to the

**Table 8.7  Adjustment of the Bank of Thailand Lending Rate, 1979–90**

| Year | Number of adjustments | Direction | | Net rate of change[a] |
|------|------|------|------|------|
|  |  | Positive | Negative |  |
| 1979 | 2 | 2 | 0 | 2.5 |
| 1980 | 6 | 3 | 3 | 0.0 |
| 1981 | 5 | 3 | 2 | 1.0 |
| 1982 | 4 | 1 | 3 | –2.0 |
| 1983 | 2 | 1 | 1 | 0.5 |
| 1984 | 1 | 0 | 1 | –1.0 |
| 1985 | 1 | 0 | 1 | –1.5 |
| 1986 | 3 | 0 | 3 | –3.0 |
| 1987 | 0 | 0 | 0 | 0.0 |
| 1988 | 0 | 0 | 0 | 0.0 |
| 1989 | 0 | 0 | 0 | 0.0 |
| 1990 | 2 | 2 | 0 | 3.0 |

a. Percent.
*Source*: Calculated from Bank of Thailand, *Monthly Bulletin*, various issues.

budgetary surplus. In 1990 the bank rate was adjusted upward twice, by a total of three percentage points (table 8.8), to curb the overheated economy.

As tables 8.7 and 8.8 suggest, a positive difference between the bank rate and the Eurodollar rate induces capital inflow, since it is cheaper to borrow from abroad than from the domestic money market. At such times, the ratio of Thai commercial bank's borrowings from the Bank of Thailand in relation to foreign banks is likely to decline. Given the size of the central bank's lending, a negative sign on this ratio indicates capital inflow, while a positive sign indicates capital outflow.

In 1979 the Bank of Thailand provided considerable credit for commercial banks for liquidity purposes. In 1985 commercial banks tried to reduce the outstanding amount of foreign loans due to excess liquidity. Except for the above two years, there was a negative correlation between the differential between domestic and foreign rates and the rate of change of the commercial banks' borrowing ratio. Table 8.8 indicates that adjustments in the Bank's lending rate can be employed to affect the balance of payments position.

## Adjustments of Interest Rate Controls

Aside from intervening in the short-term money market, the Bank of Thailand has set maximum interest rates on both lending and borrowing. As with the exchange rate between the U.S. dollar and the baht, which remained unchanged in the 1960s

**Table 8.8  Adjustments in the Bank Rate and Capital Movements, 1970–90**

| Year | Bank rate[a] (1) | Eurodollar rate[b] (2) | Differential [(1) − (2)] (3) | Commercial bank borrowings[c]/ foreign borrowing[d] (4) | Rate of change of column 4 (5) |
|------|------|------|------|------|------|
| 1970 | 9.00 | 8.52 | 0.48 | 0.25 | — |
| 1971 | 9.00 | 6.58 | 2.42 | 0.39 | 60.87 |
| 1972 | 8.00 | 5.46 | 2.54 | 0.36 | −8.20 |
| 1973 | 10.00 | 9.24 | 0.76 | 0.42 | 15.26 |
| 1974 | 11.00 | 11.01 | −0.01 | 0.53 | 25.95 |
| 1975 | 10.00 | 6.99 | 3.01 | 0.91 | 72.26 |
| 1976 | 9.00 | 5.58 | 3.42 | 0.60 | −33.88 |
| 1977 | 9.00 | 6.05 | 2.95 | 0.40 | −32.45 |
| 1978 | 12.50 | 8.78 | 3.72 | 0.33 | −18.93 |
| 1979 | 12.50 | 12.01 | 0.49 | 0.47 | 43.94 |
| 1980 | 13.50 | 14.06 | −0.56 | 0.65 | 37.93 |
| 1981 | 14.50 | 16.82 | −2.32 | 0.67 | 2.89 |
| 1982 | 12.50 | 13.16 | −0.66 | 0.81 | 21.24 |
| 1983 | 13.00 | 9.60 | 3.40 | 0.61 | −25.41 |
| 1984 | 12.00 | 10.78 | 1.22 | 0.52 | −14.19 |
| 1985 | 11.00 | 8.34 | 2.66 | 0.66 | 26.28 |
| 1986 | 8.00 | 6.77 | 1.23 | 1.29 | 96.99 |
| 1987 | 8.00 | 7.11 | 0.89 | 1.44 | 10.96 |
| 1988 | 8.00 | 7.91 | 0.09 | 1.09 | −24.12 |
| 1989 | 8.00 | 9.10 | −1.10 | 0.59 | −45.80 |
| 1990 | 12.00 | 8.28 | 3.72 | 0.44 | −25.42 |

a. Bank rate or loan rate.
b. Eurodollar rate in London.
c. Commercial bank borrowings from Bank of Thailand.
d. Borrowings from banks abroad.
*Source*: Calculated from Bank of Thailand, *Monthly Bulletin,* and International Monetary Fund, *International Financial Statistics,* various issues.

and 1970s, the Bank of Thailand did not change the maximum interest rates on lending and borrowing over the same period until the first oil price shock. The maximum rates were effective; commercial banks usually paid their depositors at the maximum rate prescribed by law. Despite the ceilings on bank deposit and lending rates, real interest rates usually remained positive (table 8.8) and high enough to attract financial savings.

The ratio of bank deposits to GDP has increased over time, reflecting financial deepening in Thailand from 1970 to 1990 (figure 8.10). The increased availability of financial resources enhanced the quantity and quality of investment. Bank credits, as a percentage of GDP, also grew considerably, following the rapid rise in bank deposits. In an economy where financial intermediaries efficiently perform the role of savings mobilization and credit allocation, the ratio of investment to GDP can be high, since investors are not limited by self-finance.

The two oil shocks significantly disrupted this regulatory system by raising the rate of inflation and driving domestic interest rates to negative levels. During the first oil shock, inflation rose from 4.9 percent in 1972 to 15.4 and 24.3 percent in 1973 and 1974, respectively. In 1975, it dropped to 5.3 percent. Similarly, during the second oil shock in 1979, inflation rose sharply from 9.9 percent to 19 percent in 1980 before falling to 12 percent in the following year. We may thus summarize the record of inflation in Thailand over the past two decades as being a normal rate in the single-digit range, interrupted by two brief periods of between one and two years where the rate surged to about 20 percent in response to external price shocks.

**Figure 8.10.  Financial Deepening, 1970–90**

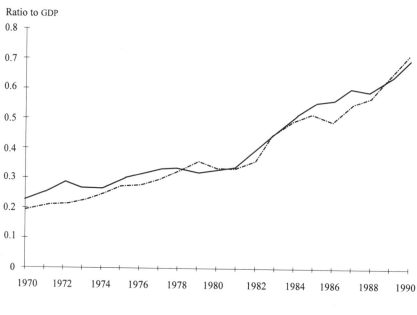

*Source:* Bank of Thailand, *Monthly Bulletin,* various issues, and authors' calculations.

Table 8.9 shows that real interest rates were significantly negative in 1973, 1974, and 1980. As a result, the growth of the volume of bank deposits slowed. External financial shocks, in the form of rising foreign interest rates, discouraged commercial banks' foreign borrowing and the credit shortage in the world money markets was thus transmitted to domestic credit markets. The illiquidity of the money market can be seen from the high growth rates of bank credit in relation to

**Table 8.9  Maximum Interest Rates and Real Deposit Rates, 1970–90**

*(percent)*

| Year | Loan rate | Time deposit rate | | Interest tax rate | Net deposit rate | Inflation rate[a] | Real net deposit rate |
|------|-----------|-------------------|--|-------------------|------------------|-------------------|----------------------|
| 1970 | 14.00 | 7.00 | | 0.00 | 7.00 | –0.09 | 7.09 |
| 1971 | 14.00 | 7.00 | | 0.00 | 7.00 | 0.44 | 6.56 |
| 1972 | 14.00 | 7.00 | | 0.00 | 7.00 | 4.91 | 2.09 |
| 1973 | 14.00 | 7.00 | | 0.00 | 7.00 | 15.47 | –8.47 |
| 1974 | 15.00 | 8.00 | | 0.00 | 8.00 | 24.30 | –16.30 |
| 1975 | 15.00 | 8.00 | | 0.00 | 8.00 | 5.30 | 2.70 |
| 1976 | 15.00 | 8.00 | | 0.00 | 8.00 | 4.20 | 3.80 |
| 1977 | 15.00 | 8.00 | | 10.00 | 7.20 | 7.60 | –0.40 |
| 1978 | 15.00 | 8.00 | | 10.00 | 7.20 | 7.90 | –0.70 |
| 1979 | 15.00 | 9.00 | | 10.00 | 8.10 | 9.90 | –1.80 |
| 1980 | 18.00 | 12.00 | | 10.00 | 10.80 | 19.70 | –8.90 |
| 1981 | 19.00 | 13.00 | | 10.00 | 11.70 | 12.70 | –1.00 |
| 1982 | 19.00 | 13.00 | (12.50)[b] | 12.50 | 10.94 | 5.20 | 5.74 |
| 1983 | 17.50 | 13.00 | (12.50) | 12.50 | 10.94 | 3.80 | 7.14 |
| 1984 | 19.00 | 13.00 | (12.50) | 12.50 | 10.94 | 0.90 | 10.04 |
| 1985 | 19.00 | 13.00 | (11.00) | 12.50 | 9.63 | 2.40 | 7.23 |
| 1986 | 15.00 | 9.50 | (7.25) | 15.00 | 6.16 | 1.90 | 4.26 |
| 1987 | 15.00 | 9.50 | (7.25) | 15.00 | 6.16 | 2.50 | 3.66 |
| 1988 | 15.00 | 9.50 | (8.63) | 15.00 | 7.34 | 3.85 | 3.49 |
| 1989 | 15.00 | 9.50 | (9.88) | 15.00 | 8.40 | 6.31 | 2.09 |
| 1990 | 19.00 | — | (13.75) | 15.00 | 11.69 | 5.35 | 5.65 |

a. The real net deposit rate is the difference between the nominal time deposit rate and current inflation rate.

b. The figures in parentheses are the actual rate of interest paid by commercial banks. Before 1982, the banks' deposit rates were equal to the maximum rates.

*Source*: Bank of Thailand, *Monthly Bulletin*, various issues.

bank deposits. In 1974 inflation reached 24 percent, and The Bank of Thailand responded by raising the maximum lending rate from 14 to 15 percent. To keep the interest spread intact, the ceiling on time deposits was also raised by one percentage point, from 7 to 8 percent. In 1980 inflation reached 20 percent and the maximum lending rate was raised by 3 and 1 percentage points in 1980 and 1981, respectively, while the maximum deposit rate was raised by 3 percentage points, to 12 percent from the 9 percent ceiling established in 1979.

These regulatory responses can be considered late and inadequate. The ex-post real rates of deposit were still substantially negative in both periods. More rapid restructuring of interest rates to establish a realistic positive rate was clearly necessary to alleviate the burden of external shocks and to restore private savings. As can be inferred from figure 8.7 the ratio of quasi money to GDP actually declined from its rising trend after the real interest rate became negative. The introduction of interest income tax on time deposits in 1978 further delayed this return to the preshock path. The restructuring of interest rates to reestablish positive real rates resulted in an escalating real rate of interest between 1981 and 1984. The outcome was a sharp increase in the ratio of time and saving deposits to GDP after 1982.

Demand conditions permitting, a surge in the growth rate of quasi money is likely to be followed by a sharp increase in credit expansion. The slowdown in the growth rate of deposits between 1977 and 1979 led to a sharp decline in the credit expansion between 1978 and 1980 but a sharp rise in credit growth between 1981 and 1983.The rapid credit expansion is said to have contributed to a deterioration in the current account balance (Chaiyawat 1984). The Thai monetary authorities applied a credit restraint policy by requiring commercial banks to restrict the growth rate of credit in the first half of 1984 to 9 percent, and for the whole year to 18 percent of 1983's credit outstanding.

From 1980 to 1983, the ceiling on the deposit rate remained at 13 percent. Since 1982, and for the first time in decades, commercial banks paid their depositors below the ceiling. After 1982 the real rate of return from deposits at banks was relatively high. The escalating real rate of interest between 1981 and 1982 resulted in a sharp increase in bank deposits. The monetary authorities hesitated to reduce the interest rate ceiling, despite the well-known downward rigidity of interest rates caused by the oligopolistic structure of the Thai banking industry. As a result, commercial banks were not willing to reduce deposit rates even though the real rate of interest went up to 11.6 percent in 1984. With a credit restraint program being implemented, commercial banks were not able to rid themselves of excess liquidity.

In 1985 the time deposit rate was reduced from 12.5 percent to 11 percent. It took three years before the deposit rate finally came down. The implementation lag of interest rate policy thus retarded economic growth. The growth rate of real investment in 1985 was negative 5.2 percent. Finally, in 1986 the Bank of Thailand came to the important realization that it had underestimated the downward rigidity of interest rates.[8] The bank decided to reduce the maximum interest rate on loans by 4 percent and on deposits by 3.5 percent. Commercial banks followed suit by reducing the deposit rate from 11 to 7.25 percent.

The experience of the two oil price shocks brings home two important points. First, at a time of a negative external shock, the combination of "sticky" interest rate controls and above-normal inflation discourages private savings, stimulating rather than retarding aggregate absorption. Unless the shock is viewed as strictly temporary, this is the opposite of the adjustment that is required. Second, in such an environment, inflation control becomes doubly important. High inflation will produce negative real interest rates and undermine the supply of private domestic and foreign savings. In the Thai case, further damage was averted by the rapidity with which inflation was contained, following each of the two oil price shocks.

## The Performance of Monetary Policy

Consider now the performance of Thailand's monetary policy adjustments in stabilizing output growth and the price level. Two internal balance targets are obviously involved, with the possible additional importance, from time to time, of issues of external balance. This raises the possibility of conflict between objectives. Precisely this conflict can be observed in the responses to the two oil price shocks. No single pattern emerges from the Thai experience as to how these conflicts have been resolved, but inflation typically became the dominant concern of monetary policy whenever the rate of inflation rose above roughly six percent. Below that level of inflation, stability of income growth seems to have been a more important objective of monetary policy.

To facilitate discussion of these issues we standardize actual growth and inflation rates, along with the values of other macroeconomic variables. A subscript Z will subsequently be used to indicate the standardized value of a variable: the value of that variable minus its mean, all divided by its standard deviation. For example, $Y_Z$ is defined as the standardized value of the variable $Y$ and is given by

$$(8.15) \qquad Y_Z = (Y - \overline{Y})/\sigma_Y$$

where $\overline{Y}$ is the mean of $Y$ and $\sigma_Y$ is its standard deviation.

In table 8.10, the years 1971 to 1990 are classified according to whether the standardized values of their growth rates ($G_z$) and inflation rates ($P_z$) were above average, (corresponding to $G_z$ and $P_z$ positive), or below average ($G_z$ and $P_z$ negative). The change in the level of the domestic credit component of the monetary base as a percentage of GDP will be used as a measure of the direction of monetary policy. Changes in domestic credit, expressed as a proportion of GDP, have been standardized into the variable denoted $M_z$. If $M_z$ is positive (negative), the monetary policy stance is considered expansionary (contractionary). The standardized values of growth rates and inflation are summarized in the scatter diagram in figure 8.11.

## Table 8.10  Macroeconomic Performance and Policy Stance

| Year | Real growth $(G_z)$ | Inflation $(P_z)$ | CAD/GDP $(C_z)$ | Fiscal stance $(F_z)$ | Monetary stance $(M_z)$ |
|---|---|---|---|---|---|
| *High growth and high inflation* | | | | | |
| 1973 | 0.943 | 1.380 | −1.244 | −0.791 | 0.207 |
| 1977 | 0.957 | 0.088 | 0.638 | 0.407 | 0.512 |
| 1978 | 1.142 | 0.150 | 0.362 | 0.533 | 1.184 |
| *Low growth and high inflation* | | | | | |
| 1974 | −0.997 | 2.689 | −1.173 | −1.035 | −1.255 |
| 1979 | −0.652 | 0.467 | 1.402 | 0.047 | 1.712 |
| 1980 | −0.841 | 2.020 | 0.967 | 1.761 | 1.367 |
| 1981 | −0.288 | 0.905 | 1.310 | 0.772 | 0.649 |
| *Low growth and low inflation* | | | | | |
| 1971 | −0.778 | −1.107 | −0.535 | −0.826 | 0.574 |
| 1972 | −1.099 | −0.380 | −1.181 | −0.482 | 0.247 |
| 1975 | −0.819 | −0.292 | 0.096 | 0.434 | 0.072 |
| 1982 | −1.102 | −0.295 | −0.396 | −1.179 | 0.892 |
| 1984 | −0.007 | −1.075 | 0.465 | 0.255 | −0.808 |
| 1985 | −1.302 | −0.787 | 0.114 | 0.389 | 0.522 |
| 1986 | −0.794 | −0.902 | −1.627 | −1.743 | −0.529 |
| *High growth and low inflation* | | | | | |
| 1976 | 0.777 | −0.511 | −0.454 | 0.860 | 0.185 |
| 1983 | 0.036 | −0.561 | 1.277 | 0.170 | 0.479 |
| 1987 | 0.809 | −0.770 | −1.118 | −1.426 | −0.814 |
| 1988 | 2.080 | −0.548 | −0.417 | −0.768 | −2.208 |
| 1989 | 1.741 | −0.287 | −0.439 | 0.425 | −1.909 |
| 1990 | 0.194 | −0.184 | 1.930 | 2.198 | −0.354 |

*Note*: Subscript $z$ indicates that the variable is standardized by subtracting its mean value and dividing the resulting difference by its standard deviation.

$G_z$ = real GDP growth rate.

$P_z$ = inflation rate (CPI).

$C_z$ = current account deficit( ratio to GDP).

$F_z$ = changes in public investment (ratio to GDP); $F_z$ is used as an indicator of the direction of fiscal policy .

$M_z$ = changes in domestic credit of the Bank of Thailand (ratio to GDP); $M_z$ is used as an indicator of monetary policy stance.

**Figure 8.11.  Growth and Inflation,  1971–90**

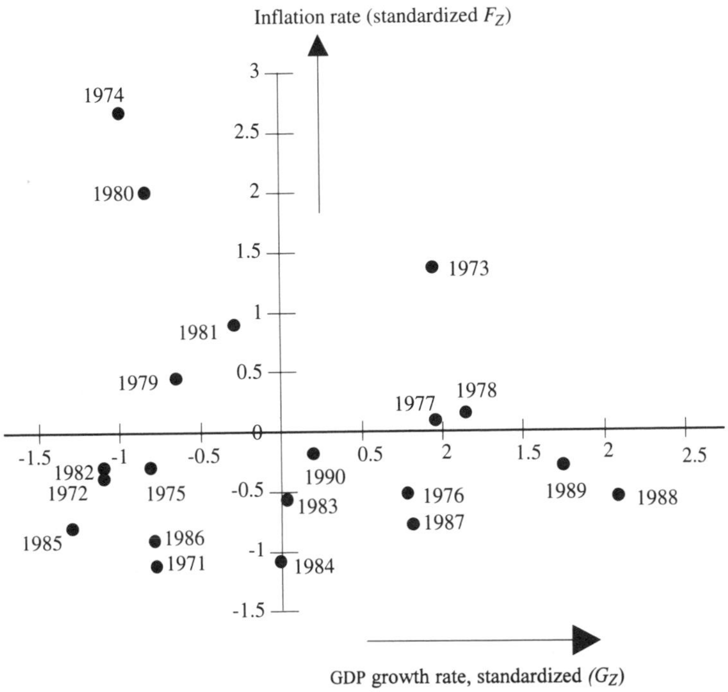

Inflation rate (standardized $F_Z$)

GDP growth rate, standardized ($G_Z$)

*Source:* Table 8.10.

## Growth and Monetary Policy Stance

We summarize the relationship between monetary growth and income growth in figure 8.12, where $M_z$ is shown together with $G_z$. Countercyclical observations will lie in the northwest and southeast quadrants—a negative relationship between growth and monetary stance. Procyclical (accommodative) observations will lie in the other two quadrants—a positive relationship. Inspection indicates that monetary policy can be characterized as both accommodative and countercyclical for different periods, but that countercyclical observations predominate.

Procyclical observations in the northeast quadrant of the diagram are observed for 1973, and during the period of 1976–78. In 1973, the positive external shocks in the price of export commodities such as rice, rubber, and maize produced a surplus in the current account (corresponding to $C_z$ negative in table 8.10). The boom in export demand created strong growth and a rising price level (in the northeastern quadrant of figure 8.11). The Bank of Thailand accommodated the demand for credits from commercial banks as a result of the rapid growth in exports. During the period 1976–78, the growth rate in credits extended by the cen-

**Figure 8.12. Monetary Policy Stance and Growth, 1971–90**

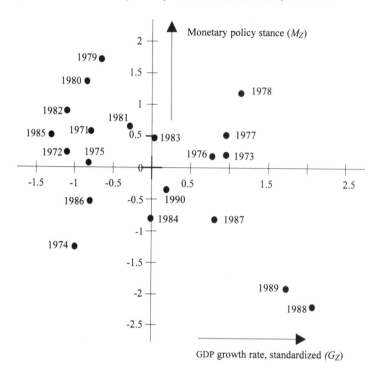

*Source:* Table 8.10.

tral bank to finance the budget deficit was enormous. While inflation in 1976 was below its average, it was slightly above average in 1977 and 1978.

The southwestern region of figure 8.12 includes two years, 1974 and 1986. In 1974, Thailand suffered a cost- and push-led recession as a result of the first oil price shock. Inflation, rather than unemployment, was considered the primary policy concern, however, and the monetary policy response was restrictive rather than expansive. Although 1986 was a year of both low inflation and low economic growth, monetary policy was restrictive, according to our measure. As discussed in chapter 7, in 1986 the Bank of Thailand's credits to the government declined substantially because of a significant shift in the method of budget deficit financing from inflationary to noninflationary methods. This fact, more closely related to long-term fiscal issues than to stabilization policy, explains why the growth rate of domestic credit was unusually low in 1986.

It should be noted that the response of monetary policy during the second oil price shock was different from the first. The monetary response was restrictive during the first oil price shock in 1974, when inflationary effects on price and output lost were more severe than after the second shock. But monetary policy was expansionary between 1979 and 1981, a period of low growth and high inflation.

During the second oil price shock, the central bank gave priority to stabilizing income rather than maintaining price stability, and this decision led to a deterioration in the current account deficit (table 8.10). The growth rate of GDP could have been even lower had the Bank of Thailand adopted a similar strategy to that employed during the first shock.

The northwestern region of figure 8.12 contains the period 1987–90, when Thailand enjoyed a period of high growth and relatively low inflation. Although inflation during this period was below its mean, it was creeping upward. The monetary authorities anticipated a rising price level and adopted an anticyclical policy response, thereby reducing the growth rate of domestic credit. The rapid income growth was driven by exports and private investment, implying increased demand for money, but the Bank of Thailand did not exacerbate inflation by fully accommodating this growth with its own credit supply.

In some cases, monetary policy has been procyclical with respect to income growth: the commodity boom year of 1973 and the period between 1976 and 1978 were periods of high growth and monetary expansion, while the years 1974 and 1986 recorded low growth and monetary contraction. Aside from these episodes, the negative overall relationship between normalized GDP growth and monetary stance suggests that monetary policy was on balance countercyclical with respect to income; expansionary measures were associated with a slowdown in economic growth, and contractionary measures with strong growth.

*Inflation and Monetary Policy Stance*

The relationship between monetary stance and inflation is summarized in figure 8.13. Again, the two variables are expected to have a negative relationship, but the situation is more mixed than that seen for income stabilization. The number of countercyclical observations (those in the northwest and southeast quadrants) is exceeded by the number of procyclical observations (northeast and southwest quadrants).

The northeastern region of the diagram contains the years 1977 and 1978. Inflation rates were marginally higher than average, and the Bank of Thailand could afford to expand its credit to accommodate the increase in the demand for money. More important, this was a period of highly authoritarian military government. Having seized power through a coup, following the democratic period of 1973–76, this government was not about to have its authority challenged by bureaucrats. The independence of the Bank of Thailand was significantly weakened during this period and was not restored until the Prem government of 1981. Price stability was not high on the monetary policy agenda in the late 1970s and credits extended to financial institutions and the central government increased substantially in those years.

In 1980, when inflation remained high as the result of the second oil price shock, the monetary policy stance was still expansionary. This monetary policy response in 1980 was in sharp contrast to the response in 1974, the sole point in the

### Figure 8.13. Monetary Policy Stance and Inflation, 1971–90

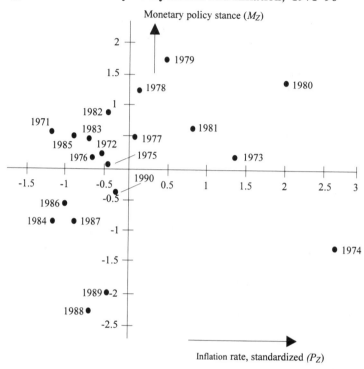

*Source:* Table 8.10.

southeastern region, when the monetary policy was contractionary. In 1980 the expansion of the monetary base was due mainly to the large increase in the money-financed deficit through borrowing from the Bank of Thailand. When the new government came to power in 1981, inflationary means of deficit financing were discouraged strongly.

Figure 8.13 also indicates the pattern of the monetary policy response in the high inflation years of 1973, 1974, 1981, and 1979. Here, except for 1980, monetary contractions were larger when inflation was most severe. Inflation in 1979 was not as serious as in 1981, and the monetary response was not as strong. In the northeastern region of figure 8.13, inflation was not considered a major problem and the central bank gave priority to achieving a higher growth rate by increasing the level of domestic lending.

In the southwestern region, the price level increased less rapidly than on average, but the policy stance was still restrictive. As noted earlier, inflation gradually gained momentum during the late 1980s, with the rapid expansion in the Thai economy. The expectation of an overheated economy prompted the central bank to slow the increase in bank credit. The years 1984 and 1990 also saw a huge current account deficit, and priority shifted to some extent from internal stability to external stability. The central bank attempted to control its lending to avoid an excessive current account deficit. The reduction in money deficit financing in 1986 and 1987 also prompted the central bank to slow down lending.

On balance, the contribution of monetary policy to short-run stabilization of the price level is significantly less impressive than its contribution to the stabilization of income growth. This is somewhat surprising, because of Thailand's obvious success in using monetary policy to control inflation over the long run. The evidence indicates that monetary policy has been much less effective in controlling inflation in the short run.

## Conclusions

To a limited extent, discretionary monetary policy in Thailand operated effectively in the short run in a stabilizing, countercyclical manner over the period 1970–90. This occurred even though Thailand simultaneously pursued a fixed exchange rate. The key to the apparent paradox is the limited degree of capital mobility that existed in Thailand over most of these two decades. The operation of discretionary monetary policy was limited by offsetting capital flows, and the implementation of monetary policy was complicated by lags in the response of the key target variables—inflation, income growth, and external balance—to changes in monetary policy.

Short-term deviations from interest rate parity occurred because of the limited substitutability between domestic and foreign assets and liabilities, capital, and foreign exchange controls, as well as uncertainty regarding the exchange rate and the possibility of changes to capital controls. The forward premium exchange rate adjusted to the interest rate gap, thus providing an insulating mechanism that discouraged offsetting capital flows. The withholding tax rate was another insulating instrument available for regulating capital flows. The outcome was that long-term capital flows, which have represented a large proportion of total capital flows, were insensitive to interest rate differentials. Although the interest rate elasticity of short-term flows was statistically significant, it was still small.

Evidence on the behavior of the components of the monetary base suggests that the Thai monetary authorities were able to exert some short-term control over domestic interest rates. Although capital movements did occur in response to differences between domestic and foreign interest rates, the degree of international capital mobility in Thailand has been far from perfect. The Bank of Thailand has thus possessed some degree of autonomy in conducting monetary policy, in spite of its fixed exchange rate policy.

Short-run discretionary monetary policy has apparently contributed to Thailand's macroeconomic stability. Surprisingly, the success of monetary policy in achieving short-run economic stabilization is clearer in the case of income stabilization than price-level stabilization. Nevertheless, Thai monetary policy is not a story of short-run discretionary adjustment at all, but one of long-run monetary discipline in pursuit of long-term price stability. In this, monetary policy operated jointly with the long-run fiscal discipline described in chapter 7.

The coordination of monetary policy with fiscal policy was particularly important during the economic boom of the late 1980s. The reason for the moderate increase in the monetary base during this period, despite the large surplus in the balance of payments, was that the government also ran a budget surplus. Instead of spending the increased revenue resulting from the boom, the government used it to retire external government debt, thus mitigating the expansion of the monetary base that would otherwise have been induced by the rising level of international reserves.

Thailand's interest rate controls caused serious problems during periods of rapid inflation. Following each of the oil price shocks, domestic inflation rose to about 20 percent. In combination with interest rate controls, which were adjusted belatedly and insufficiently, this pushed real interest rates to negative levels and undermined private savings. Long-term damage was averted only because inflation was quickly brought under control. This must be considered an impressive achievement, aided as it was by the credibility of monetary policy in Thailand.

Financial liberalization has been undertaken gradually in Thailand. All kinds of interest rate ceilings had been abolished by 1992. But even with controls, as long as inflation remained low, real interest rates remained positive and full liberalization could reasonably proceed slowly. In the meantime, it was thought that the Bank of Thailand should strengthen its supervision of commercial banks to ensure that financial liberalization did not create instability in the banking system. The Thai experience must be considered a reasonably successful example of the gradualist approach to financial liberalization.

With the abolition of the ceiling interest rate on lending, the central bank lost another policy instrument for controlling the domestic interest rate. Less direct means of affecting the domestic interest rate still exist, by altering the liquidity conditions in the money markets through loan windows and the markets for repurchasing government bonds. The effectiveness of such sterilization is limited, however, by the availability of government bonds. Furthermore, in the long run the central bank cannot sterilize the effects of capital inflows as long as capital mobility is near-perfect and the exchange rate remains essentially fixed.

The liberalization of capital market controls in the early 1990s has removed much of the basis for Thailand's monetary autonomy. Financial liberalization can be expected to have important economic benefits and will advance Thailand's attractiveness as a regional financial center. But by allowing international capital to have greater mobility, it will also limit the capacity of the Bank of Thailand to pursue an independent monetary policy. The commitment to a fixed exchange rate has not abated; indeed, some observers have suggested that the determination to defend a stable exchange rate in relation to the U.S. dollar is stronger than ever. The monetary strategy of the bank must adjust to the policy-induced changes in capital mobility unless Thailand decides instead to pursue a more flexible exchange rate system.

# Chapter Nine

# The Role of Exchange Rate Policy

Thailand's record of monetary conservatism has been accompanied by a great reluctance to use the exchange rate as an instrument of discretionary macroeconomic management. From the 1950s until 1984 the baht was pegged to the U.S. dollar. Exchange rate policy since 1984 has been officially described as a managed float, but approximate fixity to the U.S. dollar still continues. Devaluation, which in Thailand means devaluation in relation to the U.S. dollar, has been seen as a capitulation to inflation. It has occurred infrequently, in response to serious problems of external balance, and then usually only when other corrective measures have already been tried and failed. It is essential to recognize that exchange rate policy and monetary policy are intimately linked; Thailand's record of exchange rate stability has been possible only because of the sustained monetary restraint described in chapter 8.

This chapter examines exchange rate management in Thailand and its relationship to the movement of relative prices. This analysis is motivated by the so-called Australian model of the balance of payments, which stresses the distinction between traded and nontraded goods. The results strongly confirm that monetary and exchange rate policy in Thailand have the power to influence relative domestic prices. They also confirm the relevance of the traded- versus nontraded-goods analytical model as a tool for understanding issues of macroeconomic adjustment.

## The Record of Exchange Rate Policy

From 1961 to 1980 Thailand's exchange rate remained at roughly 20 baht per U.S. dollar. The long history of stable exchange between the baht and the U.S. dollar had been accepted as a normal feature of Thailand's international trade. Successive devaluations in the early 1980s raised this rate to 27 baht to the dollar at the end of 1984 (table 9.1).

**Table 9.1 Dates and Magnitudes of Devaluations**
*(baht/U.S. dollar rate)*

| Date | Percentage increase |
|------|---------------------|
| May 1981 | 1.1 |
| July 1981 | 8.7 |
| November 1984 | 14.9 |
| December 1985 | 1.9 |

*Source*: Bank of Thailand.

*Timing of Devaluations*

For summary purposes, these events may be collapsed into two significant devaluations: one in mid-1981 of roughly 10 percent; and one in late 1984 of roughly 15 percent. The objectives of the 1981 and 1984 devaluations were to reduce the existing balance of payments deficits. Economists at the Bank of Thailand had concluded that the cause of the deficit lay in the overvalued baht. Although the rate of exchange between the baht and U.S. dollar had scarcely changed, the dollar itself appreciated in relation to other currencies. Thus the baht, pulled by a strong dollar, appreciated against other currencies as well. Figure 9.1 shows the movement of the effective exchange rate between the baht and the currencies of Thailand's seven major trading partners: Japan, the United States, the United Kingdom, the former Federal Republic of Germany, Hong Kong, Malaysia, and Singapore. The series shown uses quarterly data, and the country weights are total trade shares, imports plus exports, over the fifteen-year period 1976–90. Note that the devaluations of 1981 and 1984 were small in comparison with the exogenous movements in Thailand's effective exchange rate induced by movements in other countries' exchange rates in relation to the U.S. dollar. Second, the two devaluations were each immediately preceded by appreciations of the effective exchange rate of the baht, induced by appreciations of the U.S. dollar in relation to other currencies.

In the year before the 1981 devaluation, the baht depreciated marginally in relation to the U.S. dollar, Japanese yen, and Singapore dollar, but it appreciated substantially when compared with the British pound and the German mark. For the same reasons, one year before the 1984 devaluation the appreciating dollar caused the baht to appreciate significantly against the pound and the mark. The devaluations of the baht in 1981 and 1984 can thus be seen as corrections for the overvalued baht. They were policy responses intended to restore Thailand's international competitiveness, but they were also long-term responses to the deteriorating terms of trade that began in 1974 with the first oil shock.

A further decline in the terms of trade occurred in 1985. In early December 1985 the baht was devalued further by 1.9 percent. The objective of this minidevaluation was again to recapture Thailand's competitiveness. One year before the 1985

**Figure 9.1. Nominal and Real Effective Exchange Rates, 1970–90**

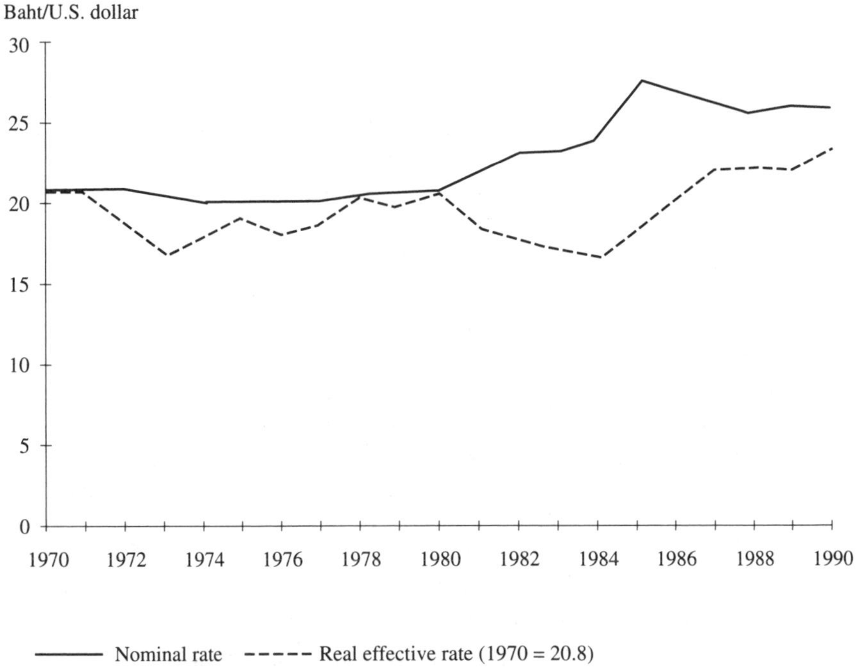

Baht/U.S. dollar

——— Nominal rate    - - - - - Real effective rate (1970 = 20.8)

*Source:* Bank of Thailand, *Monthly Bulletin,* various issues, and authors' calculations.

devaluation the baht depreciated against the pound, mark, and yen and marginally appreciated against the U.S. dollar, Hong Kong dollar, and the Malaysian ringgit.

The 1.1 percent devaluation of May 1981 reflected a decision on the part of the monetary authorities to devalue the baht by small amounts, but this was to be done repeatedly, rather than by devaluing by a single large percentage. It was believed that the latter course would generate greater public protest. Although this minidevaluation caused little such protest, it did result in devaluation speculation. As was widely recognized, the 1.1 percent devaluation was not commensurate with the appreciation of the dollar and the baht against other currencies (figure 9.1). The exchange equalization fund was required to continue selling dollars for fourteen working days until the baht was devalued once again, this time by 8.7 percent. During these fourteen days, there were seldom any sellers of dollars to the exchange equalization fund.

The deterioration in the terms of trade and the overvalued baht led to a persistent balance of trade deficit before the 1981 and 1984 devaluations. In particular, the 1983 current account deficit was alarmingly high (see table 3.4), and the domestic rate of interest was higher than the world rate by a full five percentage points. This contrasted with the situation in 1981, when the domestic rate of interest was about 2.5 percent below the world money market rate. In early 1981 the domestic money market rate was about 2.5 percentage points below the LIBOR rate and capital began to flow out in large amounts. The rise in the foreign rate of interest can be seen as a form of external shock, adversely affecting the balance of payments position. Since a ceiling rate of interest was in place, establishing a positive rate of interest—and thereby preventing capital outflow—was seen as a necessary policy response.

The appreciation of the U.S. dollar can be seen as another type of external shock, in addition to those discussed in chapter 5. Since the baht was pegged to the U.S. dollar, its value also appreciated. In addition to the expectation of further devaluation following the 1.1 percent devaluation of May 1981, the rising foreign rate of interest caused commercial banks to rush to pay foreign debts in an effort to accumulate foreign assets. Between the May and July devaluations of 1981, the value of foreign assets held by commercial banks increased by 20 percent.

The level of Thailand's international reserves declined from 1979 to 1985 (figure 9.2), although if the adequacy of reserves is taken into account, as measured by the number of months of imports covered, the declining trend started long before 1979. Although seven to eight months of reserve-covered imports were quite high, the precipitous drop in early 1981 contributed to the expectation of further devaluation. The months of import coverage series shown in figure 9.2 provides a potential explanation for the timing of the mid-1981 and late 1984

**Figure 9.2. Value of Reserves and Months of Import Coverage, 1975–90**

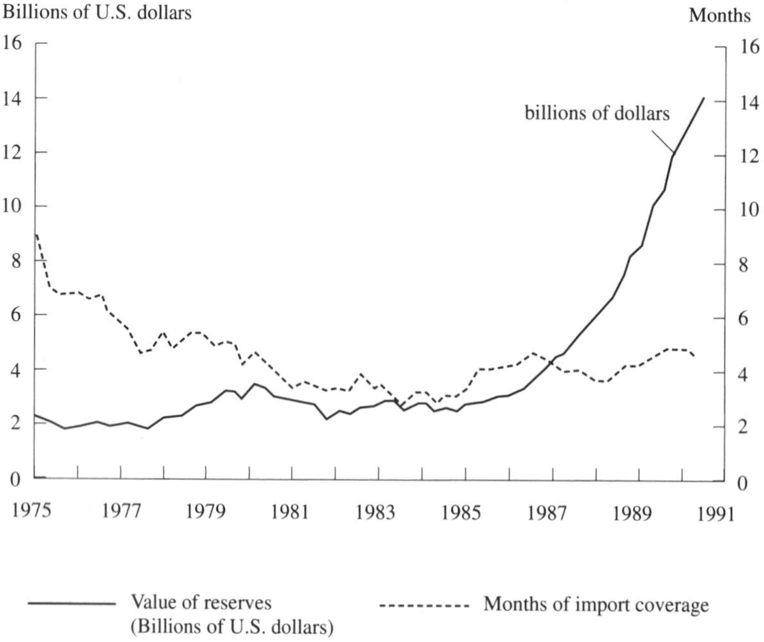

Value of reserves
(Billions of U.S. dollars)          ......... Months of import coverage

*Source:* Bank of Thailand, *Monthly Bulletin*, various issues; IMF, *International Financial Statistics,* various issues; and authors' calculations.

devaluations. In both periods, the number of months of coverage represented by reserves were historically low and had been declining for several quarters. The absolute value of reserves (shown in billions of U.S. dollars) had been declining in the quarters before the 1981 devaluations and had been rising only slightly prior to the 1984 devaluation. Moreover, the premium for the forward rate of the dollar was exceptionally high in the first half of 1981 and in early 1984.

In the cases of both the 1981 and 1984 devaluations, the policy response was applied belatedly and reluctantly. This was true not only of exchange rate policy, but also of interest rate policy, as described in chapter 8. During the first oil shock in 1974, the deposit and loan interest rate ceilings were raised by one percentage point, notwithstanding a 15 percent inflation rate in 1973. As a result, real interest rates were substantially negative. During the second oil price shock, the rate of inflation increased to 19 percent in 1980, an alarming rate by Thai standards, although smaller than the 24 percent inflation of 1974, following the first oil shock. The ceilings on interest rates were adjusted upward by 3 percentage points, but this still produced a negative 6.7 percent real interest rate.

As a consequence of Thailand's long-term exchange rate stability in relation to the U.S. dollar, the Thai price level has been closely tied to the U.S. price level. This relationship is closest in the case of the wholesale price indices for the two countries, because traded goods are more dominant in these price indices than is the case for consumer prices (figure 9.3). Thai devaluations had only a small effect on the close relationship between the two price indices.

**Figure 9.3. Thai and United States' Wholesale Price Indices, 1960–92**

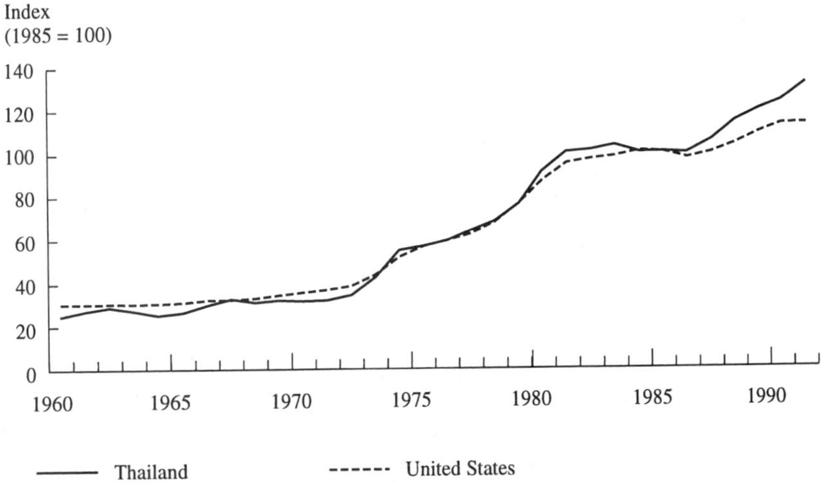

*Source:* Bank of Thailand, *Monthly Bulletin,* various issues; IMF, *International Financial Statistics,* various issues; and authors' calculations.

## The Policy Environment of Devaluation

Devaluations inevitably have unpopular political consequences. They create hardships for those depending on imported raw materials as well those holding debts denominated in foreign currencies. In Thailand, devaluations have usually been employed only after other methods of coping with trading imbalances have already been attempted. These other means have included an increase in import tariffs, contractionary fiscal and monetary policies, and credit controls. This response reflects the strong aversion of Thai monetary authorities to the inflation that devaluation causes. But its cost may well be that when devaluation finally becomes an inevitable means of correcting the balance of payments problem it must then occur at a higher rate than would have been required had action occurred earlier.

An example of such a pattern of policy response was the limit on the credit growth of commercial banks that began in 1984. This was a considerable shift in monetary policy since it was the first time that a quantity control was imposed together with a price control (that is, the interest ceiling). The shift in the policy stance was attributed to the conditions set by the IMF for the stand-by loans agreed in that year (Robinson, Yangho, and Ranjit 1991). Alarmed by the huge current account deficits of 1983, the Bank of Thailand decided to take this drastic measure against the expansion of imports. The commercial banks were subject to the maximum credit expansion at 18 percent of the 1983 level of credit.

The Bank of Thailand's credit ceiling was blamed for causing extensive failures among small and medium-size businesses. From January to June 1984 the conservative Thai Farmers Bank reported a 70 percent increase in the number of dishonored checks, compared with the previous year, and an 86 percent increase in their value. In August 1984, Prime Minister Prem Tinsulanonda canceled the credit ceiling after seven months of operation. Before the decision was made, the government had to face mounting criticism from the press, opposition parties, and some parties in the ruling coalition. A special working group, appointed by the Council of Economic Ministers to study the issue, recommended scrapping the credit ceiling on the grounds that the negative political effects outweighed the supposed positive economic benefits. The working group included the governor of the Bank of Thailand, Nukul Prachuamoh; secretary of the National Economic and Social Development Board, Snoh Unakul; and the prime minister's chief economic adviser, Virabongsa Ramangkura.

The credit ceiling was considered unnecessary since the two largest banks, Bangkok Bank, and Krung Thai Bank wanted to reduce their lending growth owing to the excessive lending in 1982. In the first half of 1984 their lending growth rate fell to only 3.0 and 0.5 percent, respectively. Before implementing the credit ceiling, the Bank of Thailand had contemplated other measures, such as raising banks' reserve requirements and controlling the issuance of letters of credit (LCs). These measures were in fact undertaken at the end of 1983. The banks had to maintain the value of LCs issued between December 1983 and November 1984 at the same level as in the preceding year. When these measures failed to reduce the balance of trade deficit, a ceiling was imposed on the volume of credit in general. Devaluation was postponed to avoid its adverse political consequences. By applying other indirect measures (such as credit controls) to correct the external deficit, the Bank of Thailand had complicated the problem.

Large and unanticipated devaluations bring more resistance and dissatisfaction than small and anticipated ones. Nevertheless, small-step devaluation cannot be undertaken frequently since speculation on further devaluation will develop. The November 1984 devaluation was not anticipated. The forward premium for U.S. dollars was very low. Thus 1984 contrasted sharply with the 1981 devaluation in terms of timing and magnitude. There was no massive run on international reserves. Government officials repeatedly stated that there would be no devaluation since other policies such as the 18 percent credit ceiling were working out. The ceiling was abandoned in August 1984 since credit monetary growth was in line with the target. On October 24, 1984, the government announced a six-month extension of the control of LCs. The combined effect of these measures was an 18 percent reduction in the trade deficit from January to September 1984. That is why the November devaluation surprised most people.

The timing of policy implementation was crucial. Inflation was high in 1980 and 1981, at 19.7 and 12.7 percent, respectively. As a result, the authorities were reluctant to devalue at a high rate. The 1.1 percent devaluation in May 1981 can be viewed as a preliminary corrective measure to avoid fueling inflation. In contrast to the inflation rates of 1980 and 1981, those in 1983 and 1984 were only 3.8 and 0.9 percent, respectively. The decision to devalue by 14.9 percent, the highest in modern Thai history, was thus considered acceptable.

At the time of the 8.7 percent devaluation in July 1981, the opposition parties were strong and Parliament was in session. Thus it was easy to form a coalition and use Parliament as a forum to attack the government in protest at the devaluation. In contrast, in November 1984, when the 14.9 percent devaluation was announced, Parliament was in recess. It was difficult for political parties to oppose the government. In any case, the opposition parties were weak and unpopular. In 1984, the government had sufficient time to make its case clear to the public.

The redistributive effects of the devaluation were also involved in the timing of its announcement. At the time of the July 1981 devaluation, Thailand had accumulated unusually large stocks of unsold agricultural products such as rice, cassava, maize, and rubber. Exporters were waiting for an upturn in the world prices, while importers tried to pay the bills that high interest rates had imposed on them. Devaluation was seen as a means of helping exporters dispose of their unsold stocks. Finance Minister Sommai Hoontrakul announced that the November 1984 devaluation would help the farmers, since their products were still in their possession. The annual export crop season was from December to March. If devaluation took place after November, the windfall would accrue primarily to middlemen.

The devaluation in 1981 taught economic policy planners several lessons. The political cost of the adjustment to a realistic exchange rate led the government to postpone devaluation. In addition, opposition parties as well as some members of the coalition attacked the devaluation. Fear of inflation was one of their great concerns, although some members were opposed to devaluation because they failed to understand devaluation per se. The record of Parliament in July 1981 also indicated that some members were afraid that the budget would be invalid since the value of the baht had eroded by 8.7 percent. Others suggested alternative policies such as totally banning imports, increasing tariffs, or asking the Bank of Thailand to assume the monopoly role of foreign exchange dealer. Other members regarded devaluation as equivalent to lèse majesté since the value of the bank notes that bear the king's picture had been reduced. There was also concerted opposition from the press. The deputy finance minister, Paichitr Uathavikul, pictured as the main culprit, resigned.

The 1981 devaluation was opposed mainly by politicians. The 1984 devaluation brought a confrontation between the prime minister and the commander in chief of the army, General Athit Kamlangek. In a public broadcast, the army commander called for the cancellation of the devaluation and the reshuffling of the cabinet, which implied the removal of the finance minister responsible for the devaluation. The finance minister had earlier strongly opposed the military's plan to purchase sixteen F16-A tactical fighters, arguing that it would substantially increase Thailand's external public debt. He had thus incurred the hostility of the military leadership. Devaluation was seen as a further threat to the plan to modernize the Thai military since the jet fighters would now cost 14.9 percent more in nominal baht terms.

The real possibility of a coup against the government made the overt opposition of the military particularly ominous. Prime Minister Prem had acknowledged his involvement in the decisionmaking process leading to the devaluation. He also strongly defended the devaluation on the grounds that it would maintain the country's financial stability. Prem's position was therefore also under attack, but he later gained the public's support, as well as that of other generals. Prem satisfied the military by promising to find the 3 billion baht needed to cover the impact of the devaluation on the purchasing of military equipment. In addition, he promised that the government would control the price of oil and some other necessities. These latter measures were designed primarily to placate the nonmilitary opposition to the devaluation. Five days later, the army commander backed away from his opposition, announcing that the dispute had all been "a misunderstanding."

Despite some strikes of railworkers, coup rumors, and attempts by the opposition to call an extraordinary session of Parliament to debate the devaluation, the government survived. Devaluations are serious matters in Thailand; they are not undertaken lightly.

## Effects of Devaluation: Wages, Balance of Payments, Inflation

Wage earners tend to be worse off as a result of devaluation if their money wage rate does not rise by the same proportion as the inflation rate induced by devaluation. The effectiveness of devaluation in improving the trade balance, however, depends in part on the extent to which the real wage is reduced. Such a reduction is required, but for this to occur nominal wages must not rise by the full extent of the price rise caused by the devaluation. Labor unions in Thailand have not been a powerful pressure group as far as wage determination is concerned, but minimum wage regulations do have an impact on rates of inflation. The Prem government increased the minimum wage rate by 12 and 6 percent in the years following the 1981 and 1984 devaluations, respectively. Since the rate of inflation was high in 1981, the real minimum wage rate decreased marginally; however, the adjustment in the minimum wage rate in January 1985 represented a real increase of 4.3 percent over the previous year.

As table 9.2 suggests, increases in the minimum wage were usually small, especially the adjustments following devaluation. Consequently, the inflationary effects of devaluation were contained, in that the government was able to hold inflationary expectations below the percentage change in the exchange rate. From January 1985 to December 1989, the minimum wage was raised only once, by 4.3 percent in 1987. Inflationary expectations can also be controlled by other methods, accompanying devaluations, such as freezing electricity tariffs, reducing import duties and income taxes, and setting maximum prices for vital commodities. After the devaluation of July 1981, devaluation speculation and the run on dollar international reserves came to a halt. The forward premium of the dollar declined to its normal level. More important, the devaluation induced capital inflows and improved the current account imbalance considerably. From figure 9.2, it can be seen that the level of international reserves, measured in months of import coverage, reversed its declining trend.

**Table 9.2  Minimum Wage Rate in Bangkok Area, 1977–87**

| *Effective*[a] | *Wage rate (baht/day)* | *Percentage increase* | *Real wage rate*[b] | *Percentage change* |
|---|---|---|---|---|
| 1977 | 28 | 12.0 | 39.6 | 6.0 |
| 1978 | 35 | 25.0 | 45.6 | 15.2 |
| 1979 | 45 | 28.6 | 53.7 | 17.6 |
| 1980 | 54 | 20.0 | 54.0 | 0.6 |
| 1981 | 61 | 12.3 | 53.3 | −1.3 |
| 1982 | 64 | 4.9 | 51.9 | −2.6 |
| 1983 | 66 | 3.1 | 51.8 | −0.2 |
| 1985 | 70 | 6.1 | 54.0 | 4.3 |
| 1987 | 73 | 4.3 | 54.9 | 1.7 |

a. The effective date usually was on 1 October, except in 1985 and 1987, the effective dates were set on January 1 and April 1, respectively.

b. The real wage rate at 1980 price level calculated from the CPI.

*Source*: Data from the Interior Ministry.

The short-run effect of the July 1981 devaluation is shown in table 9.3, which measures the percentage change of the components of the balance of payments six months before and after the devaluation. Whereas the value of exports rose substantially, the value of imports declined, compared with the corresponding period a year before, and the result was an improvement in the current account. The authorities have tended to overestimate the inflationary impact of devaluation. As table 9.4 indicates, the actual inflation rates in 1981 and 1985 were 2 to 3 percentage points below the predicted rates. It is not certain whether the authorities would have postponed devaluation had they correctly estimated the impact of this measure on inflation.

## Table 9.3  Short-Run Effects of the July 1981 Devaluation

| Item affected | January-June 1981 | July-December 1981 |
|---|---|---|
| *Percentage change* | | |
| Exports | 8.1 | 22.0 |
| Imports | 20.2 | 9.8 |
| Imported oil | 14.3 | 7.5 |
| | | |
| *Change in millions of baht* | | |
| Trade balance | −12.3 | +5.0 |
| Balance of payments | −19.7 | +17.1 |

*Note*: Change from the corresponding period in the previous year.
*Source*: Bank of Thailand, *Monthly Bulletin,* February 1982.

## Table 9.4  Government Expectations of Devaluation Consequences
*(billions of baht)*

| Devaluation | Predicted consequence | Actual consequence |
|---|---|---|
| *July 1981 (8.7 percent)* | | |
| Inflation (percent) | 14–15 | 12.7[a] |
| Balance of payments | −10 | +2.5 |
| Balance of trade | −68 | -65.8 |
| | | |
| *November 1985 (14.9 percent)* | | |
| Inflation (percent) | 5–6 | 2.4[b] |
| Balance of payments | 0 | +10.6 |
| Balance of trade | 70 | −68.8 |

a. 1980 = 19.7.
b. 1984 = 0.9.
*Source*: The forecast for 1981 was made publicly by the Minister of Finance in the Parliament. The forecast for 1985 was made by the Bank of Thailand.

## Post-1984 Exchange Rate Setting

Since the November 1984 devaluation, the Thai exchange rate system has officially been described as a managed float. The baht has been pegged to a basket of currencies, the composition of which is secret. From the stability of the baht/U.S.
dollar rate, in spite of the volatility of the U.S. dollar in relation to most other currencies, it is obvious that the dollar represents a large share of the basket. It has
been conjectured among Thai economists that the share of the U.S. dollar within
the basket may have increased since the basket system was introduced. The analysis that follows attempts to determine the implied composition of the basket and
its change over time by studying the behavior of exchange rate data since 1985.

Exchange rate data for ten countries were used in the regression analysis. These
are the ten major trading partners of Thailand: Australia, Belgium, France, Germany,
Hong Kong, Japan, Malaysia, Singapore, United Kingdom, and the United States.[1] It
is hypothesized that the baht is pegged to a basket of currencies whose composition by
shares changes linearly over time. The share coefficient for each currency in the basket
therefore has two components: an intercept component for that currency and a component that summarizes the rate of change in that currency's share through time.

The share coefficient for each currency is thus defined as

$$(9.1) \qquad a_t^i = a_0^i + a_1^i t$$

where $a_t^i$ is the overall coefficient for currency $i$ at time $t$, $a_0^i$ is the country intercept, and $a_1^i t$ is the time-dependent component of the coefficient for country $i$. In
the empirical application of this analysis, the sum of the share coefficients across
countries, $a_t^i$, is constrained to be equal to unity at each time period.

The results of the regression analysis are summarized in table 9.5. The independent variables used in explaining the baht/SDR rate are the SDR rates of the Japanese yen; Singapore dollar; U.S. dollar; an aggregated "others" variable obtained
by using a geometric mean of the SDR rates of the remaining currencies; a dummy
variable (to take into account the small devaluation of the baht in November 1985),
denoted D below; and time, denoted $t$. The three main explanatory currencies were
manipulated by dividing them by the "others" variable. The coefficient for the others variable can be recovered by subtracting the sum of the other three explanatory
variables from unity. The formula for the regression was thus:

$$(9.2) \quad \ln\left(\frac{\text{Baht}}{\text{Others}}\right) = a_0 + a_1 D + a_2 t + (a_0^1 + a_1^1 t)\ln\left(\frac{\text{US\$}}{\text{Others}}\right) + (a_0^2 + a_1^2 t)\ln\left(\frac{\text{Yen}}{\text{Others}}\right)$$
$$+ (a_0^3 + a_1^3 t)\ln\left(\frac{\text{Singapore \$}}{\text{Others}}\right)$$

The regression results confirm that the U.S. dollar is a major component in
the basket of currencies and that its share is increasing over time. The estimated
implicit weights at the midpoint of the series (January 1989) were U.S. dollar, 66
percent; Japanese yen, 9 percent; Singapore dollar, 16 percent; and others, 9 per-

**Table 9.5  Estimated Composition of Exchange Rate Setting Basket**

| Variables | Coefficient value[a] | Currency intercept[b] | Currency slope |
|---|---|---|---|
| Constant | 2.45 | — | — |
| | (29.36) | | |
| Dummy | 0.02 | — | — |
| | (4.70) | | |
| Time | 0.24 | — | — |
| | (0.13) | | |
| U.S. dollar | 0.66 | 0.52 | 0.28 |
| | (26.31) | (13.81) | (6.90) |
| Japanese yen | 0.09 | 0.07 | 0.04 |
| | (10.02) | (2.92) | (0.90) |
| Singapore dollar | 0.16 | 0.20 | –0.06 |
| | (4.91) | (4.86) | (–1.56) |

a. Coefficient value is the value of $a_t^i$ in equation 9.1 and is equal to the currency share evaluated at the sample mean.

b. Currency intercept is the value of $a_0^i$ in equation 9.1.

*Note*: $\overline{R}^2 = 0.99$; Durbin-Watson statistic = 1.83; and log of likelihood function = 386.25.

*Source*: Authors' calculations with data drawn from IMF, *International Financial Statistics*, various issues.

cent. The estimated shares for the U.S. dollar, Japanese yen, and Singapore dollar were all significantly different from zero at the 5 percent level of significance. Figure 9.4 simulates the composition of the exchange rate setting basket implied by the results shown in table 9.5. The figure clearly demonstrates the growing importance of the U.S. dollar in the currency basket to which the Thai baht is pegged. The estimated share for the U.S. dollar rose from 52 percent at the beginning of the data period (January 1985) to 79 percent at its end point (December 1992). Parallel to the growth of the U.S. dollar in the basket is the decline in the importance of other currencies. At the same time, the Japanese yen and the Singapore dollar have maintained steady shares in the basket.

## Exchange Rate Policy and Relative Prices

What role did exchange rate and demand management policy have in directing the macroeconomic adjustments Thailand made through the 1970s and 1980s? The discussion now turns to the role of relative price movements within Thailand in regulating the adjustment process. A simple theoretical model is used to illustrate the respective roles of external shocks, exchange rate policy, and domestic relative prices in balance of payments adjustment. Attention is also given to the actual be-

**Figure 9.4. Simulated Composition of Exchange Rate Setting Basket, 1985–93**

OLS prediction with time trend (percent)

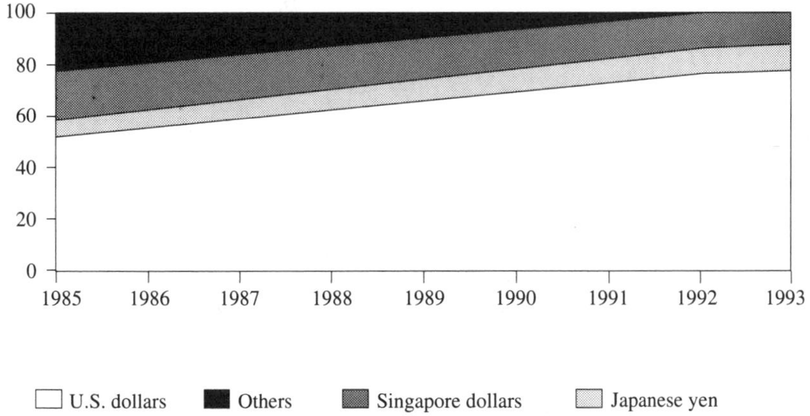
100
80
60
40
20
0
1985
1986
1987
1988
1989
1990
1991
1992
1993
U.S. dollars
Others
Singapore dollars
Japanese yen

*Source:* Authors' calculations.

havior of key relative prices within Thailand and to the degree to which their movements explain the course of Thai macroeconomic adjustment.

### *A Model of the Balance of Payments and External Shocks*

The simple two-commodity model of the balance of payments used in this analysis is known as the Australian model. The fundamental distinction in this theory is between goods that are exchanged internationally, termed tradables, and those that are not, termed nontradables. Many (but not all) primary commodities and manufactured goods are examples of tradables, while many (but not all) services are examples of nontradables. The point of distinguishing between them is that the nominal domestic prices of tradables are determined by their international prices, the exchange rate, and any subsidies, tariffs, or other taxes that may be applied to them. In contrast, the nominal prices of nontradables are determined by domestic supply and demand conditions.

According to the Australian model, a shock to the balance of payments such as a resource boom, a change in the terms of trade, or a transfer of foreign aid, will lead to equilibrating adjustments in the relative prices of traded and nontraded goods. For example, a manufacturing boom that adds to foreign exchange earnings will lead to a reduction in the price ratio of domestic traded goods versus nontraded goods. This price movement induces the domestic adjustments in demand and resource allocation that cause the increased foreign exchange earnings to be absorbed domestically. Furthermore, the Australian model analyzes the mechanism by which policy instruments such as exchange rate adjustments affect the balance of payments by focusing on their effects on the domestic relative prices of traded and nontraded goods.

The role of the domestic prices of tradables in relation to nontradables in influencing the balance of payments is depicted in figure 9.5. Value-weighted aggregated quantities of tradables are shown on the vertical axis and a similar aggregate of nontradables is shown on the horizontal axis. The schedule PP shows production possibilities for these two categories of goods, and social preferences regarding aggregate "absorption" of them are shown by indifference curves such as $U_1$ and $U_0$. They are assumed to have the usual regularity properties. The distinction between investment and consumption is not important for this analysis. Thus for simplicity both are treated as absorption.

The crucial difference between tradables and nontradables in this analysis is that the absorption of nontradables must be matched by domestic production, but the same does not apply to tradables. If more of a particular tradable good is ab-

**Figure 9.5. Tradables, Nontradables, and Balance of Payments**

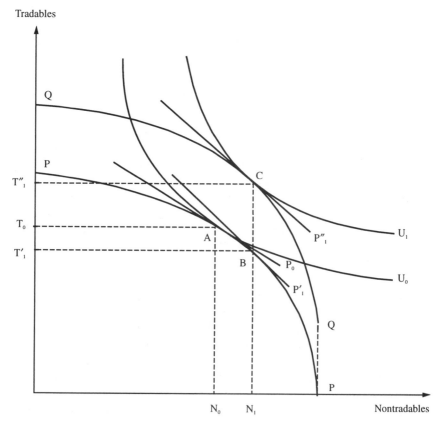

*Source:* Authors' compilation.

sorbed than is produced, then this good is a net import. The reverse is a net export. If in total more tradables (by value) are absorbed than are produced, this corresponds to a current account deficit, since the difference between absorption and production of tradables must correspond to an excess of net imports over net exports. A current account surplus is the reverse. By definition, nontradables cannot be either imported or exported, so their domestic absorption cannot exceed their production.

Current account balance is indicated by point A in figure 9.5. At this point, consumption and production are equal for both tradables and nontradables. The slope of the price line $P_0$ gives the prices of nontradables in relation to tradables. Now consider a current account imbalance. We assume production possibilities to remain at PP, disregarding the schedule QQ for the moment. Suppose that the price of nontradables in relation to tradables rises above $P_0$, say, to $P_1$. This new price ratio is indicated by the slopes of lines $P_1'$ and $P_1''$, which are drawn parallel to each other. We will discuss the possible causes of this event presently. Production of nontradables now rises and that of tradables falls. Production will now occur at point B. At this higher price ratio, however, tradables will no longer be consumed in the same quantities in which they are produced. The lower price of tradables encourages their absorption in relation to nontradables, but has the reverse effect on production.

As already explained, a divergence between absorption and production can only occur in the tradables market; absorption and production of nontradables cannot differ. The possible absorption outcomes that might occur under price $P_1$ thus lie along a vertical line drawn through the production point, B. These are the points at which the production and absorption of nontradables are equal. The actual solution will be that point along this line at which an indifference curve has a slope equal to that of $P_1$, say, point C. At point C, absorption of tradables exceeds their production. The difference is a current account deficit, equal to the vertical distance between point B and C.

How might a current account deficit like that occurring at point C arise? The key lies in the way the prices of tradables and nontradables are determined. Suppose that domestic monetary expansion occurs with a fixed exchange rate. The monetary expansion will raise domestic demand and thus increase domestic prices. But these price increases will be concentrated in nontradables rather than tradables because the nominal prices of tradables are determined by international prices expressed in foreign exchange, the exchange rate, and any subsidies, tariffs, or other taxes that may be present. Thus the monetary expansion bids up the prices of nontradables in relation to tradables and thereby produces a current account deficit.

Now consider an external shock such as a reduction in petroleum prices. Because of the importance of petroleum as an intermediate good, we represent this shock as a vertical shift in the production possibilities frontier, to QQ. That is, for a petroleum importer like Thailand we represent a reduction in international petroleum prices as a quantum increase in the economy's net capacity to produce traded goods. For convenience in the diagram, we choose an external shock that has the same foreign exchange value as the current account deficit arising in our previous analysis. There will now be no current account deficit if production and absorption both occur at point C. Point C is now an equilibrium with zero current account deficit and a price ratio given by the slope of $P_1$.

Several conclusions can be drawn from this analysis. First, the theory is clear on what an increase in the price of an export good in relation to the prices of other traded goods will mean for the relative prices of traded versus nontraded goods. There will be an income effect and a substitution effect, and both will lead to an increased demand for nontradables. The prices of nontradables should rise in relation to all tradables prices other than the export good whose price rose.

Second, the theory is more equivocal on the effect of an increase in the international price of an importable. When the price of an import good rises, there will be a similar substitution effect to the one discussed above, but an income effect that operates in the reverse direction. Depending on the relative strengths of these two effects, nontradables prices could rise or fall in relation to the prices of tradables other than the import good whose price rose. The greater the share of the value of net imports of the good in national income and the greater the income elasticity of demand for nontradables, the greater the likelihood that the relative price of nontradables will fall.

Third, assuming that an increase in an import price requires a reduction in the domestic price of nontradables, then under a fixed exchange rate policy inflation at home must be lower than inflation abroad, at least temporarily. As long as the exchange rate remains fixed, inflation abroad determines the rate of increase of tradables prices. For nontradable prices to decline in relation to them, the average price level at home must rise more slowly than the average level abroad. Under a fixed exchange rate policy, this requires lower inflation domestically than the rate abroad, thus putting severe pressure on domestic monetary and fiscal policies.

Fourth, this lower-than-normal rate of inflation, consistent with adjustment to the worsening in the terms of trade, is temporary. Once the required domestic price ratio has been attained, inflation at the world rate will sustain the required nontradables/tradables price ratio.

Fifth, the Dutch disease phenomenon, under which tradables sectors such as agriculture and manufacturing are harmed by absorption of the benefits of the improvement in the terms of trade, has a monetary component as well. Suppose there is an increase in export prices. The rate of absorption of the benefits of this improvement in the terms of trade depends on the rate at which the nontradables/tradables price ratio rises, which in turn depends on domestic aggregate demand.

The likely relative price effects of a devaluation can be inferred from figure 9.5. A devaluation will raise the nominal prices of tradables and will do so relatively quickly. The subsequent behavior of nontradables prices will be strongly affected by monetary and fiscal policy. If the initial position was one of an unsustainable current account deficit and the views of those government officials and advisers arguing for monetary and fiscal restraint prevail, then the initial increase in the prices of tradables in relation to nontradables may be sustained for some time. But if domestic aggregate demand grows at a higher rate and thus leads to continued rapid inflation, the price ratio will steadily decline from its post-devaluation peak.

## Relative Price Movements within Thailand

Suppose for a moment that "traded goods" refer to an index of all traded goods, including the ones whose prices changed. This distinction will be important in some cases. In the Thai case, for example, the temporary commodity boom of 1973 would have caused the domestic prices of those traded goods whose prices increased in international markets to rise in the short run in relation to nontraded goods, and then to decline as the boom passed. But the prices of nonbooming commodities should fall in relation to the prices of nontraded goods through the Dutch disease mechanism. The longer-term implications of the positive income effects caused by this boom would be to accentuate the decline in the prices of traded goods in relation to those of nontraded goods.

A rise in international petroleum prices would ordinarily produce an increase in local petroleum product prices, but then the negative income effects resulting from this deterioration in the terms of trade should produce an increase in traded goods prices in relation to those of nontraded goods. Similar results to this latter affect would be expected from 1979–80 oil price increases and the interest rate increases of the early 1980s.

To investigate the actual behavior of traded and nontraded goods prices, indices of the two have been constructed as follows. The index of traded goods prices was constructed from thirty-three individual commodities included in the wholesale price index. Monthly data were obtained from January 1968 to January 1988 for the nominal prices of each of these commodities. This gave 241 observations for each commodity. The particular commodities chosen for inclusion in the index were those that seemed to satisfy the standard economic definition of traded goods—they are traded internationally and their domestic prices are determined by international prices and the exchange rate.

The index then took the form:

$$(9.3) \qquad P_t^T = \sum_{i=1}^{33} \alpha_i P_{it}^T / P_{i\tau}^T$$

where $P_t^T$ is the value of the traded goods price index in period $t$, $\alpha_i$ is the weight applying to commodity $i$ in index form in the construction of the wholesale price index, $P_{it}^T$ is the price of traded commodity $i$ in period $t$, and $P_{i\tau}^T$ is the same price in period $\tau$. Dividing by the price in period $\tau$ normalizes the price series for commodity $i$ and this is necessary because the commodity weights apply to indexed prices, not to nominal prices. June 1976 was chosen for $\tau$ because this is the month in which the commodity weights were estimated.

The index of nontraded goods prices was constructed from forty-two individual components of the consumer price index. They were selected on the criteria that the commodities or services concerned are not traded internationally and that their domestic prices are not controlled. The period of coverage was the same as for the traded commodities discussed above. The index was thus

$$(9.4) \qquad P_t^N = \sum_{j=1}^{43} \beta_j P_{jt}^N / P_{j\tau}^N$$

where $P_t^N$ is the value of the nontraded goods price index in period $t$, and all other terms are analogous to those appearing in (9.3). June 1976 was again chosen for $\tau$. Tables 9.6 and 9.7 list the commodities used in the construction of the two indices and their respective weights. The results are shown in figures 9.6 and 9.7. The series are each indexed so that the value in August 1973 is 100. Figure 9.8 shows the behavior of the traded and nontraded goods price ratio $P_t = P_t^T / P_t^N$, which is formed from the separate $P_t^T$ and $P_t^N$ series and is thus automatically indexed such that the value in August 1973 is unity.

Before discussing figures 9.6 to 9.8, it is important to qualify the methodology used. Some arbitrariness enters the specification of the set of commodities in-

**Table 9.6  Composition of Index of Prices of Traded Goods**

| Commodity number | Commodity name | Index weight | Commodity number | Commodity name | Index weight |
|---|---|---|---|---|---|
| 1 | Ammonium sulphate | 0.061 | 18 | Gunny bag | 0.017 |
| 2 | Tanned leather | 0.005 | 19 | Coffee powder | 0.005 |
| 3 | Tetron fiber | 0.083 | 20 | Tea | 0.004 |
| 4 | Cotton with synthetic | 0.099 | 21 | Refrigerator | 0.005 |
| 5 | Silk yarn | 0.004 | 22 | Cassava | 0.125 |
| 6 | Cotton yarn | 0.050 | 23 | Super kenaf | 0.002 |
| 7 | Broken white rice | 0.049 | 24 | Kenaf | 0.003 |
| 8 | Farm tractor | 0.023 | 25 | Maize | 0.016 |
| 9 | Air conditioner | 0.003 | 26 | Coffee beans | 0.005 |
| 10 | Television set | 0.007 | 27 | Rice (100%) | 0.031 |
| 11 | Shoes | 0.003 | 28 | Rice (5% broken) | 0.039 |
| 12 | Briefcase | 0.002 | 29 | Steel | 0.040 |
| 13 | Kerosene | 0.010 | 30 | Paint | 0.006 |
| 14 | Super gasoline | 0.055 | 31 | Cement | 0.052 |
| 15 | Regular gasoline | 0.060 | 32 | Diesel | 0.136 |
| 16 | Penicillin | 0.003 | 33 | Plastic blocks | 0.032 |
| 17 | Shirt | 0.002 | | | |

*Source*: Department of Business Economics, Ministry of Commerce, Bangkok.

## Table 9.7  Composition of Index of Prices of Nontraded Goods

| Commodity number | Commodity name | Index weight | Commodity number | Commodity name | Index weight |
|---|---|---|---|---|---|
| 1 | Vermicelli | 0.003 | 22 | Duck egg | 0.015 |
| 2 | Pork | 0.059 | 23 | Lard oil | 0.011 |
| 3 | Cured meat | 0.005 | 24 | School fee | 0.054 |
| 4 | Chicken | 0.025 | 25 | Shrimp paste | 0.003 |
| 5 | Dressed duck | 0.001 | 26 | Salt | 0.001 |
| 6 | Serpent-head fish | 0.008 | 27 | Soda water | 0.001 |
| 7 | Catfish | 0.016 | 28 | Ice | 0.004 |
| 8 | Mackerel | 0.004 | 29 | Rice curry | 0.343 |
| 9 | Steamed mackerel | 0.011 | 30 | Women's patoong | 0.006 |
| 10 | Fresh shrimp | 0.011 | 31 | Laundry | 0.006 |
| 11 | Dried fish | 0.004 | 32 | Mattress | 0.001 |
| 12 | Kale | 0.007 | 33 | Mosquito net | 0.003 |
| 13 | Chinese mustard | 0.005 | 34 | Electricity | 0.088 |
| 14 | Cucumber | 0.003 | 35 | Charcoal | 0.021 |
| 15 | Sweet potato | 0.001 | 36 | Water supply | 0.022 |
| 16 | Garlic | 0.006 | 37 | Hospital fee | 0.044 |
| 17 | Fresh chili | 0.007 | 38 | Man's haircut | 0.011 |
| 18 | Fresh peanuts | 0.001 | 39 | Woman's haircut | 0.010 |
| 19 | Coconut | 0.009 | 40 | Bus fare | 0.080 |
| 20 | Pineapple | 0.014 | 41 | Cinema admission | 0.036 |
| 21 | Chicken egg | 0.011 | 42 | Newspaper | 0.021 |

*Source*: Department of Business Economics, Ministry of Commerce, Bangkok.

cluded in the two indices, and the results would presumably change somewhat if these decisions were made differently. Also, the results shown do not exclude commodities whose international prices have been changing. For example, petroleum-based products are included in the set of traded goods, as are rice, cassava, and other agricultural products whose international prices have been highly volatile over the period discussed. Indices could be constructed that excluded these commodities.

Figure 9.8 shows the broad features of peaks in the traded/nontraded goods price ratio in 1974 and 1978. The 1974 peak quickly vanished and within two years the price ratio had returned to roughly its value before the peak. The 1978 peak also vanished, but only after it was sustained for almost five years. The two peaks fit the theoretical predictions reasonably well. The 1974 peak corresponds to the first oil shock while the 1978 to 1982 peak corresponds to the second oil shock followed

**Figure 9.6. Traded Goods Price Index Monthly, 1968–88,**
(August 1973 = 100)

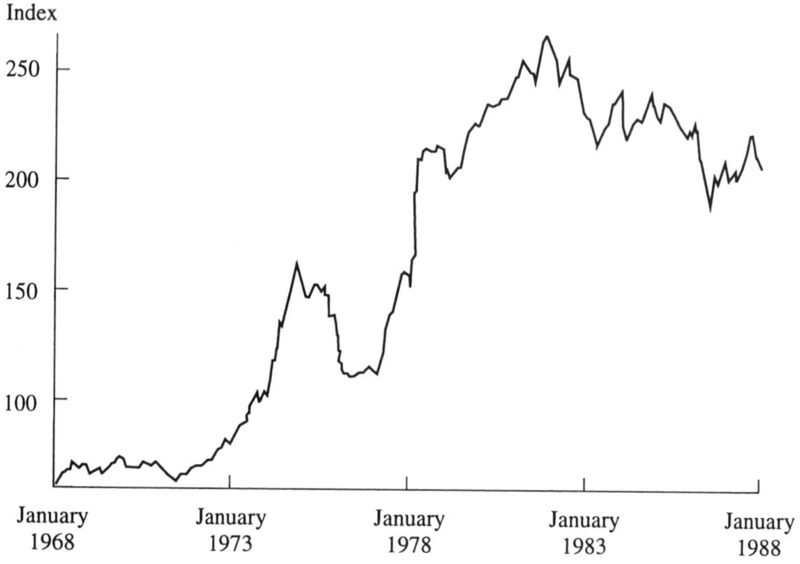

*Source:* Table 9.6 and Department of Business Economics, Ministry of Commerce.

by the debt crisis induced by high interest rates. The puzzle is, what caused the relative price declines from 1975 to 1977 and from 1983 to the present?

Before that question can be explored, a statistical worry concerning the traded goods price series that we have used needs to be cleared up. An index of traded goods prices excluding petroleum products has been constructed by assigning zero weights to commodities 13 to 15, inclusive, in table 9.6. Otherwise, the relative weights are unchanged. The behavior of this traded goods price index both considered separately and in relation to the nontradables index described previously is similar to those shown in figures 9.6 and 9.8, respectively. Excluding petroleum products from the tradables price series does not make any substantive difference to our qualitative results.

It is helpful now to turn to two separate nominal price series of traded and nontraded goods prices shown in figures 9.6 and 9.7, respectively. Taking traded goods prices first, we shall employ the usual assumption of the "law of one price": namely, the domestic prices of traded goods are determined by international prices and the exchange rate. The first oil shock followed a primary commodity price boom that began in 1972 (see the terms-of-trade series in table 3.4). Tradables prices rose, and this was reinforced by the subsequent rise in petroleum prices. The commodity boom had vanished by 1976 and the average price of tradables had fallen. By 1976, roughly half the increase in tradables prices occurring between

**Figure 9.7.  Nontraded Goods Price Index, 1968–88**

(August 1973 = 100)

Index

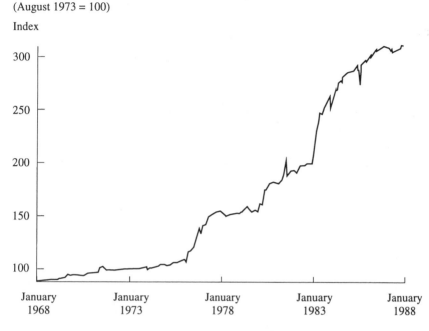

*Source:* Table 9.7 and Department of Business Economics, Ministry of Commerce.

1972 and the peak in 1974 had vanished. The second oil shock sent the average price of tradables upward again, beginning in 1978.

Significant declines in commodity prices occurred in the early 1980s, but their effects on the average prices of tradables were partly counteracted by the four devaluations we have discussed: 1.1 percent in May 1981, 8.7 percent in July 1981, 14.9 percent in November 1984, and 1.9 percent in December 1985. It must be stressed that these devaluations are measured in terms of the U.S. dollar only, not in terms of a trade-weighted index of currencies. As figure 9.1 revealed, from early 1978 to the end of 1984 the trade-weighted effective exchange rate of the baht scarcely changed.

As for the nontradables prices in figure 9.7, a monetary expansion occurred from 1972 to 1973 (see chapter 8), but the price effects of this expansion were confined mainly to tradables, whose prices were rising dramatically in relation to nontradables. Nontradables prices rose only moderately, even though inflation reached 16 percent in 1973. A severe monetary and fiscal contraction followed, from 1973 to 1974. Inflation peaked at 24 percent in 1974 but had declined dramatically to only 5 percent by 1975. Nontradables prices continued their steady rate of increase from before the external price shocks.

A monetary expansion began in 1975, and in the following year nontradables prices began to rise more rapidly. This was reflected in a rise in the rate of inflation,

**Figure 9.8.  Traded/Nontraded Goods Relative Price Index, 1968–88**

(August 1973 = 100)

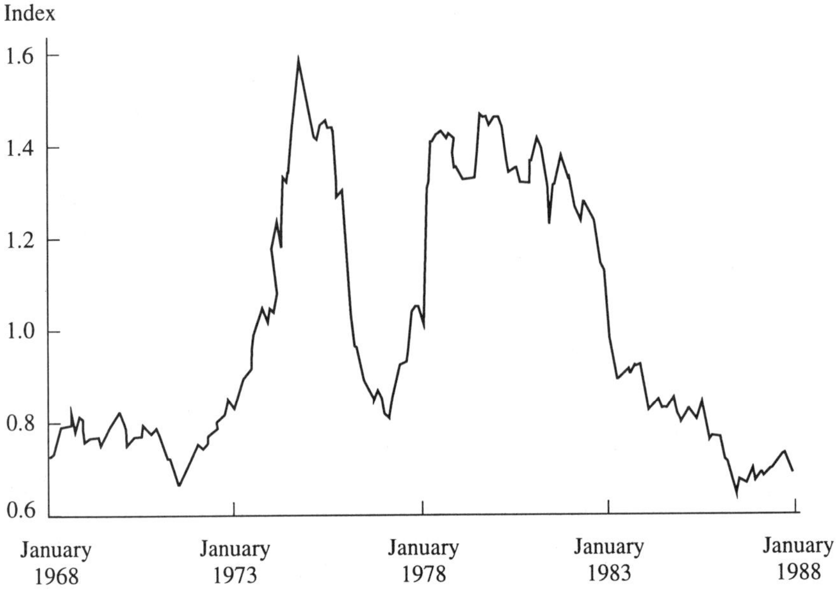

Index

*Source:* Figures 9.6 and 9.7.

from 4 to 7 percent from 1976 to 1977. A monetary, but not a fiscal contraction began in 1978, continuing to 1981. The rate of increase of nontradables prices declined accordingly. The second oil shock produced a surge in inflation, but this was concentrated in tradables prices. The recession of 1981–82 provoked a monetary expansion from 1982 to 1983. The prices of nontradables again surged, beginning at the end of 1982.

One other matter seems worth raising. As noted earlier, the 15 percent devaluation of November 1984 caught most observers by surprise. From figure 9.8, it does not seem surprising. By late 1984 the price ratio of Thailand's tradables to nontradables had fallen to levels not seen since the early 1970s, except for a brief period in 1977. "Exchange rate protection," a devaluation intended to restore the domestic competitiveness of traded goods producers, may well have played a role. Nevertheless, balance of payments considerations were undoubtedly important in the timing of the devaluation, as was the decline in the rate of inflation to only about 1 percent in 1984, which made a large devaluation at that time politically more acceptable.

## Conclusions

Since the 1950s Thailand has followed essentially a fixed exchange rate policy with respect to the U.S. dollar. The reluctance to use the exchange rate as an instrument of discretionary macroeconomic policy has coincided with a long-term commitment to low inflation. The government has been able to maintain a stable exchange rate with respect to the U.S. dollar, in combination with adequate levels of international reserves, only through monetary and fiscal discipline. The capacity to maintain a stable exchange rate has been seen as a barometer of macroeconomic stability in Thailand. Devaluations have been seen as a surrender to higher rates of inflation, and when they have occurred they have been politically costly to the government.

Significant devaluations with respect to the U.S. dollar occurred in 1981 (roughly 10 percent) and 1984 (roughly 15 percent). These devaluations occurred only when (a) the level of reserves was declining, (b) the ratio of traded goods prices to nontraded goods prices within Thailand had declined, and (c) other policy instruments, directed at these matters, had been tried and failed. These devaluations were a consequence of the external shocks of the 1970s, together with the failure of monetary policy to adjust to them, especially in the late 1970s.

After the devaluation of 1984, Thailand officially adopted what was described as a "managed float" exchange rate policy. Since then, however, the baht has remained closely linked to the U.S. dollar, despite the dollar's volatility with respect to other major currencies. Thailand's exchange rate with respect to currencies other than the U.S. dollar has thus been driven by the exchange rate policy of the United States. Wholesale prices in Thailand have closely followed those in the United States. Econometric analysis of relative exchange rate behavior since 1984 shows that the share of the U.S. dollar in the Bank of Thailand's implicit exchange rate setting basket has averaged more than two thirds and has been rising over time.

# Chapter Ten

# Conclusions: Thailand's Miracle?

A feature of traditional Thai culture, especially apparent in its classical music and dance, is its emphasis on slow, controlled lightness of movement. Sudden, jerky movements are abhorred. Thai macroeconomic policy seems to display a similar characteristic. The emphasis is on steadiness, predictability, and stability. This does not mean laissez-faire. Control is used, but it is kept to a minimum. What is more important is to avoid sudden changes of policy whenever possible. The reluctance to shift course at short notice has often been described as a weakness of Thai economic policy. In the area of macroeconomic policy, this weakness has been apparent in several instances, especially where interest rate control and exchange rate adjustment have been involved. But on the whole there can be little doubt that the cautiousness of Thai macroeconomic management has served the nation well.

The pattern of Thailand's macroeconomic responses to the major external shocks of the past two decades is of particular interest because of the way in which *discretionary* changes in government policy and the cautious and conservative economic policy stance of successive administrations of seemingly different orientation contributed to the country's stable adjustment. The central question explored in this concluding chapter is how well did Thailand really adjust to the external shocks it experienced, and how miraculous was Thailand's performance, after all?

## Pattern of Response to Shocks

For convenience, Thailand's pattern of response to the shocks of 1970–90 can be divided into three episodes:

*Episode A.* The 1972–74 temporary commodity price boom (shock 1), followed by the 1973–75 oil price increase (shock 2).

*Episode B.* The 1978–79 oil price increase (shock 3), followed by the 1980–82 interest rate increases.

*Episode C.* The 1987–90 boom in the volume of labor-intensive manufactured exports (shock 4).

The policy responses to the above episodes have reflected three primary goals: the countercyclical stabilization of national income; avoidance of inflation; and protection of Thailand's international reserves under its fixed exchange rate system. The first of these is a short-term goal, while the other two are medium-term goals; but they are potentially in conflict.

The pattern of events in response to episodes A and B was similar in several respects. Both shocks reduced income from trend, and both increased inflation in at least one year to about 20 percent. This inflation was concentrated almost exclusively in the prices of traded goods, determined internationally. There was an increase in money supply sufficient to accommodate these price rises without requiring nominal declines in nontradable prices, but not sufficient to increase nontradable prices. In response to this inflation, the authorities contracted monetary policy, and this action produced a recession that lasted for about two years. These were the years 1974–75 (shock 2) and 1980–82 (shock 3). The rate of inflation dropped quickly. The price ratio of tradables to nontradables had almost doubled since the year before the shock.

Following that recession, there was a monetary expansion that lasted for two or three years. This expansion caused the prices of nontradables to rise in relation to tradables to levels seen before the respective shocks. At that time—late 1977 to early 1978 in the case of episode A and 1983 to 1984 in episode B—a devaluation was a possibility. The trade deficit had become high and international reserves, measured in months of imports, were falling.

At this point, the pattern of events differs in an important way. A devaluation occurred in 1984 (following Episode B) but not in 1978 (the corresponding date following Episode A). Why the difference? In 1978 Thailand had a relatively new and very conservative military government that was especially averse to devaluation. Inflation was already high (8.4 percent), partly as a result of the monetary expansion promoted by this very government. Reserves were falling but still corresponded to six months of import coverage. The government decided to defend the exchange rate, even when the second OPEC oil price shock intervened (shock 3).

In 1981, when reserves fell to only 2.2 months of import coverage, there was a new, less doctrinaire government. Two devaluations occurred, amounting to roughly 10 percent. In 1984, inflation was low (1 percent) and reserves fell to only 2.4 months of import coverage. After trying other policy instruments unsuccessfully, the government chose a politically opportune moment to devalue by roughly 15 percent. This devaluation provoked a confrontation between the government and the military leadership. Although the devaluation was not rescinded, as initially demanded by the military, the government was obliged to compensate the military for the impact of the devaluation on the cost of its imported equipment.

Episode C had a more important internal component than A or B, but it was still driven primarily by external events: the migration of labor-intensive manufacturing away from the newly industrializing economies of East Asia (Korea, Taiwan (China), Hong Kong, and Singapore), in response to rising wages. Thailand's boom was fueled by unprecedented levels of foreign and domestic investment. Overheating was avoided by means of a fiscal contraction in which large fiscal surpluses offset the domestic monetary expansion that would otherwise have resulted from the conversion into baht of the large current account surpluses in the hands of the private sector. After 1990 this boom slowed, because of domestic political conflict and also the growing congestion of infrastructure facilities overburdened by the pressures resulting from the boom.

### Were Fiscal and Monetary Policy Stabilizing?

To what extent has government policy been responsible for Thailand's economic stability? This is a central question of our study and we have attempted to explore it in depth.

The ex-post fiscal deficit of the government has behaved countercyclically in the short run. This is also true of the main instrument of Thai monetary policy, the bank lending rate set by the Bank of Thailand. Both fiscal and monetary aggregates seem to have been expansionary during periods of low inflation and low growth, and contractionary in the reverse.

Two competing interpretations of these facts are possible. On one hand, it may be that fiscal and monetary and policy have been implemented in a deliberate countercyclical fashion, in line with the declared objectives of Thailand's macroeconomic managers; the observed stabilization would not have occurred in the absence of these policy decisions. On the other hand, it may be that automatic stabilizing adjustments have operated to induce the observed adjustments to the budget deficit and the observed interest rate adjustments; these automatic stabilizers, rather than deliberate policy decisions, resulted in the observed stabilization.

In the case of fiscal policy, the argument for the first interpretation—policy-induced stabilization—would stress the importance of discretionary variations in public expenditure and their role in determining the budget deficit. Less emphasis would be placed on policy-induced variations in revenue receipts, but the possibility that they could also play a role would not be excluded. In the case of monetary policy, this line of argument would emphasize impediments to capital mobility, at least in the short run. The existence of persistent differentials between Thai and foreign real interest rates for prolonged periods and their positive relation with the Bank's monetary stance lends further support to this view. It would point out that domestic lending and borrowing rates have been regulated by ceilings imposed by the Bank of Thailand and that actual borrowing and lending rates have been equal to these ceiling rates during almost all of the period under discussion. It would also point to the rhetoric of Bank of Thailand officials, emphasizing a countercyclical role in their behavior.

The argument in support of the second interpretation—automatic stabilization—would explain the observed negative correlation between the size of the budget deficit and the rate of income growth by pointing to structural features of the fiscal system driving changes in government revenue and expenditure. When incomes grow, government revenue grows, through commodity taxes and trade taxes, while expenditures may be less sensitive to income growth. The greatest emphasis would be placed upon the stabilizing behavior of government revenues, rather than expenditures. The observed negative correlation between the government budget deficit and the trade deficit would be interpreted as a reflection of this automatic stabilization because of the government's reliance on trade taxes and because the trade deficit increases with income growth.

The main argument for automatic stabilization in the case of monetary policy is that in the presence of a fixed exchange rate the domestic money supply is at least partly endogenous, depending on the degree of international capital mobility. Despite the impediments to capital mobility, in this view international capital movements are still possible to a sufficient extent to enable movements in the uncontrollable components of the monetary base to dominate the controllable ones. The behavior of the Bank of Thailand's lending rate would thus be interpreted as a response to endogenous changes in the supply of money, rather than as a reflection of exogenous (policy-determined) changes in its supply. Somewhat differently, it may be argued that the reason for the positive correlation between income growth and changes in the bank's lending rate is that when incomes grow the demand for money rises, and interest rates rise accordingly. Under this argument, the bank's rate is thus again a reflection of market forces.

In our view, the evidence supports the interpretation that a more important stabilizing force than the behavior of the government or the Bank of Thailand has been the behavior of the household sector, in particular, the responsiveness of household savings to changes in income. Beyond this, the evidence suggests that countercyclical monetary management plays a genuine role in the short run, but that automatic stabilizers, both in fiscal and monetary behavior, are a far more significant explanation for Thailand's observed short-run stability of both fiscal and monetary outcomes. In the case of monetary policy, discretionary stabilization on the part of the Bank of Thailand appears to occur, but only in the short run, and only with respect to income growth.[1] With regard to the short-run stabilization of inflation, the record of monetary policy has been surprisingly mixed.

The importance of automatic stabilizers is particularly clear in the case of fiscal outcomes. Stabilization through fiscal outcomes is more attributable to the behavior of revenues than expenditures. On the revenue side, automatic stabilizers are a consequence of the structure of the tax system, especially the reliance on business taxes and import duties and the elastic response of imports to changes in national income. On the expenditure side, they are a consequence of the government's fixed rules for planning expenditure and the consequent slow response of expenditure to changes in income. A strong negative relationship can be observed between capital spending and inflation, and this relationship can be attributed to the government's expenditure rules. When inflation occurs in the prices of capital goods, the budgeted funds may be insufficient to purchase the planned capital items, with the result that the expenditures may have to be deferred for at least a year.

The stabilizing behavior of Thailand's fiscal aggregates can be fully explained by the properties of its automatic stabilizers. Discretionary fiscal policy, as revealed by the behavior of planned adjustments to fiscal aggregates, did not contribute to fiscal stabilization; but the outcome of discretionary fiscal behavior was not significantly destabilizing either. This could well be the most significant feature that distinguishes the Thai adjustment experience from the unstable outcomes experienced in so many other developing countries.

It is important to note that although automatic stabilization through adjustments to public investment clearly contributed to macroeconomic stability in Thailand, this form of stabilization can be harmful for long-run growth. When a sustained boom in private investment and growth occurs, a contraction in public investment can produce infrastructure bottlenecks that can choke off the sustainability of the growth, as was the case in Thailand in the late 1980s and early 1990s. The sustainability of the export and investment-led boom of that period was seriously threatened by the increasingly congested public roads, ports, and telecommunications. Public investment in these infrastructure areas was contracting at the very time that the demand for them was greatest.

The structural features of the fiscal and monetary systems that contributed to automatic stabilization can always be described as the outcome of policy. But these are long-term policy outcomes, not to be confused with discretionary adjustments to policy in the short run. Indeed, the economic literature on Thailand's adjustment miracle has placed undue emphasis on the importance of short-run policy adjustment and has thereby overlooked those long-term structural features of the policy environment that have facilitated smooth adjustment. With the partial exception of monetary policy, short-term adjustments to discretionary economic policy have been unimportant sources of stabilization. Thailand's outstanding record of macroeconomic stability can be understood properly only when the long-term sources of policy stability are emphasized.

## Why the Macroeconomic Conservatism?

Aversion to inflation and a commitment to financial prudence has a long history in Thailand. The Thai kings of the nineteenth century believed financial stability was essential to keeping foreign gunboats—especially those of the French and British—from forcing colonial rule onto their people. Until 1950, foreign financial advisers—always British, and usually from the Bank of England—were employed to assist the kings in this respect. The policy recommendations of the financial advisers were highly conservative and were influential.

Thailand's only experience of sustained high inflation occurred during and immediately after World War II. This experience coincided with the foundation of the Bank of Thailand, which was assigned the task of controlling inflation and was granted considerable independence from political interference. Interestingly, this independence has subsequently continued to be respected, in spite of frequent turmoil in the political sphere. With minor exceptions, the bank has been allowed to pursue its inflation-control mandate single-mindedly.

At the first sign of high inflation, the Thai monetary authorities endeavored to contract monetary policy and sustained this monetary stance until inflation fell below 6 percent. The monetary contractions of 1973–74, 1979–80, and 1980–82 are cases in point. These contractions were not especially prolonged because inflation responded quickly. It must be emphasized that the past record of Thailand's conservative monetary management has been such that its monetary policy remains highly credible. When the Bank of Thailand starts raising its lending rate, inflationary expectations start to abate.

Exchange rate policy has largely been driven by attitudes to inflation. Devaluations have been avoided because they are seen as capitulations to inflation. They have occurred only when the following conditions have *all* been met: the effective exchange rate has suddenly appreciated as a result of currency realignments among Thailand's trading partners; the price ratio of tradables versus nontradables has been falling; the level of reserves, measured in months of import coverage, has been declining for several quarters; the current level of reserves is inadequate to defend the existing exchange rate; the current rate of domestic inflation is low; and other measures to correct the trade imbalance have already been tried (including tariff increases, credit controls, and domestic monetary contraction).

Why has the Bank of Thailand been so successful in pursing its sound money policies? Individuals are part of the story. Two early governors of the Bank— Prince Wiwattanachai Chaiyan (Prince Wiwat) and Puey Ungphakorn—each played a crucial role in developing the bank's traditions and professionalism. But why were successive governments willing to grant them the political independence they needed to accomplish their anti-inflation mandate?

Thailand's policy formation process has been dominated by its civil servants. This is especially true of the Bank of Thailand. The rapid inflation of the 1940s had devastating effects on the real incomes of Thailand's civil servants, causing genuine hardship and increased corruption. These civil servants were the very group who were subsequently to administer Thailand's financial policies and dominate the formation of policy as well. But the economic conservatism of the civil servants is only the first component of what must be explained. The greater puzzle is why successive governments consistently empowered the civil service to set the constraints on economic policy and not merely to implement them.

Technocrats have no inherent political authority. If they have power, it is only because politicians grant it to them. Recent developments in political science offer a potential explanation as to why they do so. It centers on a game-theoretic analysis known as the politician's dilemma.[2] Its basic assumption is that politicians are motivated primarily by the desire to remain in office. There is constant pressure on them to approve the spending of public money in ways that benefit this or that special interest group. The self-interest of the politicians, it is argued, tends to favor giving in to these pressures. But when all politicians behave in this way, the accumulated economic effect will be large budgetary deficits, and the problems of financing these deficits may threaten the survival of the regime as a whole.

It is therefore in the interests of the politicians to find a way to tie their own hands so as to restrain them from this ultimately self-defeating form of behavior. If this analysis is valid, two manifestations of this mechanism can be identified in Thailand: the empowerment of technocrats and legislated fiscal rules.

EMPOWERMENT OF TECHNOCRATS. By investing technocrats with the power to say "no" to politicians, a state can institutionalize long-term fiscal and monetary restraint, despite the short-term incentive for politicians to act otherwise. The power of the Bank of Thailand to decline to finance government budgetary deficits by purchasing government bonds, thereby expanding the money supply and promoting inflation, is an example; the power of the Bureau of the Budget to resist expenditures demanded by politicians, or at least to delay them, is another.

LEGISLATED FISCAL RULES. Laws introduced during the Sarit government of 1958–63 constrained subsequent government behavior regarding such matters as the magnitudes of planned deficits in relation to planned revenues and the magnitudes of the government's foreign borrowing, in any one year.[3] These laws were amended somewhat by subsequent governments, but the point is that they were not ignored or repealed, even though governments changed frequently, sometimes through violence, and sometimes replaced the constitution at the same time. Now and then these fixed rules have acted as binding constraints on government policy. They could have been changed radically or repealed, but it seems that once laws of this kind existed and were accepted, the political cost of disposing of them was prohibitive. Their existence and wide acceptance, especially within the bureaucracy, generated a political inertia that helped constrain subsequent fiscal behavior for at least three decades.

The theory of the politician's dilemma is an abstract notion that may provide an explanation for the otherwise puzzling outcomes of the Thai experience. But if it is basically correct, then its manifestation in a particular setting will reflect the circumstances of the time, and particular individuals may play an important role. The theory does not provide a convincing account of the mechanism by which politician-constraining institutions actually come into existence in one particular environment and not in another, nor could a general theory of this kind be expected to do so. What it may provide is an underlying rationale for the tendency for *some* politicians voluntarily to introduce institutional constraints on their own behavior and then for subsequent politicians to permit the continued existence of these constraints.

## How Well Has Thailand Adjusted?

The terms-of-trade changes represented by negative external shocks reduced Thai national income in the long term. How did Thailand adjust? Before 1985, Thailand's adjustment had been unspectacular. The reasons for this judgement are, first, that the income effects of the adverse terms-of-trade movement were financed entirely by increased external borrowing and by depletion of international reserves; second, that the ratio of tradables prices to nontradables, which should have risen if Thailand was to have restructured its economy in response to the price shocks, had not done so. By 1985 this price ratio had returned to its level *before* the first oil shock.

Thailand had avoided the short-run crises that so many other oil-importing countries had suffered. Macroeconomic stability had been preserved. Despite the apparent success of short-term management, the fact remains that the long-term adjustment of the Thai economy necessitated by the change in its external environment had been deferred. The increased cost of Thailand's petroleum imports was matched by an increase in external debt and a depletion of reserves. In this respect, the record of post-1970 economic management in Thailand is significantly different from the ultracautious pre-1970 emphasis on building the country's reserves and avoiding indebtedness. Was the change a mistake? The answer depends on how well the external savings absorbed by Thailand were used. The result could have been better, but on the whole the resources were used productively. The resulting economic growth led to a sustained improvement in economic welfare for the vast mass of the population.

Our account of the Thai experience is in a sense negative. When compared with other developing countries, many severely destabilized by exogenous shocks similar to those experienced by Thailand, the Thai case resembles Sherlock Holmes's "dog that did not bark." The dog did not bark because the intruder was not really such an inherent threat. It was possible to adjust to international price shocks of the 1970s and 1980s without drama. The Thai experience proves that. It was also possible to allow these events to cause macroeconomic havoc, resulting in widespread human suffering. The experience of Thailand's near-neighbor, the Philippines, which has a similar economic structure and was hit by almost identical shocks, proves that.

In one important respect, Thailand was fortunate. Efforts at policy-led adjustment were implemented in the early 1980s, but by the middle of the decade these efforts had produced little apparent effect. If the externally-driven export and investment boom of the late 1980s had not occurred, Thailand would have faced a difficult adjustment from the mid-1980s onward. The events that led to Thailand's boom in the late 1980s produced simultaneous booms in Indonesia, Malaysia, and the southeastern corner of China. This fact shows the importance of external forces in producing the boom. But there were no such booms in the Philippines or Sri Lanka. Investors—domestic and foreign—were not willing to risk their capital in such unstable and unpromising environments. Thus internal factors also played a role.

It would be wrong, however, to attribute Thailand's macroeconomic success simply to fortuitous circumstances. The same good fortune that assisted Thailand in the late 1980s was available to others as well. There is more to be extracted from the Thai experience than the importance of good luck. The principal lesson here is that giving priority to long-term macroeconomic stability promotes economic growth. It does so because macroeconomic stability is a necessary condition for attracting the domestic and foreign investment needed to exploit economic opportunity. When governments postpone action on inflation control, the cost of controlling it will eventually be higher, not least because high inflation means that the intellectual resources of the government must then constantly be devoted to thinking of ways to contain it. The Thai experience also illustrates the value of relying principally on market solutions to resolve problems of resource allocation, supplemented by cautious public investment in productive infrastructure and human capital.

A miracle is something that is unusual, beneficial, and inexplicable. Thailand's experience of stable growth has been miraculous in the first two senses, but not the third. There was nothing particularly brilliant, farsighted, or mysterious about the way Thailand adjusted to its changing environment: it was nothing that other developing nations could not emulate or even improve upon if they chose to do so.

# Notes

## Chapter Two

1. An important example has been the traditional role of senior military figures in controlling Thailand's public enterprises. Critics have attributed much of the corruption and inefficiency associated with these organizations to military domination of their controlling Boards.
2. The following account is based primarily on Bank of Thailand (1962) and Ingram (1971).
3. Prince Wiwattanachai Chaiyan, popularly known as Prince Wiwat, was born in 1899, the son of Prince Mahisra Raj Haruetai. Prince Wiwat was a graduate of Cambridge University and Ecole des Sciences Politique in Paris. In 1938 he was appointed the first adviser to the minister of finance and in 1940 he became the director of the National Banking Bureau.
4. This recommendation was in his August 1944 report on postwar monetary reconstruction, as contained in *Wiwatchaiyanusorn* (Wiwat memorial) (see Bank of Thailand 1961).
5. This appeared in his lecture notes published in *Thanakhan Haeng Prathet Thai (Bank of Thailand)*, a memorial volume issued at the cremation of Gen, Phao Bariphanyutthakit (Bank of Thailand 1970).

## Chapter Four

1. The only exception to this pattern was the change in the structure of effective protection between 1984 and 1987, which showed a weak positive relationship to changes in export performance.
2. Note that the revenues of the public enterprises include the total proceeds from their sale of goods and services, which somewhat distorts the comparison with the rest of the public sector.

## Chapter Five

1. In this autoregressive model, the usual $DW$ statistic has reduced power and is biased toward 2. The relevant test for autocorrelation is Durbin's $h$-statistic. Under the null hypothesis of no autocorrelation, $h$ is asymptotically normal with 0 mean and unit variance. Our estimate of Durbin's $h$-statistic is 0.74, which is less than the critical value of 2.756 (at the 99 percent significance level) and indicates the absence of significant autocorrelation.

## Chapter Six

1.    This taxonomy has benefited greatly from discussions with W. M. Corden.

## Chapter Seven

1.    Thailand's fiscal year begins on October 1 and ends on September 30 of the following calendar year. We shall subsequently write, for example, fiscal 1990 to mean the fiscal year 1989–90, ending on September 30 1990.
2.    By "inflation" we mean, as elsewhere in this book, the rate of change of the consumer price index. The mechanism by which inflation retards expenditure growth is discussed in a subsequent section of this chapter.
3.    This interpretation differs from that of Robinson and others (1991: 16). This important study mentions automatic stabilizers in passing but emphasizes what is assumed, without supporting evidence, to be the stabilizing role of discretionary fiscal policy.
4.    This interpretation is further supported by the evidence on the behavior of the current account, discussed above.
5.    An estimate of zero would have meant that real expenditures remained constant as the price level rose and thus that nominal expenditures rose with the price level; an estimate of $-1.0$ would indicate that nominal expenditures remain exactly constant as the price level increases.
6.    On the basis of data for 1970–89, the correlation coefficient between the private investment/GDP ratio and the public investment/GDP ratio was $-0.66$.
7.    If $(E - R) = 0.2E$, then $E = 1.25R$ and $(E - R)/R = 0.25$.

## Chapter Eight

1.    Only ten countries reported lower average rates of inflation than Thailand over the twenty-five years from 1965 to 1990: Ethiopia, Chad, Burundi, Honduras, Panama, Hungary, Singapore, Germany, Canada, and Switzerland (World Bank 1992: table 1).
2.    Relaxed in 1990 to fifteen days, following the acceptance by Thailand of IMF article XIII.
3.    The negative effect of the premium forware exchange rate on short-term capital flows will be confirmed by regression (8.13).
4.    The latter variables were computed from the domestic consumer price index and the world import price index from IMF, *International Financial Statistics*, various issues.
5.    It was only in 1986 that the annual current account was in surplus.
6.    When market capitalization grew, portfolio investment also grew as a proportion of the monetary base and became more volatile.
7.    Following the discussion in chapter 7, it is essential to distinguish between fiscal *outcomes*, as referred to here, and fiscal *intentions*. As already demonstrated, they are not necessarily the same.
8.    See Naris (1993) for a discussion of this issue as it relates to the collusive determination of interest rates within the oligopolistic structure of Thailand's commercial banking sector, combined with the major banks' difficulty in agreeing on interest rate reductions.

# Chapter Nine

1. The data for the regression were obtained from the International Monetary Fund, *International Financial Statistics*, various issues. The series used is denoted "aa" and is the ratio of the end-of-period national currency value of the special drawing right (SDR).

# Chapter Ten

1. To a lesser extent, the Ministry of Finance also plays a role in monetary stabilization, through adjustments to the withholding tax on foreign borrowing.
2. The name derives from the famous game-theoretic analysis known as the prisoner's dilemma. See Williamson (1994).
3. Examples include the 1959 Budgetary Law, which limited any excess of planned spending over planned revenue to no more than 25 percent of the planned revenue; and the 1960 External Public Debt Law, which set a 5 percent ceiling on the government's debt service ratio and limited the size of foreign debt service to less than 13 percent of the level of exports.

# Bibliography

Aghevli, Bijan B., and S. Mohsin Khan. 1978. "Government Deficit and Inflationary Process in Developing Counties." *IMF Staff Papers* 25 (September): 383–416.

Aliber, Robert Z. 1973. "The Interest Rate Parity Theorem: A Reinterpretation." *Journal of Political Economy* 81 (November/December): 1451–59.

Ammar Siamwalla. 1975. "Stability, Growth and Distribution in the Thai Economy." In Puey Ungphakorn and others, eds., *Finance, Trade and Economic Development in Thailand: Essays in Honour of Khunying Suparb Yossundra.* Bangkok: Sompong Press.

———. 1978. "Farmers and Middlemen: Aspects of Agricultural Marketing in Thailand." *Economic Bulletin for Asia and Pacific* 29(1):38–50.

Ammar Siamwalla, and Prayong Nettayarak. 1990. "Estimating the Cost of Subsidies for Agricultural Credit." Thailand Development Research Institute, Bangkok. Processed.

Ammar Siamwalla, and Suthad Setboonsarng. 1989. *Trade, Exchange Rate and Agricultural Pricing Policies in Thailand: Comparative Studies on the Agricultural Pricing Policy.* World Bank, Washington, D.C.

Ammar Siamwalla, Suthad Sethboonsarng, and Direk Patamasiriwat. 1993. "Agriculture." In Peter G. Warr, ed., *The Thai Economy in Transition.* Cambridge: Cambridge University Press.

Amnuey Saengnoree. 1984. *Comparative Analysis of Market Structure, Economies of Scale and Profit Behavior of Thai Commercial Banks and Finance and Security Companies.* Bangkok: King Mongkut Institute of Technology. (In Thai.)

Anat Arbhabhirama, Dhira Phantumvanit, J. Elkington, and Phaitoon Ingkasuwan, eds. 1988. *Thailand Natural Resources Profile.* Bangkok: Thailand Development Research Institute.

Argy, Victor. 1971. "Monetary Policy and Internal and External Balance." *IMF Staff Papers* 18 (November): 508–27.

Armatonoff, G. L. 1965. *State Owned Enterprises of Thailand.* Bangkok: Agency for International Development.

Asjana Watananukij. 1985. "Foreign Debt of Public Enterprises." Paper presented at the seminar Foreign Debt Crisis of the Thai Government, February 11–12, Faculty of Economics, Thammasat University, Bangkok. (In Thai.)

Bandid Nijathaworn, and Madee Weerakitpanich. 1987. "Economic Fluctuations and Stability of the Commercial Banking System." Symposium paper on the stability of financial institutions, Thammasat University, Bangkok. (In Thai.)

Bank of Thailand. 1961. *Viwatchaiyanusorn (Wiwat Memorial)*. Bangkok: Sivaporn. (In Thai.)

———. 1962. *Twentieth Anniversary of the Establishment of the Bank of Thailand, 10 December 1962*. Bangkok. (In Thai).

———. 1970. *Thanakhan haeng Prathet Thai (Bank of Thailand)*. Memorial volume issued at the cremation of Gen. Phao Bariphanyutthakit. Bangkok: Sivaporn. (In Thai.)

———. 1986. *Financial Institutions in Thailand*. Bangkok.

———. 1992. *50 Years of the Bank of Thailand, 1942–1992*. Bangkok.

———. Various issues. *Monthly Bulletin*. Bangkok.

———. Various issues. *Monthly Economic Report*. Bangkok. (In Thai.)

———. Various issues. *Quarterly Bulletin*. Bangkok.

Barker, Randolph, Robert W. Herdt, and Beth Rose. 1985. *The Rice Economy of Asia*. Washington D.C.: Resources for the Future.

Beltz, P. A., and B. P. McCormack. 1982. "The Origins of the Banking Industry in Thailand." *Thai-American Business* 14(6): 7–11.

Bertrand, Trent J., and Lyn Squire. 1980. "The Relevance of the Dual Economy Model: A Case Study of Thailand." *Oxford Economic Papers* 32(3): 480–511.

Bhagwati, Jagdish. 1984a. "Splintering and Disembodiment of Services and Developing Nations." *The World Economy* 7(2): 133–44.

———. 1984b. "Why Are Services Cheaper in the Poor Countries?" *Economic Journal* 94 (June): 279–84.

———. 1989. *Protectionism*. Cambridge, Mass: MIT Press,

Bhanupong Nidhiprabha. 1993. "Monetary Policy." In Peter G. Warr, ed., *The Thai Economy in Transition*. Cambridge: Cambridge University Press.

Bhanupong Nidhiprabha and Atchana Wattananukit. 1987. "Asset Holding Behavior and the Stability of Thai Commercial Banks." Paper presented at the symposium The Stability of Financial Institutions, Thammasat University, Bangkok. (In Thai.)

Blinder, A. S., and R. M. Solow. 1974. "Analytical Foundations of Fiscal Policy." *Economics of Public Finance*. Washington, D.C.: Brookings Institution.

Block, Peter, Sirilaksana Chutikul, and Nipon Poapongsakorn. 1986. "Public Sector Employment in Thailand: Civil Service and State Enterprises." Background Paper for World Bank Economic Report on Thailand. Washington, D.C.

Buiter, W. H. 1977. "Crowding Out and the Effectiveness of Fiscal Policy." *Journal of Public Economics* 7(3): 309–28.

———. 1983. "Measurement of Public Sector Deficit and Its Implications for Policy Evaluation and Design." *IMF Staff Papers* 30(2): 306–49.

Caldwell, J. C. 1967. "The Demographic Structure." In T. H. Silcock, ed., *Thailand: Social and Economic Studies in Development*. Canberra: Australian

National University Press.

Central Statistical Office. 1935. *Statistical Yearbook of Siam 1933–35.* Bangkok.

Chaipat Sahasakul. 1993. "Fiscal Policy." In Peter G. Warr, ed., *The Thai Econo-my in Transition.* Cambridge: Cambridge University Press.

————. 1987. *Features of the Tax System in Thailand.* Bangkok: Thailand Devel-opment Research Institute.

Chaipat Sahasakul, Thongpakda Nattapong, and Kraisoraphong Keokam. 1989. *Lessons from the World Bank's Experience of Structural Adjustment Loans (SALs): A Case Study of Thailand.* Bangkok: Thailand Development Research Institute.

Chaiyawat Wibulswasdi. 1984. "Formulation and Implementation of Monetary Policy: A Study of Thailand Monetary Experience during 1983–1984." Paper for the 15th SEANZA Central Banking Course, Kathmandu, Nepal.

Chaiyong Pativintranond. 1984. "Lending Behavior of Commercial Banks in Thailand." Master's thesis, Thammasat University, Bangkok. (In Thai.)

Chalongphob Sussangkarn. 1993. "Labour Markets." In Peter G. Warr, ed., *The Thai Economy in Transition.* Cambridge: Cambridge University Press.

Chand, S. K. 1973. "Summary Measures of Fiscal Influence." *IMF Staff Papers* 20(3): 405–47.

Chelliah, R. J. 1973. "Significance of Alternative Concepts of Budget Deficit." *IMF Staff Papers* 20(3): 741–77.

Chesada Loohawenchit. n.d. "State Enterprises and Their Impact on the Govern-ment Budget." Thammasat University, Bangkok. (In Thai.) Processed.

————. 1984. "Public Enterprises in the Thai Economy." Paper presented at the seminar Thai Public Enterprises: Past, Present, and Future, January 26–27, Bangkok. (In Thai.)

Chirmsak Pinthong. 1977. "A Price Analysis of the Thai Rice Marketing System." Ph.D. diss., Stanford University.

————. 1984. "Distribution of Benefit of Government Rice Procurement Policy in 1982/1983." *Thammasat University Journal* 13(2): 166–87. (In Thai.).

Corden, W. M. 1967. "The Exchange Rate System and the Taxation of Trade." In T. H. Silcock, ed., *Thailand: Social and Economic Studies in Development.* Canberra, Australian National University Press.

————. 1987. "Relevance for Developing Countries of Recent Developments in Macroeconomic Theory." *World Bank Research Observer* 2(2): 171–88.

Corden, W. M., and H. V. Richter. 1967. "Trade and the Balance of Payments." In T. H. Silcock, ed., *Thailand: Social and Economic Studies in Development.* Canberra: Australian National University Press.

Cumby, Robert E., and Maurice Obstfeld. 1984. "International Interest Rate and Price Level Linkages Under Flexible Exchange Rates: A Review of Recent Ev-idence." In John F. Bilson and Richard C. Marston, eds., *Exchange Rate The-ory and Practice.* Chicago: University of Chicago Press.

Direk Patamasiriwat, and Suewattana Sakeddao. 1990. "Sources of Growth of Ag-ricultural Production 1965–1985: Analysis Based on TDRI Model." *Warasarn Settasat Thammasat* 8(1): 43–69. (In Thai.)

Direk Patamasiriwat, and Supaporn Prompongsri. 1987. "Financial Centralization and the Setting of Economic Policies." Paper presented at the symposium The Stability of Financial Institutions, Thammasat University, Bangkok. (In Thai.)

Direk Patmasiriwat, and Pairoj Benjamanon. 1982. "Concentration and Mobility of Commercial Banking System in Thailand." *Journal of National Institute of Development Administration* 22(2): 278–304. (In Thai.)

Dooley, M. P., and Peter Isard. 1980. "Capital Controls, Political Risk, and Deviations From Interest Rate Parity." *Journal of Political Economy* 88: 370–84.

Dornbusch, Rudiger, and Stanley Fischer. 1992. *Macroeconomics*. New York: McGraw-Hill.

Driscoll, Michael J., and Asok K. Lahiri. 1983. "Income Velocity of Money in Agricultural Developing Economies." *Review of Economics and Statistics* 65(3): 393–401.

Emery, R. F. 1970. *The Financial Institutions of Southeast Asia: A Country-by-Country Study*. New York: Praeger.

Enrique, R. S., and others. 1985. "Thailand: Poverty Review." World Bank, East Asian and Pacific Division, Washington, D.C. Processed.

Feder, Gerschon, Tongroj Onchan, Yongyuth Chalamwong, and Chira Hongladarom. 1988. *Land Policies and Farm Productivity in Thailand*. Baltimore, Md.: Johns Hopkins University Press.

Feldstein, Martin. 1983. "Domestic Savings and International Capital Movements in the Long Run and the Short Run." *European Economic Review* 21(March): 129–51.

Feldstein, Martin, and Charles Horioka. 1980. "Domestic Saving and International Capital Flows." *Economic Journal* 90: 314–29.

Frankel, Jacob A., and Michael L. Mussa. 1981. "Monetary and Fiscal Policies in an Open Economy." *American Economic Review* 71(May): 253–58.

Friedman, Milton. 1968. "The Role of Monetary Policy." *American Economic Review* 58(1): 1–17.

Fuller, T. D., Prathet Kamnuansilpa, P. Lightfoot, and Samakhom Rathanamongkolmas. 1983. *Migration and Development in Thailand*. Bangkok: Social Science Association of Thailand.

Goldfeld, Stephen M., and Lester V. Chandler. 1986. *The Economics of Money and Banking*. New York: Harper and Row.

Herring R. H., and R. M. Marston. 1977. *National Monetary Policies and International Financial Markets*. Amsterdam: North-Holland.

Hewison, Kevin. 1989. *Bankers and Bureaucrats: Capital and the Role of the State in Thailand*. Yale Center for International and Area Studies, Monograph Series 34. New Haven, Conn.: Yale University.

Industrial Management Corporation. 1984. *A Study of Fiscal Implications of Investment Incentives and Promotion Efficiency*. Bangkok.

————.1985. *Industrial Restructuring Study for the NESDB*. Bangkok.

Ingram, James C. 1971. *Economic Change in Thailand: 1850–1970*. Stanford, Calif.: Stanford University Press.

International Labour Office, Asian Regional Team for Employment Promotion. 1984. *Employment Issues in Thailand's Sixth Plan.* Bangkok.

International Monetary Fund (IMF). Various years. *International Financial Statistics.* Washington, D.C.

Inthapanya Wutdhithep, and Jumlong Atikul. 1988. "Urban Self-Employment in Bangkok." A Report for the National Economic and Social Development Board of Thailand, New Delhi, India.

Jamison, D. T., and L. J. Lau. 1982. *Farmer Education and Farm Efficiency.* Baltimore, Md.: Johns Hopkins University Press.

Jones, L. P. 1975. *Public Enterprise and Economic Development: The Korean Case.* Seoul: Korean Development Institute.

———. ed. 1982. *Public Enterprise in Less Developed Countries.* Cambridge: Cambridge University Press.

Juanjai Ajanant, Supote Chunanuntatham, and Sorrayuth Meenaphant. 1986. *Trade and Industrialization of Thailand.* Bangkok: Social Science Association of Thailand.

Kosit Panpiemras, and Somchai Krusuansombat. 1985. "Seasonal Migration and Employment in Thailand." In T. Panayotou, ed., *Food Policy Analysis in Thailand.* Bangkok: Agricultural Development Council.

Kouri, Penti. 1975. "The Hypothesis of Offsetting Capital Flows: A Case Study of Germany." *Journal of Monetary Economics* 1: 21–39.

Kouri, Penti, and Michael Porter. 1974. "International Capital Flows: A Portfolio Equilibrium." *Journal of Political Economy* 82(May/June): 443–67.

Kraiyudht Dhiratayakinant. 1987. "Privatization: An Analysis of the Concept and Its Implementation in Thailand." Bangkok: Thailand Development Research Institute.

———. 1989. "Privatization of Public Enterprises: The Case of Thailand." A research report commissioned by Asian and Pacific Development Centre, Kuala Lumpur.

———. 1993. "Public Enterprises." In Peter G. Warr, ed., *The Thai Economy in Transition.* Cambridge: Cambridge University Press.

Krueger, Anne O., Maurice Schiff, and Alberto Valdés. 1988. "Agricultural Incentives in Developing Countries: Measuring the Effect of Sectoral and Economywide Policies." *World Bank Economic Review* 2(3): 255–71.

Lee, S. Y., and Y. T. Jao. 1982. *Financial Structures and Monetary Policies in Southeast Asia.* Hong Kong: Macmillan.

Leff, Nathaniel, and Kazuo Sato. 1980. "Macroeconomic Adjustment in Developing Countries: Instability, Short-Run Growth and External Dependency." *Review of Economics and Statistics* 62(2): 170–79.

Llewellyn, David T. 1980. *International Financial Integration.* London: Macmillan.

Mabry, Bevars D. 1984. "The Development of Labor Institutions in Thailand." Southeast Asia Program, Drake Paper 112. Cornell University, Ithaca, N.Y.

Martin, Will, and Peter G. Warr. 1990. "Explaining Agriculture's Declining Share of Thai National Income." *Chulalongkorn Journal of Economics* 2 (August): 178–224. (In Thai.)

———. 1994. "The Declining Economic Importance of Agriculture: A Supply Side Analysis for Thailand." *Agricultural Economics* 11 (November): 219–35.

Mathana Phananiramai, and Andrew Mason. 1988. "Enrollment and Educational Cost in Thailand." Paper for the seminar Demographic and Economic Forecast for Thailand, July 2–3, Bangkok.

Mathana Phananiramai, and Aphichart Chamrasrithirong. 1984. "Poverty in the Northeast: A Study of Low-Income Households in the Northeastern Region of Thailand." A Research Report Submitted to the Council for Asian Manpower Studies, Manila.

Medhi Krongkaew. 1993. "Poverty and Income Distribution." In Peter G. Warr, ed., *The Thai Economy in Transition.* Cambridge: Cambridge University Press.

Medhi Krongkaew, and Chintana Chernsiri. 1975. "The Determination of the Poverty Level in Thailand." *Thammasat University Journal* 5(1): 48–68. (In Thai.)

MedhiKrongkaew, and others. 1988. *Financing Public Sector Development Expenditure in Selected Countries: Thailand.* Asian Development Bank, Manila.

Medhi Krongkaew, Pranee Tinakorn, and Suphat Suphachalasai. 1991. "Priority Issue and Policy Measure to Alleviate Rural Poverty: The Case of Thailand." Economic Development Resources Center, Asian Development Bank, Manila.

Meltzer, Allan H. 1987. "Limits of Short-Run Stabilization Policy." *Economic Inquiry* 42(January): 1–14.

Mishkin, F. S. 1976. "Illiquidity, Consumer Durable Expenditure, and Monetary Policy." *American Economic Review* 66(4): 642–54.

———. 1984. "Are Real Interest Rates Equal Across Countries? An Investigation of International Parity Conditions." *Journal of Finance* 39: 1345–58.

Modigliani, Franco. 1977. "The Monetarist Controversy or, Should We Forsake Stabilization Policies?" *American Economic Review* 67(2): 1–19.

Moerman, Michael. 1968. *Agricultural Change and Peasant Choice in a Thai Village.* Berkeley, Calif.: University of California Press.

Monadjemi, M. 1990. "Testing the Degree of International Capital Mobility." *Australian Economic Papers* (June) 30–39.

Muangchai Tajaroensuk. 1975. "Educational Planning in Thailand: Status and Organization." *Bulletin of the UNESCO Regional Office for Education in Asia* 16: 128–40.

Mundell, Robert A. 1962. "The Appropriate Use of Monetary and Fiscal Policy for Internal and External Stability." *IMF Staff Papers* 9: 70–79.

Muscat, Robert. 1966. *Development Strategy in Thailand.* New York: Praeger.

Myers, C. N. 1986. "Quality of Human Resources in Human Resources Management." Paper prepared for TDRI Year-End Conference, December, Bangkok.

Myers, C. N., and Chalongphob Sussangkarn. 1989. "Economic Transformation and Flexibility of the Education System." Paper prepared for Human Resource

Problems and Policies, February 24–25, Hua-Hin.

Nalinee Homasawin. 1984. "A Regional Analysis of Financial Structure in Thailand: Growth and Distribution." Master's thesis, Thammasat University.

Naris Chaiyasoot. 1993. "Commercial Banking." In Peter G. Warr, ed., *The Thai Economy in Transition*. Cambridge: Cambridge University Press.

Naris Chaiyasoot, Varakorn Samakoses, and Cheunruthai Pornpatrakul. 1987. "Structure and Problems of Financial Institutions in the Thai Economy." Paper presented at the symposium The Stability of Financial Institutions, Thammasat University, Bangkok. (In Thai.)

Narongchai Akrasanee. 1973. "The Manufacturing Sector in Thailand: A Study of Growth, Import Substitution, and Effective Protection, 1960–1969." Ph.D. dissertation, Johns Hopkins University.

————. 1977. "The Structure of Effective Protection in Thailand: A Study of Industrial and Trade Policies in the Early 1970s." Report prepared for the Ministry of Finance, the National Economic and Social Development Board of the Government of Thailand, and the International Bank for Reconstruction and Development, Washington, D.C.

————. 1983. *Rural Off-farm Employment in Thailand: Summary and Synthesis of the Rural Off-farm Assessment Project*. Bangkok: Industrial Management Consultants.

Nimit Nontapanthawat. 1976. "Foreign Borrowing of Commercial Banks in Thailand." In Narongchai Akrasenee and Rangsan Thanapornpun, eds., *Rak Muang Thai*. Bangkok: Thailand Social Science Association. (In Thai.)

Obstfeld, Maurice. 1986. "Capital Mobility in the World Economy: Theory and Measurement." Carnegie-Rochester Conference Series on Public Policy. *Journal of Monetary Economics* Suppl. Amsterdam: North-Holland.

Oey Meesook. 1979. *Income, Consumption and Poverty in Thailand, 1962/63 to 1975/76*. World Bank Staff Working Paper 364. Washington D.C.

Otani, Ichiro, and Siddharth Tiwari. 1981. "Capital Controls and Interest Rate Parity: The Japanese Experience, 1978–91." *IMF Staff Papers* 28 (December): 793–816.

Pairote Wongwuttiwat. 1975. "The Structure of Differential Incentives in the Manufacturing Sector: A Study of Thailand's Experience during 1945–1974." Master's thesis, Thammasat University.

Paisan Chaimonkol. 1976. *Public Enterprises*. Bangkok: Thai Watana Panich. (In Thai.)

Paitoon Wiboonchutikula, Rachain Chintayarangsan, and Nattapong Thongpakde. 1989. "Trade in Manufactured Goods and Mineral Products." The 1989 TDRI Year-End Conference. Thailand Development Research Institute, Bangkok.

Pannee Bualek. 1986. *An Analysis of Thai Commercial Bank Capitalists: B.E. 2475–2516*. Bangkok: Chulalongkorn University. (In Thai.)

Pasuk Phongpaichit. 1980. *Economic and Social Transformation of Thailand 1957–1976*. Bangkok: Chulalongkorn University Social Science Research Institute.

————. 1982. *From Peasant Girls to Bangkok Masseuses*. Geneva: International Labour Office.

Pasuk Pongpaichit, and Samart Chiasakul. 1993. "Services." In Peter G. Warr, ed., *The Thai Economy in Transition*. Cambridge: Cambridge University Press.

Poonsin Ingavala. 1989. "Privatization in Thailand: Slow Progress Amidst Much Opposition." *Asean Economic Bulletin*, March.

Praipol Koomsup. 1993. "Energy Policy." In Peter G. Warr, ed., *The Thai Economy in Transition*. Cambridge: Cambridge University Press.

Prateep Sondysuvan, ed. 1975. *Finance, Trade and Economic Development in Thailand*. Bangkok: Sompong Press.

Prayuth Thongtheppairot. 1972. "Return on Investment in Thai Bank." *Business in Thailand* 3(8):19–20.

Reynolds, Clark. 1978. "Why Mexico's Stabilizing Development Was Actually Destabilizing (with Some Implications for the Future)." *World Development* 6(7/8): 1005–18.

Riggs, F. W. 1966. *Thailand: The Modernization of a Bureaucratic Policy*. Honolulu: East-West Center Press.

Rizwanul, Iwan. 1984. "Poverty, Income Distribution and Growth in Rural Thailand." In A. R. Khan and E. Lee, eds., *Poverty in Rural Asia*. Bangkok: International Labour Office, Asian Regional Team for Employment Promotion.

Robinson, David, Yangho Byeon, and Ranjit Teja. 1991. "Thailand: Adjusting to Success, Current Policy Issues." Occasional Paper 85. International Monetary Fund, Washington, D.C.

Rozental, A. A. 1970. *Finance and Development in Thailand*. New York: Praeger.

Rungsan Thanapornan. 1985. *Tax Buoyancy and Tax Elasticity in Thailand: The State of Knowledge*. Bangkok: Thammasat University, Faculty of Economics. (In Thai.)

Sataporn Jinachitra. 1987. "Efficiency, Stability, Supervision of the Financial Institutions." In Nopporn Ruengsakul and others, eds., *Money and Banking and Implementation of National Economic Policies*. Bangkok: Chulalongkorn University Press. (In Thai.)

Schlossstein, Steven. 1991. *Asia's New Little Dragons: The Dynamic Emergence of Indonesia, Thailand, and Malaysia*. Chicago, Ill.: Contemporary Books.

Silcock, T. H. 1967. "Promotion of Industry and the Planning Process." In T. H. Silcock, ed., *Thailand: Social and Economic Studies in Development*. Canberra: Australian National University Press.

————. ed. 1967. *Thailand: Social and Economic Studies in Development*. Canberra: Australian National University Press.

————. 1970. *The Economic Development of Thai Agriculture*. Canberra: Australian National University Press.

Sirilaksana Chutikul-Khoman. 1988. "The Burden of Expenditure on Higher Education in Thailand and the Role of the Private Sector." In Nipon Poapongsakorn and Rangson Thanapornpun, eds., *The Economy: On the Path of Peace and Social Justice*. Bangkok: Thammasat University Press. (In Thai.)

————. 1993. "Education Policy." In Peter G. Warr, ed., *The Thai Economy in Transition*. Cambridge: Cambridge University Press.

Skully, M. T. 1984. *Financial Institutions and Markets in Southeast Asia.* London: Macmillan.

Somchai Jitsuchon. 1987. "Sources and Trend of Income Inequality: Thailand 1975/76 and 1981." Master's thesis, Thammasat University.

Sompop Manarungsan. 1989. *Economic Development of Thailand, 1850–1950: Response to the Challenge of the World Economy.* Institute of Asian Studies Monograph 042. Chulalongkorn University.

Somsak Tambunlertchai, 1977. *Japanese and American Investment in Thailand's Manufacturing Industries.* Tokyo. Institute of Developing Economies.

————. 1993. "Manufacturing." In Peter G. Warr, ed., *The Thai Economy in Transition*, Cambridge: Cambridge University Press.

Somsak Tambunlertchai, and Chesada Lohawenchit. 1981. "Labour-Intensive and Small-Scale Manufacturing Industries in Thailand." In Ahmed Rashid, ed., *The Development of Labour-Intensive Industry in ASEAN Countries.* Geneva: International Labour Organisation.

Somsak Tambunlertchai, and I. Yamazawa. 1983. *Manufactured Export Promotion: The Case of Thailand.* Institute of Developing Economies Joint Research Program Series 38, Tokyo.

Suehiro, Akira. 1985. *Capital Accumulation and Industrial Development in Thailand.* Bangkok: Chulalongkorn University Social Research Institute.

————. 1989. *Capital Accumulation in Thailand: 1855–1985.* Tokyo: Centre for East Asian Cultural Studies.

Suganya Hutaserani, and Somchai Jitsuchon. 1988. "Thailand's Income Distribution and Poverty Profile and Their Current Situations." Paper prepared for the 1988 TDRI Year-End Conference, Thailand.

Supote Chunanunthatham. 1978. "The Binding of the Exchange Rate Between Thai Baht and U.S. Dollar." In *Current Economic Situation and Policy Analysis of Thailand, Economics Symposium.* Bangkok: Faculty of Economics, Thammasat University. (In Thai.)

Swoboda, A. K. 1973. "Monetary Policy under Fixed Exchange Rates: Effectiveness, the Speed of Adjustment, and Proper Use." *Economica* 40: 136–45.

Tanzi, Vito. 1986. "Fiscal Policy Responses to Exogenous Shocks in Developing Countries." *American Economic Review* 76(2): 88–91.

————. 1989. "Fiscal Policy, Growth, and the Design of Stabilization Programs." In Mario I. Blejer and Ke-young Chu, eds., *Fiscal Policy, Stabilization, and Growth in Developing Countries.* Washington, D.C.: International Monetary Fund.

Tarisa Derethinan. 1987. "The Development of Thai Financial Institutions." In Nopporn Ruengsakul and others, eds., *Money and Banking and Implementation of National Economic Policies.* Bangkok: Chulalongkorn University Press. (In Thai.)

Terwiel, B. J. 1983. *A History of Modern Thailand: 1767–1942*. St. Lucia: University of Queensland Press.

Thailand, Ministry of Finance. 1990. *A History of Government Salary in Thailand: 100th Anniversary of the Department of the Comptroller-General*. Bangkok: Borpit Printing.

Thailand, National Economic and Social Development Board. 1983. "Summary of the Financial Situation and Operation of 60 Public Enterprises during the First Two Years of the Fifth Development Plan." B.E. 2525 and 2526. Bangkok. Processed.

Thailand, National Statistical Office. 1988. *Report of the 1988 Household Socio-Economic Survey: Whole Kingdom*. Bangkok.

Thompson, Virginia. 1941. *Thailand: The New Siam*. New York: Macmillan.

Tobin, James. 1978. "Monetary Policy and the Economy: The Transmission Mechanism." *Southern Economic Journal* 44(3–4): 421–31.

Trairong Suwankiri. 1970. "The Structure of Protection and Import Substitution in Thailand." Master's thesis, University of the Philippines.

Trairong Suwankiri, and others. 1975. "The Determination of Minimum Wages in Thailand and Their Economic Impact." *Thammasat University Journal* 5(1): 2–47. (In Thai.)

Trescott, P. B. 1971. *Thailand's Monetary Experience: The Economics of Stability*. New York: Praeger.

United Nations Development Programme. 1992. *Human Development Report*. New York: Oxford University Press.

Usher, Dan. 1967. "The Thai Rice Trade." In T. H. Silcock, ed., *Thailand: Social and Economic Studies in Development*. Canberra: Australian National University Press.

Vares Oupatiga. 1986. *Roles of Financial Institutions in Thailand in Savings Mobilization and Credit Allocation*. Bangkok: Thammasat University, Faculty of Economics. (In Thai.)

Virabongsa Ramangkura. 1975. "A Macroeconomic Model for Thailand: A Classical Approach." In Prateep Sondysuvan, ed., *Finance, Trade and Economic Development in Thailand*. Bangkok: Sompong Press.

Warr, Peter G. 1993. "The Thai Economy." In Peter G. Warr, ed., *The Thai Economy in Transition*. Cambridge: Cambridge University Press.

———. ed. 1993. *The Thai Economy in Transition*. Cambridge: Cambridge University Press.

Warr, Peter G., and Bandid Nijathaworn. 1987. "Thailand's Economic Performance: Some Thai Perspectives." *Asian-Pacific Economic Literature* 1:60–74. Reprinted (in Chinese) in *Jingjixue Yicong* (Economic translations) 10(1988): 59–66.

Williamson, John. 1994. "In Search of a Manual for Technopols." In John Williamson, ed., *The Political Economy of Policy Reform*. Washington, D.C.: Institute for International Economics.

Wilson, Constance M. 1983. *Thailand: A Handbook of Historical Statistics*.

Boston: G. K. Hall.

Wilson, D. A. 1960. *Politics in Thailand.* New York: Cornell University Press.

World Bank. 1959. *A Public Development Program for Thailand.* Baltimore, Md.: Johns Hopkins University Press.

———. 1992. *World Development Report 1992.* New York: Oxford University Press.

———. 1993. *East Asia's Economic Miracle.* New York: Oxford University Press.

Wyatt, David K. 1984. *Thailand: A Short History.* New Haven, Conn.: Yale University Press.

# Index